KT-547-881

HOLLYWOOD COMEDIANS,
THE FILM READER

Despite the cult status enjoyed by star performers such as Charlie Chaplin, Buster Keaton, the Marx Brothers and Woody Allen, comedians and the contexts within which they worked have not always received their due in scholarly discussions of cinema culture. *Hollywood Comedians, The Film Reader* seeks to redress the balance, combining distinguished work on comedian comedy produced since the early 1980s with more recent material that explores the genre's contemporary revival.

Grouped in thematic sections, the articles explore the central issues and debates in the study of comedian comedy, providing a comprehensive guide to a range of comedians, themes and contexts:

- Genre, narrative and performance – considers the interaction between fictional representation and comic performance;
- Approaches to silent comedy – examines the silent films of Chaplin and Keaton and their historical and cultural contexts;
- Sound comedy, the vaudeville aesthetic and ethnicity – explores the exploitation of variety entertainment traditions in the early sound comedy of the Marx Brothers and their contemporaries;
- Comedian comedy and gender – discusses the gender dynamics of comedy, focusing upon the careers of Mae West, Hope and Crosby, Lucille Ball and Jerry Lewis;
- Post-classical comedian comedy – assesses the changing nature of comedians and comedian comedy in the era of Steve Martin, Eddie Murphy, Jim Carrey and Chris Rock.

Contributors: Steven Cohan, Philip Drake, Tom Gunning, Bambi L. Haggins, Henry Jenkins III, Peter Krämer, Patricia Mellencamp, Steve Neale, William Paul, Joanna E. Rapf, Kathleen Rowe, Steve Seidman, Mark Winokur.

Frank Krutnik is Professor in Film Studies at Sheffield Hallam University. He is the author of *Inventing Jerry Lewis* (Smithsonian University Press 2000), *In a Lonely Street: Film Noir, Genre, Masculinity* (Routledge 1991) and, with Steve Neale, *Popular Film and Television Comedy* (Routledge 1990).

IN FOCUS

Focus: Routledge Film Readers
Series Editors: Steven Cohan (Syracuse University) and Ina Rae Hark (University of South Carolina)

The In Focus series of readers is a comprehensive resource for students on film and cinema studies courses. The series explores the innovations of film studies while highlighting the vital connection of debates to other academic fields and to studies of other media. The readers bring together key articles on a major topic in film studies, from marketing to Hollywood comedy, identifying the central issues, exploring how and why scholars have approached it in specific ways, and tracing continuities of thought among scholars. Each reader opens with an introductory essay setting the debates in their academic context, explaining the topic's historical and theoretical importance, and surveying and critiquing its development in film studies.

Exhibition, The Film Reader
Edited by Ina Rae Hark

Experimental Cinema, The Film Reader
Edited by Wheeler Winston Dixon and Gwendolyn Audrey Foster

Hollywood Comedians, The Film Reader
Edited by Frank Krutnik

Hollywood Musicals, The Film Reader
Edited by Steven Cohan

Horror, The Film Reader
Edited by Mark Jancovich

Movie Music, The Film Reader
Edited by Kay Dickinson

Forthcoming Titles:

Marketing, The Film Reader
Edited by Justin Wyatt

Reception, The Film Reader
Edited by Barbara Klinger

Stars, The Film Reader
Edited by Marcia Landy and Lucy Fischer

THE LIBRARY
GUILDFORD COLLEGE
of Further and Higher Education

HOLLYWOOD COMEDIANS,
THE FILM READER

Edited by Frank Krutnik

Routledge
Taylor & Francis Group

LONDON AND NEW YORK

~~105033~~
791. 43028 KRU
141712

First published 2003
by Routledge
11 New Fetter Lane, London EC4P 4EE

Simultaneously published in the USA and Canada
by Routledge
29 West 35th Street, New York, NY 10001

Routledge is an imprint of the Taylor & Francis Group

Selection and editorial matter © 2003 Frank Krutnik

Designed and typeset in Novarese and Scala Sans
by Keystroke, Jacaranda Lodge, Wolverhampton
Printed and bound in Great Britain
by The Cromwell Press, Trowbridge, Wiltshire

All rights reserved. No part of this book may be reprinted or reproduced
or utilized in any form or by any electronic, mechanical, or other means,
now known or hereafter invented, including photocopying and
recording, or in any information storage or retrieval system, without
permission in writing from the publishers.

British Library Cataloguing in Publication Data
A catalogue record for this book is available from the British Library

Library of Congress Cataloging in Publication Data
Hollywood comedians, the film reader/edited by Frank Krutnik.
        p. cm. – (Film readers)
Inlcudes bibliographical references and index.
    1. Comedy films–United States–History and criticism.
    I. Krutnik, Frank, 1956– II. Series.
    PN1995.9.C55 H65 2002
    791.43'617'0973–dc21   2002013360

ISBN 0–415–23551–0 (hbk)
ISBN 0–415–23552–9 (pbk)

Contents

PART FIVE: POST-CLASSICAL COMEDIAN COMEDY   167

Acknowledgements

Steve Seidman, 'Performance, Enunciation and Self Reference in Hollywood Comedian Comedy', adapted from *Comedian Comedy: A Tradition in Hollywood Film* (Ann Arbor, UMI Research Press), pp. 15–57. © 2002 Steve Seidman. Reprinted by permission of the author.

Peter Krämer, 'Comicality and Narrative Closure in Buster Keaton's *The Blacksmith*', from *The Velvet Light Trap* no. 23 (Spring 1989), pp. 101–3, 105, 107, 111–16. © 1989 University of Texas Press. Reprinted by permission of the publisher.

Steve Neale and Frank Krutnik, 'The Case of Silent Slapstick', from *Popular Film and Television Comedy* (London and New York, Routledge, 1990), pp. 110–31. Reprinted by permission of Taylor & Francis Group Plc and Routledge, Inc.

Tom Gunning, 'Buster Keaton, or the Work of Comedy in the Age of Mechanical Reproduction', from *Cineaste* vol. 21 no. 3 (July 1995), pp. 14–16. Reprinted by permission of the author.

William Paul, 'Charlie Chaplin and the Annals of Anality', from *Comedy/Cinema/ Theory*, ed. Andrew S. Horton (Berkeley, University of California Press, 1991), 115–29. © 1991 the Regents of the University of California. Reprinted by permission of the publisher.

Henry Jenkins III, 'Anarchistic Comedy and the Vaudeville Aesthetic', from '"Fifi Was My Mother's Name . . ." Anarchistic Comedy and the Vaudeville Aesthetic', *The Velvet Light Trap* no. 26 (Fall 1990), pp. 3–9, 23–7. © 1990 University of Texas Press. Reprinted by permission of the publisher.

Mark Winokur, 'The Marx Brothers and the Search for the Landsman', from *American Laughter: Immigrants, Ethnicity, and 1930s Hollywood Film Comedy* (London, Macmillan, 1996), pp. 125–46, 150–3. Reprinted by permission of the publisher.

Kathleen Rowe, '*She Done Him Wrong*: Spectacle and Narrative', from *The Unruly Woman: Gender and the Genres of Laughter* (Austin, University of Texas Press, 1995), pp. 119–25. © 1995 University of Texas Press. Reprinted by permission of the publisher.

Patricia Mellencamp, 'Lucille Ball and the Regime of Domiculture', from *High Anxiety: Catastrophe, Scandal, Age and Comedy*, (Bloomington and Indianapolis, Indiana University Press,

1992), pp. 313–14, 322–33, 337. © 1992 Indiana University Press. Reprinted by permission of the publisher.

Joanna E. Rapf, 'Comic Theory from a Feminist Perspective: a Look at Jerry Lewis', from *The Journal of Popular Culture*, vol. 27 no. 1 (Summer 1993), pp. 192–203. Reprinted by permission of the author and the *Journal of Popular Culture*.

Steven Cohan, 'Queering the Deal: On the Road with Hope and Crosby', from *Out Takes: Essays on Queer Theory and Film*, ed. Ellis Hanson (Durham, NC, Duke University Press, 1999), pp. 23–30, 34–45. © 1999 Duke University Press. Reprinted by permission of the publisher.

Hollywood Comedians,
The Film Reader

General Introduction

Hollywood comedians may routinely strike gold at the box office but they rarely find such good fortune at the hands of film critics. Regarded as too throwaway, too vulgar or too populist to merit serious attention, comedian films have languished until quite recently among the more embarrassing and untapped byways of Hollywood cinema. A select handful of performers have certainly attained widespread renown as filmic artists – most notably Charlie Chaplin, Buster Keaton, the Marx Brothers and Woody Allen – but the vast majority of Hollywood comedians remain consigned to the ghettos of film cultism. Even the canonical performers tend to crop up far more frequently in popular biographies than in works of film scholarship. For example, comedian films were routinely bypassed in the campaigns that helped establish film studies as a critical discipline – battles waged in the name of auteurism, or genre theory, or the heady brew of Marxism, psychoanalysis, semiotics, structuralism and feminism propagated by *Screen* magazine in the 1970s. By contrast, the past two decades have witnessed a remarkable upsurge in academic discussion of popular film comedy, with the development of stimulating approaches to the aesthetics, history and ideology of the comedian-centred film.[1] Even so, with the exception of such period-based accounts as Henry Jenkins' *What Made Pistachio Nuts* and Mark Winokur's *American Laughter* (which both deal with the 1930s), there has been no book-length overview of the comedian film since Steve Seidman's groundbreaking 1981 study *Comedian Comedy: A Tradition in Hollywood Film*.

This anthology proposes to fill this gap by collecting some of the most distinguished work on comedian comedy produced since the early 1980s together with new material that explores the genre's contemporary revival. It covers a range of comedians, contexts and issues: from the silent films of Chaplin and Keaton to the early sound comedy of Mae West and the Marx Brothers; from the gender dynamics of Hope and Crosby, Lucille Ball and Jerry Lewis to the post-classical variations wrung by Jim Carrey and Chris Rock. Although it is organized within a predominantly historical framework, the Reader nonetheless illustrates the disparate critical and theoretical projects that have embraced the comedian film in recent years. Thus, besides examining issues of genre, narrative and performance, contributors to this volume also explore how comedian films manage representations of otherness that are defined through ethnicity, race, class, gender and the body.

Like the other entries in this series, this reader aims to provide a lively and invigorating educational resource that will also appeal to a wider readership interested in film and film comedy. Contributions have been selected not merely for *what* they say about comedian films but also for the manner in which they say it. The 'frivolous' comic pleasures permitted by such movies are extremely difficult to write about 'seriously' within a 'film criticism whose academic legitimacy has always been based on the distinction between serious pleasures and mere diversion (the repeated attempts to separate "high" from "mass" culture, art from "mere" commodity)' (Rutsky and Wyatt 1990: 4). Until quite recently, Steve Neale argues, critical discussion of film comedy has operated within 'evaluative paradigms compatible with liberal humanist values, hence within frameworks of concern that have tended to focus on issues of aesthetic integrity, self-expression, and direct or indirect social and cultural worth' (Neale 2000: 65). Most comedian films defy such evaluative frameworks because they delight in vicarious gags or performative spectacle, and because they display and celebrate the excesses of the body. Those comedians who have attained critical respectability are generally considered to have 'transcended' the vulgarities of low comedy, as is the case with the canonical silent clowns of the 1920s.

Contributions to this reader have been selected precisely because they succeed admirably in furthering our understanding of Hollywood, comedy and popular culture without losing sight of the fun of the films themselves.[2] A devoted fan of Jerry Lewis responded to my monograph on his hero by complaining that: '25% of the book is all footnotes that you have to keep referring to. The print seems smaller than normal and the words seem larger than normal. Very difficult reading. I believe the author is from England and he is trying to impress you with his vocabulary. Really very annoying.'[3] Given such expectations, I would not expect 'Joe548' (as he tags himself) to enjoy this reader because, like *Inventing Jerry Lewis*, it does not shirk from grappling thoughtfully with the pleasures and meanings of popular comedy. While die-hard aficionados such as Joe548 may prefer devotional approaches to their comic idols, the critics included in this reader appreciate comedian films not simply because they are fun but because they recognize that fun is itself an intricate and ideologically charged process.

The popular biography remains by far the most commonplace format for encountering discussion of Hollywood comedians. Although there are several distinguished and exhaustively researched examples of the genre – for example, David Robinson's book on Chaplin (Robinson 1985), Simon Louvish's studies of W.C. Fields, the Marx Brothers and Laurel and Hardy (Louvish 1999a, 1999b, 2001) – many biographers of film comedians find it difficult to resist either blinkered hagiography or salacious exposé. A contrasting tendency, however, is embodied by career studies that resist biographical speculation to examine the multiple contexts which shape the comedian's work and stardom. Examples include Charles Maland's study of Chaplin's role as a cultural icon (Maland 1991), Robert Knopf's book on Keaton (Knopf 1999), my own work on Jerry Lewis (Krutnik 2000), and the numerous studies of Mae West that have cropped up in recent years (Curry 1996, Hamilton 1996, Leider 1997). In general, however, scholarly work on the Hollywood comedian film may be regarded as dealing with three distinct yet by no means mutually exclusive approaches: formal, historical and ideological.

Formal approaches often focus on the operative or structural logics of comedy, particularly in regard to visual and verbal gags. Examples of such approaches include Paul Willemen's account of comic mechanisms in the work of director Frank Tashlin (Willemen 1973); Patricia Mellencamp's semiotic analysis of the way the Marx Brothers' comedy plays with language (Mellencamp 1983); Jerry Palmer's dense but rewarding examination of the logical processes of gag construction in the films of Laurel and Hardy (Palmer 1987); and Noel Carroll's analyses of gags and performance in Buster Keaton's films (Carroll 1990a, 1990b, 1991).[4] Later critics would attempt to ally such formal enquiry to a consideration of the specific historical conjunctures that give rise to diverse comic possibilities. One example of such an approach is the critical dialogue between Don Crafton and Tom Gunning concerning the relative importance of gags and narrative to early film comedy (Crafton 1995, Gunning 1995a, 1995b). Henry Jenkins' work, to be discussed more fully below, provides another example of scholarship that combines both formal and historical considerations (Jenkins 1992).

Historical approaches to the Hollywood comedian film often examine the way that comic forms and cycles illuminate the history of US cinema and culture. While orthodox histories restrict themselves to the canonical silent feature films of the 1920s, more recent studies have explored a greater range of periods, cycles and performers. Other approaches deal with the history of the comedian-centred film itself, which is conceived of either as a generic form or as a succession of cycles that are designed to exploit specific performers or teams. Although comedians have been a consistent presence within Hollywood since the 1910s, they have not always occupied the same status vis-à-vis the cinematic institution, nor have they worked under the same conditions. At any one time, moreover, the precise characteristics of screen comedy are themselves coordinated by the particular extra-cinematic environments (British music-hall, vaudeville, cabaret, broadcast radio, television and so on) in which comedians learn their craft and gain exposure prior to their cinematic show-cases. As a generic form the comedian film has also been affected by broader shifts within Hollywood cinema, such as the transition from the short format to the feature film, the displacement of the silent film by the synchronized sound movie, and the dismantling of the studio system through the 1950s and 1960s.

Ideological approaches to the study of the film comedians encompass a wide variety of priorities and agendas. The Hollywood comedian film has proved especially useful for such projects because of the way it deals consistently with relations between norms and deviance. Generally cast as an outsider or misfit in some way, the comedian presents a spectacle of otherness by serving as a conduit for energies that are marginal, non-normative or antisocial. The resultant conflicts between the comedian and the (social) world may also be played out through intrapsychic divisions, with the comedian located as an eccentric individual who (knowingly or unknowingly) disrupts conventional modes of behaviour, thought and identity. Such eccentricity is never a purely personal issue, however, for the very articulation of deviance immediately triggers awareness of the broader sets of social and representational conventions that define it as such. Hollywood comedians tend also to affiliate themselves with socially subordinated groups or identities: thus the Marx Brothers play immigrant stowaways in both *Monkey Business* (1931) and *A Night at the Opera* (1935), and in *A Day at the Races* (1937) they seek refuge among the black underclass; Jerry Lewis repeatedly plays exploited servant figures (as in *The Stooge* (1953), *The Caddy* (1953), *Cinderfella* (1960), *The Bellboy* (1960), *The Errand Boy* (1961), *The Patsy* (1964)); Mae West's 'fallen women' characters frequently battle against abusive heteromasculine authority; and in *Happy Gilmore* (1996) Adam Sandler's eponymous slacker turned pro-golfer emerges as the populist leader of a movement of social outsiders that includes workers, trailer trash, bikers and the homeless.

Comedy is fascinating for the slippery manner in which it handles ideological tensions and contradictions. It may delight in overturning conventions, but comedy can also reconfirm normative codes by reducing difference to laughter. Critics have often explored such paradoxes in their analyses of the comedian film's representations of otherness and difference. Among the many critics to examine how comedian-centred comedy deals with, or refuses to deal with women, are Patricia Mellencamp (1986, 1992), Alex Doty (1990), Lucy Fischer (1991), Henry Jenkins (1991), Pamela Robertson (1993), Kathleen Rowe (1995) and Ramona Curry (1996). The representation of masculinity within comedian texts has also been scrutinized by several critics, including Doty (1991), Rapf (1993), Sikov (1994), Sanders (1995), Krutnik (1995a, 2000, 2002) and Cohan (1999). Charles Musser (1991), Henry Jenkins (1990a) and Mark Winokur (1996) have also led valuable investigative forays into the importance of ethnicity to Hollywood comedian films of the pre-Second World War era. More recent work has also begun to tackle the representations of race and class in Hollywood comedian films (on comedy and race see Watkins 1999 and chapter 12, this volume, by Bambi Haggins, and on comedy and class see Beach 2002).

As a means of setting the stage for the work collected in this Reader, the remainder of this introduction provides a more detailed examination of some pivotal moments in the critical conceptualization of the Hollywood comedian film. I begin with an early discussion by the respected critic, screenwriter and littérateur James Agee, whose account of comedian comedy proved extremely influential upon subsequent critical discourse.[5] I will subsequently consider two contrasting examples of scholarly debate on comedian comedy by Steve Seidman and Henry Jenkins, who both take issue with the canonical assumptions of Agee's work. Where Seidman attempts to provide a general generic framework for examining the comedian film, Jenkins both extends and critiques his project by emphasizing the complex determination of a specific era within the genre's history.

Silence is golden

'The golden age of American comedy ended with the comic of the talking picture' René Clair.

(Kerr 1975: 39)

In 'Comedy's Greatest Era', an article published in *Life* magazine in 1949, James Agee argued that Hollywood's conversion to sound two decades earlier had destroyed the vibrant culture of visual comedy that flourished from 1912 to 1930. With the transition to sound, Agee suggests, a dialogue-driven mode of screen humour came to supplant the inventive artistry of silent gag-makers:

To put it unkindly, the only thing wrong with screen comedy today is that it takes place on a screen which talks. Because it talks, the only comedians who ever mastered the screen cannot work, for they cannot combine their comic style with talk. Because there is a screen, talking comedians are trapped into a continual exhibition of their inadequacy as screen comedians on a surface as big as the side of a barn.

(Agee 1974: 440)

With the absence of synchronized sound putting film at one remove from reality, comic performers of the silent era could capitalize upon their liberation from the literalism of speech. Agee contends that this context encouraged the development of a stylized poetics of physical comedy that, at its best, constituted an intricate language of visual expressiveness.

Agee's reading of silent comedy echoes long-established prejudices against the ascendancy of the Hollywood dialogue film. Since the 1920s numerous critical voices had championed the silent screen as the highest and purest form of cinematic art.[6] They objected not to synchronized, pre-recorded sound in itself but to the importation of speech, which they feared would debase cinema's essentially visual qualities and reduce it to a form of canned theatre.[7] By comparison with the silent era, Agee suggests, comedians found sound cinema a far more restrictive aesthetic milieu:

> When a modern comedian gets hit on the head . . . the most he is apt to do is look sleepy. When a silent comedian got hit on the head he seldom let it go so flatly. He realized a broad license, and a ruthless discipline within that license. It was his business to be as funny as possible physically, without the help or hindrance of words. So he gave us a figure of speech, or rather of vision, for loss of consciousness. In other words, he gave us a poem, a kind of poem, moreover, that everybody understands. The least he might do was straighten up stiff as a plank and fall over backward with such skill that his whole length seemed to slap the floor at the same instant. Or he might make a cadenza of it – look vague, smile like an angel, roll up his eyes, lace his fingers, thrust his hands palms downward as far as they would go, hunch his shoulders, rise on tiptoe, prance ecstatically in narrowing circles until, with tallow knees, he sank down the vortex of his dizziness to the floor and there signified nirvana by kicking his heels twice, like a swimming frog.
>
> (Agee 1974: 438–9)

Besides proclaiming the overall superiority of the silent screen as a medium for film comedy, Agee also celebrates the contributions of a small group of creative practitioners. He credits Mack Sennett as the 'father' of American screen comedy because the production context he established at Keystone Studios in 1912 provided an incubator for the art of silent comedy. For Agee, Keystone's rough and ready brand of knockabout slapstick – in itself influenced by earlier French and Italian comedies – possessed an intensity and vitality that was lost to the sound era:

> these people zipped and caromed about the pristine world of the screen as jazzily as a convention of water bugs. Words can hardly suggest how energetically they collided and bounced apart, meeting in full gallop around the corner of a house; how hard and how often they fell on their backsides; or with what fantastically adroit clumsiness they got themselves fouled up in folding ladders, garden hoses, tethered animals and each other's headlong cross-purposes. The gestures were ferociously emphatic; not a line or motion of the body was wasted or inarticulate.
>
> (Agee 1974: 441)

Sennett's short films may have pioneered the American visual comedy style but their vulgarity and lack of ambition disqualify them from greatness (Agee 1974: 443). Instead, Agee proposes, it was Chaplin, Keaton, Lloyd and Harry Langdon who would bring Hollywood silent comedy to a peak of artistic accomplishment.

They all learned from the Sennett style – indeed, Chaplin, Keaton and Langdon had experience of working for the legendary Keystone producer – but they also learned to move beyond his comedy of kinetic violence. By refining Sennett's raw and vicarious style, these four 'masters' of silent screen comedy were able to craft more individuated comic personae. They also developed distinctive styles of performance and gag-making (Agee 1974: 445–54). Chaplin's films combined a deftly choreographed physical comedy with a sentimental concern for the plight of his outsider figure, the Tramp. Lloyd jettisoned the stylized Chaplin clones he started with (Willie Work and Lonesome Luke), in favour of a more naturalistic persona (the 'glasses' character). His films also aspired towards a more integrated blend of narrative, gags and thrills.[8] Although Langdon's comic persona was a grotesque hybrid of baby and adult, he nonetheless proved as adept as Chaplin at 'subtle emotion and mental process' (Agee 1974: 450). Finally, Agee suggests that Keaton not only developed a deadpan style of response that was capable of 'subtle leverages of expression' but also proved himself a 'wonderfully resourceful inventor of mechanistic gags' (Agee 1974: 452–3).

Many subsequent discussions of screen comedy echoed Agee's nostalgic lament for the glories of silent cinema, including studies by Donald McCaffrey (1968), Walter Kerr (1975) and Gerald Mast (1976) (Jenkins 1992: 3). Kerr's immensely detailed and elegant book *The Silent Clowns* basically follows Agee's canon, but also devotes substantial attention to other performers such as Larry Semon, Raymond Griffith and Laurel and Hardy. Like Agee, Kerr maintains that the lack of speech renders the silent film an inherently superior aesthetic proposition:

> The less complete the canvas, the more there is for the viewer to contribute. He [*sic*] must work with hints, and the more he must do for himself, the more deeply engaged he becomes in the work. Audiences are rarely aware of how active they become in the presence of work that is created by nuance, by incomplete statement. With their own imaginations forcibly alerted, they move forward to *meet* the imagination of the man who has composed what they are watching. There is a journey and a greeting, an exchange of experience, a handshake on truth. The two make the image together. . . . Silence is not a softer form; it is a more demanding one.
>
> (Kerr 1975: 3–4)

When he describes the gradual move from one-reel short films to feature-length narratives as a 'struggle toward maturity' (Kerr 1975: 159), Kerr clearly implies the inferiority of earlier and subsequent comedies. The canonization of the 1920s as a period of creative exceptionalism in Hollywood comedy, a golden age of auteurs and masterpieces, has produced a skewed account of the history of the genre and its broader relationship to US cinema and US culture.[9] With the feature films of Chaplin, Keaton, Lloyd and Langdon accorded bench-mark status, it is not surprising that comedian movies which operate according to other logics are found to be lacking – especially those produced in the sound era. More recent critics have challenged this canonization of 1920s feature comedy. Peter Krämer and Steve Neale, for example, both argue that when viewed within the broader production context of early Hollywood these films emerge as more hybrid and unstable than their reputation as fully realized (and unified) artistic masterpieces would suggest (Krämer 1988: 101–3, Neale and Krutnik 1990: 5). Moreover, critical valuation of the narratively integrated feature comedy rests, Henry Jenkins stresses, 'on explicit appeals to classical criteria of thematic significance, character consistency, narrative unity, causal logic, and psychological realism' that are simply not relevant to many of the comedian films that appeared prior to and after the golden decade of the 1920s period (Jenkins 1992: 3). In his own exemplary consideration of early 1930s anarchistic comedy, *What Made Pistachio Nuts*, Jenkins successfully demonstrates how comedian films are shaped not simply by the signifying materials of the medium, nor from the quality of individual performers, but by a more complex interaction between the cultural, economic and industrial forces that shape popular entertainment.

Comedian comedy as generic tradition

Where many earlier discussions of comedian comedy either focused on individual performers or proclaimed the pre-eminence of the silent screen, Steve Seidman sought to map a broader generic terrain in Hollywood cinema. His 1981 book *Comedian Comedy: A Tradition in Hollywood Film* traces the persistence of certain formal and thematic preoccupations across the work of diverse comedians from the 1910s to the 1970s. Seidman approaches comedian comedy as a cohesive generic form that encompasses recurring thematic concerns and stylistic devices. As a cinematic 'tradition', it transcends the contributions of individual practitioners while at the same time relying upon their particular skills. Comedian comedy is a distinctive cinematic hybrid of presentational and representational processes that mediates between a tradition of modular entertainment spectacle (popularized through variety forms such as vaudeville, cabaret, broadcast radio and television) and the classical narrative protocols that Hollywood adapted from nineteenth-century fiction and drama. With a barrage of wide-ranging examples, Seidman shows how comedian comedy carries traces of an alternative to classical Hollywood narrative aesthetic. By seeking to approximate the interactive dynamic of US show business, the comedian film works against the effacement and hermeticism associated with the Hollywood style. In particular, it parades the speciality performer *as* a performer rather than subjugating his or her presentation to the demands of character construction. Although some comic players – such as Harold Lloyd, Joe E. Brown and Danny Kaye – do adhere more closely to the perimeters of fictional verisimilitude, the comedian film routinely abandons the pretence that the onscreen world possesses a realistic unity and wholeness. For example, where classical narrative is generally oblivious to the spectator's presence, comedian comedy frequently ruptures the self-consistent realm of fiction to address the audience directly.

The first chapter of Seidman's book, which is excerpted in this Reader, examines the extra-fictional features of the comedian comedy tradition. While other figures inhabiting the diegetic universe must act as their fictional roles decree, the comedian commonly possesses a degree of freedom from such representational constraints. Seidman illustrates how numerous comedians flaunt their disengagement from the limitations of character identity and behaviour by acknowledging the presence of the camera – through looks, bows or direct verbal address – or by exposing the constructed nature of both film and fiction. Besides employing devices that 'jam' the transmission of an orthodox story, the comedian is further differentiated from the diegetic regime through the familiarity of his or her comic persona. All Hollywood star vehicles must mediate between a fictionally specific character identity and a star image that circulates beyond the boundaries of the particular film, and beyond cinema itself. Comedian comedy exacerbates this tension, however, because its prime rationale is to provide a show-case for the star performer. The comedian film, Seidman suggests,

> is generated by two seemingly contradictory impulses: (1) the maintenance of the comedian's position as an already recognizable performer with a clearly defined extrafictional personality (and in the case of comedians from 1930 on, a *highly visible* extrafictional personality); and (2) the depiction of the comedian as a comic figure who inhabits a fictional universe where certain problems must be confronted and resolved.
>
> (Seidman 1981: 3)

Instead of reading comedian comedy as a subversive form that disrupts classical Hollywood protocols, Seidman argues that it combines interruptive devices with recurring fictional procedures. Like many Hollywood genres comedian comedy exhibits a recurring narrative tension between eccentricity and social conformity. The comedian film articulates this dialectic as a conflict between the idiosyncratic individual and the normative parameters of cultural identity, a conflict that simultaneously takes place *within* the comedian figure. The comedian frequently plays an eccentric individual who is thrown into a rule-governed fictional environment and proceeds to play havoc with its conventions. While performative expertise identifies them as someone with exceptional gifts, he or she frequently plays characters who are exceedingly stupid (as with Laurel and Hardy, Jerry Lewis or Jim Carrey), neurotic (for example, Danny Kaye) or otherwise dysfunctional. The signs of the comedian's creativity are thus simultaneously configured as indicators of the character's aberrance. As Seidman puts it, comedian comedy provides numerous instances of 'adaptability to disguise, verbal manipulation (dialects, impressions), and physical dexterity' that serve as 'the fictional translation of the comedian's performing talents into the comic figure's behavioural traits' (Seidman 1981:6).

Seidman proposes that comedian comedy functions as a generically articulated myth that mediates between individual exceptionalism and cultural obligation. 'The work of comedian comedy as a genre,' he suggests, 'is to divest the comic figure of his creativity – his difference – so that he can be incorporated into the culture depicted in the films, and to resolve in some way the particular generic problems of individual evolution and cultural initiation' (Seidman 1981: 143). The comedian figure's difference sets him in conflict with the community, a conflict that is resolved when he either learns to relinquish eccentricity – by 'evolving a coherent identity' and thereby accepting his place within the cultural order – or chooses to remain an outsider by resisting cultural assimilation (Seidman 1981: 145). Both forms of resolution require the comic misfit to sacrifice or accommodate his or her individual creativity as a means of attaining a culturally legitimate identity (Seidman 1981: 146). However, he also proposes that audiences can derive a twofold pleasure from such films, enjoying 'the counter-cultural nature of the comic figure, as well as the reaffirmation of cultural values which stress community and harmony' (Seidman 1981: 147).

Seidman's model, then, concerns itself not simply with the formal negotiation between performance and fiction but also with the thematic arbitration between the conflictual demands of social conformism and counter-cultural impulses (imagination, creativity, infantilism, excessive erotic desires and so on). In a summary of Seidman's model, Steve Neale comments that comedians:

> often portray eccentric or deviant characters, characters given to dreaming, to disguise, to regression and to bouts of madness. To that extent, the opposition between eccentricity and social conformity to be found elsewhere in Hollywood comedy is here internalized as an aspect of the comedian's character, one which is inextricably linked to his or her performance skills, and one which is therefore irresolvable.
>
> (Neale 2000: 69)

Dealing as it does with scenarios centred upon outsiders or misfits, comedian comedy provides a potentially fruitful site for exploring socially subordinated cultural identities produced through distinctions in ethnicity, race, gender and sexual preference. This potential is not necessarily realized, however – or, at least, not in an explicit or unproblematic fashion – because comedy is a notoriously double-edged sword that can simultaneously hack away at conformism while whittling down voicings of dissent or transgression. The predominantly white, male and heterosexual bias of most comedian comedy inevitably trammels the genre's ability to tackle the foreclosures of cultural hegemony. Moreover, as Seidman's model emphasizes, the comedian film frequently proposes an individualist and integrationist trajectory to the comedian-figure's battle with social convention.

Where Agee's article was carried by a prestigious magazine aimed at an enlightened general readership, Seidman's book on comedian comedy issued from the still relatively new context of academic film studies. *Comedian Comedy: A Tradition of Hollywood Film* was a version of Seidman's doctoral thesis in film studies, which he submitted to UCLA in 1979. At this time, film studies was dominated by a modernist theoretical agenda that defined itself in opposition to the easy enticements of popular cinema. The British journal *Screen* wielded a widespead influence that recalled the heady days of *Cahiers du Cinéma* twenty years earlier. Blending together Marxism, psychoanalysis, semiotics, structuralism and feminism, *Screen* theory dislodged auteurist criticism from the high ground of academic discourse on film. The *politique des auteurs* may have been radical in its time, but by the late 1960s it had become something of a critical orthodoxy – largely because the authorial concept was already such a foundational premise of literary and cultural criticism. The *Screen* paradigm certainly energized intellectual debate on film, its engagement with European critical theory helping to boost the reputation of film studies as a cutting-edge humanities discipline. At the same time, however, *Screen*'s treatment of texts, subjects and the relations between the two tended to focus more on shoring up its preferred theoretical models than with illuminating the specificities of films, their cultural contexts and audiences.

The auteurist critics of *Cahiers du Cinéma* and the British journal *Movie* had often blurred the distinctions between popular films and high art by considering the accomplishments of Hollywood directors with the same seriousness accorded canonical artists such as Shakespeare, Mozart and Joseph Conrad. Proponents of the *Screen* model, by contrast, sought legitimacy by adopting a notoriously impenetrable academic discourse that pitted itself against the very accessibility of the Hollywood films it scrutinized. Moreover, because it tended to treat such films as if they were only ever watched by generalized and abstract 'subjects', the *Screen* paradigm could not cope very easily with the manner in which film viewing is inflected by internalized formations of class, race, ethnicity, gender and so on. Thus, despite the pioneering work of vanguard feminist critics – most famously, Laura Mulvey's hugely influential article 'Visual Pleasure and Narrative Cinema' (Mulvey 1975) – *Screen*'s high-theory allegiances offered little scope for fully satisfactory conceptualizations of either difference or the popular. *Screen* theory promoted modes of criticism and film practice that contested the classical realist narrative system of mainstream cinema. Hollywood's manufactured dreams, it was argued, encouraged spectators to identify with their own subjection to bourgeois capitalist ideology. Where the classical realist text aims to deny contradiction and to mask the real circumstances of social and economic inequality, the oppositional practice of the radical critic or film-maker seeks to break the spell of illusionism and thereby to engage in the interrogation of texts and ideology.

Seidman's investigation of the comedian film may have sprung from this theoretical ground, but he simultaneously attempted to illuminate the pleasurable seductions of this most assertively popular of Hollywood genres. He demonstrates that there are striking similarities between the comedian film and the kinds of avant-garde textual practice championed by contemporary theorists. He argues that both exemplify alternatives to the hermetic mode of Hollywood's dramatic fiction:

A nonhermetic approach to narrative . . . is comprised of a more open and expansive narrative structure which acknowledges the spectator, narrative exposition that is 'spoiled' by actors who 'step out' of character, a foregrounding of its marks of production, essential artificiality, and a deconstruction of its signifying practice.

The implications of a nonhermetic approach to narrative have been discussed in relation to political and/or personal cinema, generally European. These are said to be subversive in nature – 'radical' texts – insofar as they react to the dominance of Hollywood cinema, and thus ostensibly challenge the spectator to become self-aware of his position in relation to the processes of filmic construction. It is further argued that these processes, since they are produced by a commercial cinema that is ideologically bourgeois and reactionary, subjugate the spectator to a world of fantasy and wish-fulfilment.

(Seidman 1981: 55–6)

The non-hermetic features of comedian comedy are not part of some politically or aesthetically radical agenda but derive instead from a long-established tradition of popular entertainment (which Henry Jenkins would later describe as the 'vaudeville aesthetic'). Even so, there is a logical basis for the presence of such interruptive devices in both experimental avant-garde films and popular comedian movies that are designed, as Jenkins puts it, 'for entertainment purposes only' (Jenkins 1990b: 6). Where the former use techniques of foregrounding, self-reflexivity, explicit enunciation and so on to produce active, questioning spectators, the latter similarly aim for a disengagement (momentary or otherwise) from the protocols of the 'classical realist text'. Thus, these strategies cannot be regarded as inherently 'subversive' because their role depends very much on the contexts – cinematic, cultural, institutional – in which they are employed. Moreover, the fact that they occur with such regularity in a routine Hollywood genre should be sufficient warning against holding too monolithic a conception of the operations of popular cinema.

Anarchistic attractions

Even if several critics contested aspects of his generic model, Seidman's work on comedian comedy paved the way for a productive reassessment of this Hollywood tradition.[10] Like Seidman, later film scholars gravitated towards the comedian film because it provided an amenable site for exploring alternatives to the legacy of 1970s screen theory. Instead of dealing in abstracted texts and subjects, today's most conscientious scholarship on Hollywood cinema tries to ground its enquiries in the historical particularities that coordinate the production and reception of films. It was precisely for deficiencies in his historical conceptualization of comedian comedy that Seidman drew criticism from Peter Krämer (1989) and Henry Jenkins. Jenkins praises Seidman for stressing the continuities between silent and sound comedy – thereby refuting the exceptional status of the former – but argues that Seidman fails to pay sufficient heed to the diverse cycles of comedian film and to the social, cultural and institutional contexts that have shaped them (Jenkins 1992: 11). Such criticisms are certainly valid, but it needs to be recognized that Seidman was working in a very different scholarly environment than later writers on comedian comedy – one that required him to address different sets of problems and priorities. By the time Jenkins, Krämer and others began to engage with the comedian film, the analytic paradigms had shifted. Where Seidman was in dialogue with the agendas of *Screen* theory, subsequent critics were impelled by the broader 'return to history' that has energized film studies since the mid-1980s.

The new historical approaches challenged received myths to offer invigorating perspectives on cinematic institutions, ideologies and audiences. Early cinema provided an especially fruitful site for such historical re-interrogation. Where traditional histories tended to view cinema's first decade as a primitive era that fumbled towards the development of a narrative style, revisionist historians pointed to alternative logics that supervised the activities of early film-makers and audiences. In particular, Tom Gunning proposed that in its first ten years cinema functioned less as 'a way of telling stories than . . . a way of presenting a series of views to an audience' (Gunning 1990: 57). Governed by a self-consciously presentational aesthetic, early films aimed to engage spectators by offering them discrete visual *attractions* that stimulated 'sensual or psychological impact' (through shock, surprise or laughter) (Gunning 1990: 59). The flashily performative exhibitionism of what Gunning describes as the 'cinema of attractions' went underground when narrative became established as the principal currency of mainstream cinema. Instead of simply disappearing from the Hollywood scene, however, the cinema of attractions persisted in generically codified forms that place a high premium on performance or spectacle. Feature-length comedian films, for example, often deploy visual or physical gags as semi-autonomous show-stopping attractions (Gunning 1995a: 97).

Henry Jenkins' book *What Made Pistachio Nuts? Early Sound Comedy and the Vaudeville Aesthetic* provides an especially accomplished example of such revisionist historiography.[11] Focusing upon a particularly significant yet hitherto poorly conceptualized era in Hollywood comedy, Jenkins moves beyond both the auteurist/masterpiece paradigm and the generic template offered by Seidman. Declaring that he aims to 'reconstruct the historical norms applicable to early sound comedy' (Jenkins 1992: 6), Jenkins shows that this transitional period in screen comedy provoked a momentary destabilization of the norms of classical Hollywood film-making. Through the innovation and standardization of the synchronized sound film, cinema emerged as a totalizing form that could replicate the full panoply of existing popular entertainments. To capitalize upon this potential, Hollywood film companies made extensive investments in talent from the Broadway and vaudeville stages. They did so not only to exploit the possibilities introduced to the medium by pre-recorded sound but also to illustrate the new entertainment territories that could be colonized by films with sound, speech and music. Very early in the proceedings, for example, Vitaphone – the corporation set up by Warner Brothers and Western Electric to market their sound-on-disc system – demonstrated that the synchronized sound film could provide a form of 'canned vaudeville'. The second public demonstration of the Vitaphone process, in October 1926, climaxed with an hour-long collection of shorts that one critic described as proceeding 'almost precisely as the most extravagant booker would build a show for his vaudevillle house'.[12]

Over subsequent years Hollywood would continue to showcase name performers from the variety stage in tailor-made screen vehicles – including Eddie Cantor, the Marx Brothers, Wheeler and Woolsey, Clark and McCullough, Joe Cook, Olsen and Johnson, George Burns and Gracie Allen, Mae West, W.C. Fields and Joe E. Brown. This policy was part of a broader initiative to secure the hegemony of the sound film. As Jenkins points out, 'ambitious studio executives saw sound as a means of broadening their entertainment empire and bringing Broadway and vaudeville under their corporate control' (Jenkins 1992: 159).[13] Vaudeville managed to withstand competition from the silent film because it offered an experience that was distinct from the cinematic parade of spectacle and narrative. It did not survive for long, however, once the silver screen began to purvey its glamorous extravaganzas of music and comedy – especially as American homes also enjoyed the free entertainments distributed by network radio. By the mid-1930s vaudeville was virtually eradicated by such competition, and the Broadway theatre likewise found itself in dire straits.[14]

Comedian films of the sound era may have met with a dismissive reception from the Agee camp, but there is no denying the raw euphoria exuded by the early sound comedies as they explore the comic promise of cinema's newly discovered voice. The talent raids on the variety and Broadway theatres ignited a concentrated renewal of the vaudeville style in Hollywood films, exemplified most clearly by what Jenkins describes as anarchistic comedy. Largely remembered through the films of the Marx Brothers, this style of comedy was actually shared by a much broader cohort of performers who were recruited from stage to screen to fuel the new and seemingly insatiable appetite for music, speech and song (Jenkins 1992: 9–10). Like the Marx Brothers, such teams as Clark and McCullough, Wheeler and Woolsey and Olsen and Johnson were presented as free-wheeling agents of a disintegrative entertainment spectacle that sat uneasily with the norms of classical narrative (Jenkins 1992: 22).[15]

Rejecting the narrative ambitions of the 1920s silent features, comedian films of the early sound era are impelled by a more attraction-oriented aesthetic. The Marx Brothers' Paramount vehicles, for instance, are loosely structured entertainment packages that juxtapose the performers in various combinations as a means of exhibiting their comic and musical specialisms. Marx-on-Marx interaction is interspersed with perfunctory boy-girl stuff and occasional 'action' set pieces (for example, the battle against kidnappers that concludes *Monkey Business*, the football game in *Horsefeathers* (1932), the war scenes in *Duck Soup* (1933)). The ramshackle nature of the combination underscores the degree to which narrative development is secondary to what happens *within* the scenes. Peculiar amalgams of vaudeville style and story film, these anarchistic comedies are 'neither fully contained within the classical Hollywood cinema nor fully free of its norms' (Jenkins 1992: 24). They represent instead:

> a succession of uneasy compromises, painstakingly negotiated during the production process, between two competing aesthetic systems, one governed by a demand for character consistency, causal logic, and narrative coherence, the other by an emphasis upon performance, affective immediacy and atomistic spectacle.
>
> (Jenkins 1992: 24)

To appreciate such films, and to understand them historically, Jenkins insists that 'we need to think about comedy atomistically, as a loosely linked succession of comic "bits". That the parts are more satisfying than the whole may only be a criticism if we do not like the parts' (Jenkins 1992: 5). Those critics of screen comedy who privilege a classical or 'organic' model of narrative, one that prioritizes coherence and unification as evaluative criteria, can only read such heterogeneity as a sign of ineptitude. Jenkins argues instead that the anarchistic films are fascinating precisely because they combine two opposing paradigms.[16] By incorporating the vaudeville aesthetic, anarchistic screen comedy challenges the assimilationist trajectory of classical narrative. This process, moreover, has ideological as well as formal consequences. The films of the early sound era exemplify a counter-current to the model Seidman proposes for comedian comedy because they 'often celebrate the collapse of social order and the liberation of the creativity and impulsiveness of their protagonist'.[17] Seidman, by contrast, implicitly frames comedian comedy as a conservative genre because it:

displaces narrative conflict from a social sphere into the psychic sphere, seeing comic misconduct as an outward manifestation of personality conflict, an aberration from social and textual norms. While acknowledging our pleasure in the comedian's disruptiveness, Seidman suggests that narrative resolutions contain these comic transgressions and pull the characters back into the mainstream; the emotional 'risk' posed by comic transgression is too intense to be left unresolved. Satisfactory resolution can be achieved in only two ways: (1) the 'cure' and assimilation of the comic figure into society or (2) the comic figure's rejection from society.

(Jenkins 1992: 235–6)

They may both regard comedian comedy as dealing with the individual's ambivalent relationship to social and cultural norms, but Seidman and Jenkins have divergent interpretations of what is at stake in the process. For Seidman, the comedian character ultimately faces a critical choice between subordinating his eccentricity through social integration, or preserving his eccentricity and thereby risking social exclusion. Each option privileges the determining role of social norms. For Jenkins, however, early sound comedy is driven by disintegrative rather than integrative impulses. 'Reduced to its simplest outline,' he maintains, 'anarchistic comedy explores the relationship of the "natural", uninhibited individual to the rigidifying social order, of creative impulses to encrusted habit and conventional modes of thought' (Jenkins 1992: 221). Besides celebrating the unshackling of individual creative impulses, anarchistic comedy literally gives voice to repressed cultural energies. In *Monkey Business*, for example, the Marx Brothers are cast as insurrectionist lower class immigrants who assault the orderly WASP hierarchies they encounter on board ship and in the USA. These disorderly figures are agents of otherness and difference who challenge hierarchies, not simply by overturning them but by disorientating the codes of language, logic and custom that structure them.

Entertaining others

The dominant laughter of the early 1930s was undoubtedly the belly laugh, an intense eruption that shook the entire body, an anarchic laughter that challenged the power of institutions to exercise emotional and social constraint upon individual spontaneity, a nonsensical laughter that was meaningful precisely in the way it transcended narrative meaning. Perhaps most important, it was a popular laughter, which entertained without pretenses of moral education or social reform.

(Jenkins 1992: 284)

In reading anarchistic comedy as a form that celebrates insurrectionist energies, Jenkins draws explicitly on the work of literary theorist Mikhail Bakhtin. Whether or not their narratives ultimately promote the comic outsider's social integration, comedian comedies profile alternative modes of thinking about relations between individuals and the social order. Through its assaults upon norms and hierarchies, its identification with the 'lower' social orders and its gross physicality, Hollywood comedian comedy reveals its kinship with the mode of popular cultural practice that Bakhtin has identified as the carnivalesque.[18] The carnival festivities of Medieval Europe provided a dynamic form of popular expression that reversed the prevailing social hierarchy to allow, albeit in a contained and localized manner, both the imaginative overthrow of institutional power structures and the ascendancy of the popular body (Bakhtin 1984: 18–21). For Bakhtin, carnival

> celebrated temporary liberation from the prevailing truth and from the established order; it marked the suspension of all hierarchical rank, privileges, norms, and prohibitions. Carnival was the true feast of time, the feast of becoming, change and renewal. It was hostile to all that was immortalized and completed.
>
> (Bakhtin 1984: 10)

Bakhtin coins the term 'grotesque realism' to describe the distinctive aesthetic regime of the Medieval carnival, an aesthetic characterized by 'degradation, that is, the lowering of all that is high, spiritual, ideal, abstract; it is a transfer to the material level, to the sphere of earth and body in their indissoluble unity' (Bakhtin 1984: 19–20). Through its peculiar combination of crudity and utopianism, grotesque realism unshackles the unruly body from the discipline of acculturation. Releasing the lower bodily stratum (belly, genitals, anus) from its subjection to the intellect and the spirit, the carnivalesque parades bodies of exaggerated proportions, unquenchable sensuality and revolting assertiveness (Bakhtin 1984: 21). Carnival festivity prioritizes formlessness over fixity, process over position and 'becoming' over 'being'. It not only liberates the otherness of the human body but also highlights new possibilities for the social body by stressing principles of cooperation, collectivity and community. Thus Bakhtin argues that in carnival culture:

> the bodily element is deeply positive. It is presented not in a private, egotistic form, severed from the other spheres of life, but as something universal, representing all the people. . . . [T]he body and bodily life have here a cosmic and at the same time an all-people's character; this is not the body and its physiology in the modern sense of these words, because it is not individualized. The material bodily principle is contained not in the biological individual, not in the bourgeois ego, but in the people, a people who are continually growing and renewed. This is why all that is bodily becomes grandiose, exaggerated, immeasurable.
>
> This exaggeration has a positive, assertive character. The leading themes of these images of bodily life are fertility, growth, and a brimming-over of abundance. . . . [T]he grotesque body is not separated from the rest of the world. It is not a closed, completed unit; it is unfinished, outgrows itself, transgresses its own limits.
>
> (Ibid.: 19, 26)

Bakhtin insists, however, that his model of the carnivalesque applies to a historically specific cultural and social regime that shares little in common with the contemporary Western world.[19] The medieval carnival was a participatory festival that was shaped directly by collective action: the people literally *were* the entertainment. By contrast, contemporary entertainment forms such as vaudeville, film, radio and television enforce a distinction between the professionalized performer and the generalized audience. Nonetheless, the grotesque body continues to persist as a potent signifier of the ambivalent relations between individuals and the social order, even if the contexts of commercial and technogically mediated popular culture charge it with distinctive meanings (Bakhtin 1984: 33–52, Jenkins 1992: 223). The most obvious manner in which the Hollywood comedian film reconfigures the carnivalesque process lies in the way it individuates the unruly energies of the crowd in the figure of the comedian. As an embodiment of that which is socially excessive or excluded, the comedian serves as both emissary of and scapegoat for counter-cultural impulses. Thrown into conflict with the social codifications of gender and sexuality, the body and identity, class and ethnicity, comedians inspire a disorderly rewriting of normative protocols.

Across its history the comedian film has provided Hollywood with its principal conduit for low comedy, demonstrating a persistent and fundamental affiliation with those who are socially marginalized or repressed. The comedian film operates not merely as a show-case for the display of the performer's talents but also as a generic platform for enunciating resistant identities – hence the prominence of such liminal figures as immigrants (the Marx Brothers), tramps (Chaplin), psychological misfits (Danny Kaye, Jerry Lewis) and slackers (Adam Sandler). By casting comedians as eccentric individuals who are in conflict with the demands of living by the rules, the films set up numerous opportunities for them to disrupt conventional procedures regulating activities such as work, communication, gender and sexuality. Defined as a misfit or outsider, the comedian figure resists the pressure of social conformity and transforms a context that initially demeans or represses them into a show-case for their distinctive individualism (perceived as such by the film spectator, if not necessarily by the characters inhabiting the fictional universe).

Focusing upon the play between disruption and containment or difference and conformism, the Bakhtinian approach permits an interrogation of the slippery ideological operations of comedian comedy. As Jenkins' work illustrates, such processes need to be considered not within some generalized model of the comedian film but within particular historical articulations (through the activities of particular comedians, cycles or periods). Moreover, the carnivalesque impulse can actually operate in quite distinct yet by no means mutually exclusive registers:

1   It can manifest itself through a resistance to integrative norms of Hollywood narrative. The anarchistic films, for example, reveal the persistent intrusion of the vaudeville aesthetic into Hollywood's standardized fictional paradigm. Other forms of comedian comedy similarly overturn the dominance of narrative in favour of gag logic or entertainment attractions, a good example being the series of self-reflexive *Road to . . .* films starring Bob Hope and Bing Crosby.

2   The carnivalesque can also coordinate the logic of the narrative itself. Examples of this tendency include such films as the 1954 Dean Martin and Jerry Lewis vehicle *Living it Up* (in which two hicks from a sleepy backwater outfox the city slickers of New York) and Adam Sandler's 1996 comedy *Happy Gilmore* (whose eponymous blue-collar hero invades and triumphs over an elite golfing establishment).[20] The Marx Brothers films *Monkey Business* and *A Night at the Opera* likewise present carnivalesque narratives that celebrate the ascendancy of underdogs and outsiders over the exclusionary forces of social order.

3   A third expression of the carnivalesque worth noting here involves the way comedians often incarnate an exaggerated physicality that resembles Bakhtin's concept of the grotesque body. Performers as diverse as Laurel and Hardy, W.C. Fields, Mae West, the Marx Brothers, Jerry Lewis and Jim Carrey have all adopted extremely stylized modes of self-presentation that underscore their resistance to accommodation within fiction and verisimilitude. Identifying the comedian as someone who clearly does not fit within the 'straight' diegetic universe, the carnivalesque body raises both social and aesthetic issues. Besides foregrounding the comedian *figure's* disjuncture from or resistance to everyday social codes,

THE LIBRARY
GUILDFORD COLLEGE
of Further and Higher Education

bodily exaggeration is also a sign of the comic *performer's* creative development of a trademark style (for example, the distinctive walks and costumes of Chaplin or Groucho Marx).

The comic performers who have worked in Hollywood cinema have generated multiple articulations and inflexions of the grotesque body. However, there remains a strong inter-relationship between the comic spectacle of physical otherness and forms of social or cultural otherness that are defined through class, ethnicity, race or gender. Implicitly or explicitly concerned with class identities and class relations, the carnivalesque presents a peculiar compound of crudity and utopianism. The freakish comedians showcased by the silver screen are interlopers into both straight universes and the orderly procedures of the Hollywood film. Such films certainly problematize Seidman's assimilationist model of comedian comedy because they detail the comic outsider's resistance to, and democratization of, an exclusionary and repressive social world.

Whether or not they directly engage or agree with Bakhtin, many of the contributions to this volume share his concern with exploring the cultural logics of popular festivity. William Paul's explicitly Bakhtinian reading of Chaplin's *City Lights* (1931) considers how vulgar comedy flaunts problems of the body and class that tend to be marginalized in traditional discussions of the film as a genteel masterpiece. Mark Winokur examines how the Marx brothers' comedy of social dissolution is driven by aspirations towards an alternatively imagined community, one that is formed apart from and in opposition to mainstream social identity. Kathleen Rowe explores how Mae West operates as a carnivalesque 'unruly woman' who mobilizes an ironic persona and comic style to challenge the social authority of the male gaze. Patricia Mellencamp is similarly concerned with the interplay between female unruliness and domestication in the televisual comedy of Lucille Ball.

Gender issues are also to the fore in Joanna Rapf's chapter, which focuses upon the way Jerry Lewis's grotesque comedy deforms and disarms the protocols of patriarchal masculinity. Steven Cohan discerns a similar process of carnivalesque reorientation in the homosocial hi-jinks of 1940s entertainment team Bob Hope and Bing Crosby, whose phenomenally successful comedies negotiate wartime challenges to masculinity. Bambi Haggins concentrates on the troubled relations between comedy and race, investigating the problems African American comedians of the post Civil Rights era have faced in their passage to Hollywood mainstream. Philip Drake is concerned less with questions of representation than with problems in interpreting performance, but his chapter still grapples with a group of films – the contemporary 'dumb comedies' of Jim Carrey – that have been consistently denigrated by bourgeois cultural authorities as pandering to the baser instincts of lower class audiences. Like most of the best work on comedian comedy produced over the past two decades, Drake's chapter explicitly aims to move beyond the narrow cultural prejudices that have impaired the conceptualization of performative comedy. In the way that it extends the work of Seidman, Jenkins and other writers on film comedy, Drake's chapter provides an especially fitting conclusion to this critical anthology and the variety of formal, historical and ideological approaches it presents.

Notes

1 The past two decades have witnessed a veritable explosion of scholarly articles, monographs and anthologies devoted to film comedy, including Seidman 1981, Palmer 1987, Babington and Evans 1989, Neale and Krutnik 1990, Horton 1991, Jenkins 1992, Paul 1994, Sikov 1994, Karnick and Jenkins 1995, Rowe 1995, Winokur 1996, Dale 2000, Matthews 2000, Rickman 2001, Beach 2002, King 2002.

2 Although this Reader endeavours to broaden debates on the comedian film by stressing the importance of non-canonical texts, contexts and arguments, it nonetheless makes extensive use of films that are likely to be easily obtainable (hence the focus on the Marx Brothers in Part 3 rather than more obscure contemporaries such as Clark and McCullough).

3 Posted to 'The Official Jerry Lewis Threaded Discussion Forum', *The Official Jerry Lewis Comedy Museum and Store* by Joe548, 23 April 2000 <http://www.jerrylewiscomedy.com>. Joe548 prefers the more fan-friendly opus by James Neibaur and Ted Okuda (1995) (who actually consulted Joe548 in the research), because 'It's easy reading, informative and very understandable. I use it as a reference all the time. It is my bible!' (posted on 26 May 2000).

4 Some notable antecedents that considered the work of gag in the comedian film were Charles Barr's 1967 monograph on Laurel and Hardy, Raymond Durgnat's idiosyncratic 1969 book *The Crazy Mirror* and Sylvain du Pasquier's 1970 article 'Les gags de Buster Keaton'.

5 Agee was a columnist for the *Nation*, a book and film reviewer for *Time* magazine, poet, novelist (whose *A Death in the Family* received a posthumous Pulitzer prize in 1957) and screenwriter (*The African Queen* (1951), *The Night of the Hunter* (1955)).

6 Weis, Elizabeth and John Belton (eds.) (1985): *Film Sound: Theory and Practice*, New York: Columbia University Press; 75.

7 Agee's conception of the impact of the talkie upon cinematic art resembles Rudolf Arnheim's position in the latter's 1938 essay 'A New Lacoön: Artistic Composites and the Talking Film'. Arguing, like Agee, that the silent film became an art form precisely because of the absence of speech, Arnheim asserts that film 'cannot become the servant of speech without giving up its own self' (Weis and Belton 1985: 114).

8 Adam Reilly notes that most of the Lonesome Luke shorts which Lloyd made between 1915 and 1917 'have only the thinnest plot line. They contain much kinetic, physical humour, like kicking in the seat of the pants, conking over the head, and being hit by traffic' (Reilly 1978: 17). In his subsequent work, Lloyd established a comic persona modelled upon Douglas Fairbanks' go-getting adventurers and also combined slapstick with a more plausible, character-oriented comedy that derived from the popular stage (Borger 1978: 185, Everson 1978: 168–70).

9 To be fair, Kerr acknowledges the degree to which the artistic achievements of the period were also impelled by economic considerations. With the standardization of feature-length narrative as Hollywood's dominant product in the mid-1910s, the short comedy film was rendered a subsidiary component of cinema programmes. Although the short films of certain comedians could actually prove a bigger attraction than the feature-length narratives they accompanied, film rental policies were largely biased in favour of longer movies. By extending their films to feature length, the comic auteurs could thus secure a more equitable share of the box-office pie (Kerr 1975: 160–1).

10 Critical work that directly addressed Seidman's account of the comedian film includes Krutnik 1984, 1995b, Jenkins 1986, Krämer 1989.

11   Like Seidman's book, Jenkins' study had its origins in doctoral research – it helped earn him a Ph.D. award from the University of Wisconsin, Madison.

12   Barrios, Richard (1995): *A Song in the Dark: the Birth of the Musical Film*, New York: Oxford University Press; 26. The highlight of the show was a short film in which Al Jolson gave an energetic performance of three of his most popular hits – a year before his appearance in *The Jazz Singer* propelled the Hollywood sound film into mainstream acceptance, opening the way for a torrent of talking and singing pictures (ibid.: 27).

13   As Jenkins points out, Hollywood cinema entered the sound era by appealing fervently to 'Broadwayness' in the drive to build urban audiences (Jenkins 1992: 160).

14   Nolan, Frederick (1994): *Lorenz Hart: A Poet on Broadway*, New York: Oxford University Press; 195.

15   Although the Marx Brothers entertainment team exemplifies the style of anarchistic comedy he discusses, Jenkins distances himself from the exuberant excesses of some of their highbrow enthusiasts. Instead of reading their comedy either as an expression of the performers' exceptional personalities (as do Clifton Fadiman and John Grierson) or as subversive assaults upon the order of things (as do Raymond Durgnat, Salvador Dali and Antonin Artaud), he takes pains to outline the broader entertainment context that germinated the Marx Brothers' style of comic entertainment (Jenkins 1992: 7–8).

16   Within the anarchistic comedies an 'aesthetic based on heterogeneity, affective immediacy, and performance confronted one that had long placed primary emphasis upon causality and consistency, closure and cohesiveness' (Jenkins 1992: 278). Jenkins also discusses a contrasting cycle of 1930s performer-centred comedy with a 'more conservative thematic structure' that stressed the importance of social integration (Jenkins 1992: 282). These 'affirmative comedies' – which include the screen vehicles of Joe E. Brown, one of the top box-office stars of the period – operate more closely within the terms of Seidman's model. Although he devotes special attention to anarchistic comedy, Jenkins also discusses several other contemporary models for organizing the presentation of comic performance (such as the revue film, the show-case film and the comic romance (Jenkins 1992: 132–44). Following on from Jenkins' categories, Tino Balio also notes the presence in the early 1930s of sophisticated comedies (such as *Trouble in Paradise* (1932)) that show-cased glamorous female stars and sentimental or folksy comedies (such as those Marie Dressler made for MGM, or Will Rogers and Shirley Temple starred in at Fox) (Balio 1995: 256–80).

17   This line from Jenkins' Ph.D. is quoted in Balio 1995: 263.

18   Bakhtin's work on carnival has influenced numerous writers on film comedy, including William Paul (1994), Kathleen Rowe (1995) and many of the contributors to *Comedy/Cinema/Theory*, edited by Andrew Horton (1991). This account of the carnivalesque receives more extensive treatment in Krutnik 2000.

19   '[T]he depth, variety and power of separate grotesque themes can be understood only within the unity of folk and carnival spirit. If examined outside of this unity, they become one-sided, flat, and stripped of their rich content' (Bakhtin 1984: 51–2).

20   *Living it Up* is examined closely in Johnson (1981), while *Happy Gilmore* is discussed in Krutnik (2003).

PART ONE

GENRE, NARRATIVE AND PERFORMANCE

Introduction

The opening section of this Reader is devoted to Steve Seidman's model of comedian comedy.
The first essay has been specially adapted for this volume from Seidman's (1981) book *Comedian
Comedy: A Tradition in Hollywood Film*, which is discussed at length in the General Introduction.
This particular selection is an adaptation of Seidman's initial chapter, 'Extrafictional Features of
Comedian Comedy', in which he explores how the comedian film operates as a 'stylistic
countercurrent to the narrative hermeticism' of classical Hollywood cinema. He argues that by
seeking to approximate the interactive dynamic of such show business forms as vaudeville,
cabaret, and radio and television variety shows, the comedian film uses various techniques that
work against the grain of classical narrative's stylistic self-effacement. These techniques include:
direct address to the spectator (through camera looks or verbal address); an overt acknowledgement of the iconicity of the performer as a performer; and a deconstructive approach to
fictional protocols and to the materiality of the film. Where established models for theorizing
screen performance tend to privilege the 'unaware actor' of the traditional fiction film, Seidman
highlights the degree to which popular cinema is also fed by alternative aesthetic paradigms. Like
the Hollywood musical, comedian comedy not only flaunts performative specialities but also self-
consciously addresses its very status as entertainment spectacle. In his exploration of how the
comedian film seeks to build a special relationship between the comic performer and the
audience, Seidman glides effortlessly through an impressive array of performers from the 1910s
to the 1920s (including Chaplin, Keaton, Langdon, Fatty Arbuckle, Mabel Normand, W.C. Fields,
Laurel and Hardy, the Marx Brothers, Mae West, Eddie Cantor, the Ritz Brothers, Abbott and
Costello, the Three Stooges, Jack Benny, Bob Hope and Bing Crosby, Danny Kaye, Martin and
Lewis, Mel Brooks and Woody Allen).

For Peter Krämer, the very multiplicity of Seidman's examples is a problem because it
downplays the differences that exist between these comedians and the contexts within which they
worked. Although Krämer welcomes aspects of what he terms 'the Seidman-Krutnik model', he
argues that it requires testing and redefinition. Krämer is particularly concerned here with ways
of conceptualizing the forms of interaction between fictional representation and comic
performance. He argues that Seidman's work proceeds through broad generalizations about
stylistic and fictional devices derived from an array of films from a range of periods. More work

needs to be done, he suggests, in testing Seidman's hypotheses in relation to particular instances of comic performance and narrative. I realize that I am doing Krämer a great disservice here by eliminating most of his painstaking analysis of Buster Keaton's short film *The Blacksmith* (1922), but my aim is to focus attention on the general principles of his argument in relation to Seidman's work.

Krämer's account of *The Blacksmith* suggests that although Seidman's model attributes comic effects to the distance inscribed between performer and character, the reverse is true for most of this film. *The Blacksmith* may start out with a self-conscious parody of Henry Wadsworth Longfellow's well-known poem 'The Village Blacksmith', but it subsequently forsakes such heightened narrational awareness to immerse the spectator in a self-consistent fictional world. The fictional regime does not necessarily obey the rules of the real world – it permits, for example, such magical deviations as a hyper-strong magnet – but it is governed by its own logical coherence. Comedy results not from Keaton's intrusion into this world as a performer but from the comic antics of the character he plays, namely a blacksmith's assistant. For example, Krämer notes the recurrence of two particular gag strategies: first, comic effects deriving from the contrast between intention and resulting action (as when the attempt to repair a car ends with its destruction); second, the contrast between the means and the ends in carrying out such actions (for example, repairing a watch with the blacksmith's tools) (Krämer 1989: 108). Keaton's performance, then, is not directed *against* the fictional world but *within* it, for the failures of the blacksmith's assistant operate simultaneously as a successful performance by Buster (which is generated via props, other characters and the narrative situation). Furthermore, rather than existing at the expense of narrative, comic incidents can make a semantic contribution to it at various levels.

Krämer shows clearly that this particular film, and perhaps much of Keaton's work, does not necessarily exemplify Seidman's argument about the general relations sustained between performance and narrative in comedian comedy. Nevertheless, Krämer aims not to demolish Seidman's work but to extend and refine it. As Krämer shows, rather than being characterized by one monolithic model, the comedian film may make use of various frameworks for organizing performance, gags and narrative.

1

Performance, Enunciation and Self-reference in Hollywood Comedian Comedy

STEVE SEIDMAN

This chapter will examine certain extrafictional features of comedian comedy. By extra-fictional, I mean anything that interrupts the smooth exposition of a fictional universe, or anything that intrudes upon the depiction of a 'real' fictional universe to give the sense that 'it's only a movie'. By providing relevant examples from various films I will demonstrate that comedian comedy grants the comedian a particular narrational stance that allows the articulation of these features. The examination will proceed by first suggesting that the films adapted those aspects of show business performance that acknowledged the presence of the audience. As such, the show business origins of the comedian may be seen as an influential factor in the manifestation of extrafictional features. The show business influence on film not only relates to performance per se, but also extends to the pre-filmic cultural reputation of the comedian. The preservation of that reputation will also be considered in this discussion of show business performance and film. I will then propose two further levels by which to consider the comedian's narrational stance in relation to extrafictional features: enunciation and self-reference. Finally, I will posit that these extrafictional features constitute a particular approach to narrative, one that can be seen as a counter-tendency to the general narrative approach taken by the dominant mode of the Hollywood feature film, the so-called 'classical' cinema.

Performance

Show business performing traditions have rarely been examined in terms of their possible influence on the formation of film narrative. Discussions of acting style in film have tended to situate it within overall signifying practice as one of a number of codes that facilitate smooth narrative exposition: for example, the kind of acting that denies the presence of the spectating subject and furthers the depiction of a 'real' fictional universe. Discussions of this nature are typified by the work of theorists such as V.I. Pudovkin and André Bazin, both of whom were concerned with arguing for the unique properties of film. They sought to differentiate film from theatre, extending this concern to considerations of acting as well. Pudovkin asserted, for example, that one crucial difference is that 'the direct consciousness in the actor of the multiple spectator is *completely* absent in the cinema' [italics added].[1] Bazin expanded upon Pudovkin's assertion by arguing that in theatre the actor oriented his performance towards the spectator, and because of this theatre demanded at least implicit participation from audiences. But Bazin claimed that: 'The opposite is true in the cinema. Alone hidden in a dark room we watch through half-open blinds a spectacle that is *unaware of our existence* and which is part of the universe [italics added].'[2]

One can accept these characterizations about the basic lack of reciprocity between actor and spectator in cinema insofar as they are concerned with the function of acting as it relates to the depiction of a 'real' fictional universe. The majority of actors and actresses in film represent the kind of acting discussed by Pudovkin and Bazin. They were trained in legitimate theatre, or were at least trained in its major conventions, especially that of 'becoming' another character within the context of a coherent, contoured fictional situation. In the theatre, actors and actresses did not explicitly comment on their presence to the audience until the 'curtain call', or until the fictional situation had ended. These performers were part of a classical tradition of acting – developed largely in the nineteenth-century melodramatic theatre – which respected the contours of the fiction.[3] In Greek comedies (particularly in the plays of Aristophanes) and later in Shakespeare's works, actors intruded upon fictional realism by conversing with the audience and even the stage-hands. But the nineteenth-century melodramatic theatre exerted the primary influence on narrative cinema, a kind of theatre based entirely on fictional realism.

Vaudeville, which also developed during the nineteenth century, involved a very different mode of performance. In vaudeville, and the various show business forms that grew out of it, the success of performers was dependent on first establishing a direct rapport with the audience, then continuing to relate to that audience – much in the manner of oratory. While the success of the actor or actress in nineteenth-century theatre was predicated on the performer's becoming a 'he' or a 'she', the performer's success in vaudeville and its descendants was contingent on presenting the 'I', exhibiting the self in such a way as to induce an immediate response (laughter, applause, singing along) from the audience. Moreover, many vaudeville performers integrated the audience directly into their acts. For example, the 1880s comedy team of Clooney and Ryan featured Clooney singing while Ryan, who accompanied him on the clarinet, mugged at the audience and directed his comments about Clooney's voice towards the audience.[4] Dave Marion, a 1912 vaudevillian, often jumped into the aisles and sang directly to the audience, as did Al Jolson during the 1920s.[5]

Interestingly enough, it was Bazin who noted the importance of this tradition in film:

> The greater part of French and American comedians come from the music hall or from boulevard theater. One need only look at Max Linder to see how much he owes to his theatrical experience. Like most comics of his time he plays directly to the audience, winks at them and calls on them to witness his embarrassment, and does not shrink from asides. As for Charlie Chaplin, apart from his indebtedness to the English school of mime, it is clear that his art consists in perfecting, thanks to the cinema, his skill as a music-hall comic.[6]

Part of Chaplin's music-hall 'skill' was the manner in which he ingratiated himself with his audience by bowing or smiling. It was this awareness of the spectator that Chaplin, like other vaudevillians and their show business descendants, brought to film. While direct reciprocity is of course impossible in the cinema, these comedians were nevertheless featured in films built upon the same kind of awareness of the spectator as existed in their stage performances.

Bazin's remarks about the unaware actor are relevant to most of the major film stars of the past sixty-five years, including Douglas Fairbanks, Sr., Carole Lombard, Joel McCrae, Claudette Colbert, Gary Cooper, James Stewart, Katharine Hepburn, Henry Fonda, Spencer Tracy, Ginger Rogers, Humphrey Bogart, Clark Gable, Rosalind Russell, John Wayne, Cary Grant, Doris Day and Jack Lemmon. Audiences perceived these actors and actresses in a certain way, a perception derived in part from the theatrical acting tradition they represented. Many of these performers worked in legitimate theatre (though few of them enjoyed success in it), but all of them were basically 'created' by the movies and were recognizable to audiences as such. They may be seen as filmically generated icons – by which I mean they had a particular cultural function that was correlatable to an identifiable world of filmic codes. They were not expected to conform to pre-filmic cultural reputations, other than a general one stemming from theatrical tradition – that is, to be able to play a range of roles. This expectation was coupled with the accepted practice of film acting that the actor should maintain individual personality traits from one role to the next.

Those who attended films frequently knew what these performers represented since their iconicity barely fluctuated from film role to film role. In short, these actors and actresses were eminently adaptable to various genre forms – they were the prime inhabitants of a total cinematic universe. They moved back and forth from situation comedies[7] to melodramas to action films, and audiences responded to them regardless of the type of film in which they appeared. For example, James Stewart's popularity during the 1940s rested on his appearances in situation comedies such as The Philadelphia Story (1940), but during the 1950s he maintained his position among the top ten box office stars by appearing in westerns such as The Naked Spur (1953) and Night Passage (1957).

Conversely, the iconicity of show business performers was generated pre-filmically, by what they had done in other media. Although the end of vaudeville is usually situated around 1928, when there were 200 full-week acts as opposed to 20,000 in 1906,[8] the tradition of performing it spawned was elaborated by such other show business media as radio, supper clubs, cabarets, resort hotels, television variety programmes and, of course, film. During the late 1920s and early 1930s American radio featured many vaudeville performers and enabled them to become well known after vaudeville had died. Nightclubs developed from vaudeville theatres as early as 1907, when a vaudeville agent named Jack Levy convinced several New York restaurant owners to feature vaudeville acts after show hours. In 1921 the Club Deauville on East 59th Street in Manhattan became the first establishment to be specifically advertised as a nightclub, although the Prohibition period that ensued saw supplanting of nightclubs by speakeasies. Cabaret developed during the 1920s in hotels, cafes, saloons or anywhere that served alcohol and featured entertainment as an extra attraction.

In short, some comedians were able to attain an iconic function before they appeared in front of a movie camera because of the exposure they received in vaudeville and the show business forms that grew out of it. Again, radio was a prime factor in this, insofar as the popular programmes of such former vaudevillians as Eddie Cantor, Jack Benny and Bob Hope made them 'guests' in the homes of millions of listeners. While vaudeville had been accessible to audiences who lived near circuit theatres, radio transcended such provincialism to allow increased accessibility to the performing style vaudeville generated. These comedians were attractive propositions to Hollywood not just because of their performing talents but also because of their instant identifiability. The essence of the comedian's cultural iconicity stemmed from the way he had established close contact with audiences in other show business forms. In film, the clearest manifestation of direct contact was the acknowledgement of the audience through devices such as looking and bowing at the camera and, with the advent of sound, talking to the camera.

The camera look, of course, was the functional equivalent of the vaudeville 'aside'. It is a prominent device in many of Chaplin's shorts, including *Making a Living* (1914), his very first. In *Pool Sharks* (1915) W.C. Fields glances and smiles at the camera after he hits his rival in the eye with a billiard ball. At the beginning of *Fatty and Mabel Adrift* (1916), a cross-cutting sequence shows Fatty Arbuckle and Mabel Normand within large cut-out hearts, alternating between looking at each other and looking at the camera. At the end of the film, the pair share the same heart, and after they snuggle up to each other and swoon, they look at the camera. Unlike *Making a Living* and *Pool Sharks*, there are no camera looks during the fictional situation of *Fatty and Mabel Adrift* but its utility as a device is indicated by its function in these bracketing scenes – where Fatty and Mabel use it to remove themselves from the fiction, while still showing the audience that they are both smitten by 'young love'.

The films of Laurel and Hardy are permeated by camera looks; even with the advent of sound, the pair retained the device rather than speak to the camera. Charles Barr suggests that it was Hardy who looked at the camera most frequently, noting that: 'Chaplin in his early films uses the camera look delicately, usually to express mute appeal when thwarted, or apprehension, as do other comedians including even Stan [Laurel], but no one has used the technique with such emphasis (frequent close-ups) or with such range of expression as Ollie.'[9] Barr then suggests that Hardy's camera looks may be categorized as follows: quizzical, apprehensive, conspiratorial and embarrassed. He does not categorize Laurel's camera looks, though they could be defined in much the same manner. In *Sailors Beware* (1927), as Laurel is getting beaten in a crap game with a baby, he looks at the camera with alternating expressions of surprise, dejection and disgust. The spectator here possesses information that Laurel does not – that the 'baby' is really a midget who is playing with loaded dice. Hardy's camera looks are typified by one that he gives in *Sons of the Desert* (1933), after Laurel impulsively and briefly converses like a well-educated scholar instead of the semi-moron he has been throughout the film. Hardy reacts to Laurel's sudden intelligence by staring at the camera in astonishment.

Bob Hope is an example of a comedian who did not appear in silent films but who employed camera looks frequently. When Hope is kissed by Dorothy Lamour at the end of *They Got Me Covered* (1943) he stares at the camera, then rolls his eyes lustfully. In *Road to Utopia* (1945) Hope leers at the camera while Lamour sings to him: 'You wouldn't dare be too bold, would you? . . . than to take advantage of me, would you?' In *Road to Bali* (1952) Bing Crosby asks Hope to explain how he escaped from the deadly squid and got out of his diving suit; Hope begins an explanation, then looks at the camera and hesitates. He nods towards the camera, then takes Crosby to the other end of the boat in the background of the frame. There, he gesticulates wildly, but no dialogue is heard. Crosby walks back to the foreground, then silently shrugs at the camera.

With the advent of sound, direct verbal address to the camera became the dominant way of acknowledging the spectator's presence. Although Laurel and Hardy continued to rely on the camera look in their sound films, Chaplin opted for direct address in *The Great Dictator* (1940), his first film with spoken dialogue. At the end of the film, the Jewish Barber's impassioned speech for peace and democracy alternates between his brief glances at the assembled crowd and his direct looks into the camera. While the Barber is allowed to give the speech because he is disguised as the dictator Hynkel (Chaplin's other role in the film), and thus mistaken for him, he is generally framed in extreme close-ups that keep Hynkel's uniform out of the frame (he also no longer wears the dictator's hat). Moreover, the depth and passion of the speech are clearly beyond the verbal capabilities of the shy Barber, who shares many of the same qualities with Chaplin's silent Tramp. Both the framing and the content of the monologue thus collapse the film's fictional situation, serving instead to emphasize that it is Chaplin himself who is speaking to the spectator.

Comedians such as Mae West and W.C. Fields who were known for their verbal dexterity frequently uttered asides, but rarely to the camera. Groucho Marx was perhaps the prime exponent of direct address during the 1930s. In *Cocoanuts* (1929), one of the first sound comedies, Groucho frequently steps out of character to offer sarcastic remarks to the camera about the fictional situation and the other characters. During the scene in *Horse Feathers* (1932) in which several characters continually enter, then exit, Connie's room, Groucho gets up from the couch, walks to the foreground, and says to the camera, 'I've got to stay here. But there's no reason why you folks shouldn't go into the lobby until this thing blows over.' Groucho then returns to the couch – and the fictional situation – and none of the characters acknowledge his remark to the camera. Groucho's address to the camera also extended to reflections about his own 'jokes'. In *Animal Crackers* (1930), for example, he utters a wisecrack, then faces the camera and says, 'Well, all the jokes can't be good. You have to expect that once in a while.' In *Go West* (1940) Groucho stuffs a handkerchief in a villain's mouth and says to the camera, 'You know, this is the best gag in the picture.'

During the 1940s Bob Hope was the main practitioner of direct verbal address. Like his eye-rolling leers at the camera, his comments often served to point up his sexual intentions. As Hope and Trina kiss at the end of *Where There's Life* (1947), the camera moves from medium long shot to medium close-up; Hope looks at the camera moving towards him, then says, 'Well, go home, you've seen it all.' Similarly, as Hope and Sal are walking arm-in-arm towards the background in *Road to Utopia*, Hope turns and looks behind at the camera following them, then continues walking. When Hope stops again, he turns to the camera and says, 'Aw come on folks, quit following us, will ya?' In *Road to Bali* Hope asks a bare-chested native boy if everyone on the island dresses in the same way; the boy replies in the affirmative, which causes Hope to ask Crosby leeringly, 'Do you suppose . . . ?' When Crosby replies, 'Not a chance', Hope turns to the camera and says, 'Stick around, folks, he could be wrong, you know.' In the same film, Hope also addresses the camera in a way that echoes Groucho's advice to the 'folks' in *Horse Feathers*: when Crosby goes on deck to romance Princess Lala, Hope looks at the camera and suggests: 'He's going to sing, folks; now's the time to go outside and get the popcorn.'

The films of Dean Martin and Jerry Lewis, the team who succeeded Hope and Crosby, frequently acknowledged their status as iconic entertainers. At the end of *Pardners* (1956), for example, Martin and Lewis shoot 'The End' title away from the screen with their six-guns and then talk to the camera, thanking the audience for making them popular box office stars. 'We hope you keep coming to see us because we like seeing you,' Lewis says. The comedians here refer to each other as 'Dean' and 'Jer' rather than the names of their fictional characters.

More recently, Woody Allen's films maintained the device of direct address. In the first episode of *Everything You Always Wanted to Know About Sex But Were Afraid to Ask* (1972) Allen portrays a court jester in medieval England who frequently addresses the camera. As he tries to unlock the queen's chastity belt with a lance, he turns to the camera and says, 'This is what I call beaver shooting.' *Annie Hall* (1977) opens with Allen addressing the audience, discussing his philosophy of life and his affair with Annie. Allen often talks to the camera throughout the film, notably during a sequence in which Allen waits in a movie theatre lobby and becomes annoyed with a boorish man behind him in line. Allen looks at the camera and asks, 'What do you do when you're stuck in a movie line with a guy like this behind you?' Allen and the man then both step out of line and the man proceeds to defend himself by invoking the name of Marshall McLuhan and mentioning his own position as an instructor of mass media at Columbia University. Allen counters by pulling the real Marshall McLuhan from behind a sign in the lobby; McLuhan tells the man that he doesn't know what he's talking about. Allen then remarks to the camera, 'Boy, if real life were only like this!'

Exemplifying a visible characteristic that evolved from show business performing, such camera acknowledgements permit the building of a special relationship between comedian and film spectator. The camera looks of Bob Hope allow the spectator to see what the characters in the film do not: that Hope would like to 'take advantage' of Sal, and that his desires run counter both to his fictional behaviour and to the conventional norms of onscreen man/woman relationships allowed by film industry censorship and social mores. With regard to Laurel and Hardy, Barr's categories are reasonable but inconclusive, insofar as they do not account for the way the camera looks relate to the spectator. The camera looks of both men tend to underscore their helplessness in a world in which they are continually victimized. It is a world in which the pair is unable to explain certain phenomena (such as how a 'baby' could beat Laurel in a crap game, or how Laurel can suddenly speak in learned tones), but they nevertheless *do* know that there is a camera which records their actions, and that someone is watching them perform. The camera looks thus suggest an extrafictional intelligence while at the same time perpetuating the pair's fictional stupidity, since appeals to the camera can never be answered.

Groucho Marx's use of direct verbal address allows him to question both the fictional situation and his function as a performer who tells 'jokes'. Moreover, his ability to extricate himself from the fictional universe gives Groucho a degree of superiority not afforded to the other characters in the film, not even his brothers. Hope's spoken interdictions expose the voyeuristic drive of the spectator, objectified by primary identification with the camera. At moments when the possibility of consummated desire is suggested, Hope catches the spectator in the act of watching through the 'half-open blinds' that Bazin speaks of. The use of direct address at the end of *Pardners* indicates a refusal on the part of Martin and Lewis to accept that there is any difference between performing on the stage and performing in film ('we like seeing you'). By directing a contemporary slang expression ('beaver shooting') at the camera in *Everything . . . About Sex*, Allen indicates his position as a twentieth-century culture-bearer within a fictional universe of the past. Although Allen does not step out of character in *Annie Hall* to address the camera (since the use of direct address is one of a number of ways Allen's fictional character takes the spectator into his confidence), the technique nonetheless indicates the desirability of extending fictional bonds ('Boy, if real life were only like this!').

Camera acknowledgement also contributes to the assumption of a particular narrational stance by the comedian – as a fiction-maker who can assert a degree of control over the fictional situation. In *Road to Bali* Hope not only refuses to inform the spectator how he escaped from the squid, but by advising the spectator when to 'stick around' or to go out for popcorn he indicates his possession of inside information about how the narrative will turn out. When Mae West bows at the end of *Goin' to Town* (1935), the brim of her hat obscures the screen to produce the final fade-out; thus it is her physicality that brings the film to an end. In *Pardners* Martin and Lewis not only bring the fiction to a halt in the manner of Groucho and Hope, but they also establish their power over film materiality by stalling the film's end title – and, by extension, the end of the film.

These instances of camera acknowledgement clearly indicate that, contrary to Pudovkin, 'direct consciousness . . . of the multiple spectator' was far from absent in cinema, and was in fact incorporated into many films. Camera acknowledgement was just one device that the comedian employed to indicate his awareness of the audience. Reference to the pre-filmic performing career was another. Just as, say, Sonja Henie played an ice-skater or Esther Williams portrayed a swimmer, comedians drew on their pre-filmic cultural reputations by portraying characters who were 'like' the show business performers they began their careers as. While it was chiefly through the rise of mass media that comedians attained vast cultural recognizability,[10] certain vaudeville performers who made the transition to silent film – particularly Keaton and Fields – were known to audiences who frequented the vaudeville circuits in urban centres and large towns, and these performers integrated that familiarity into their silent films.[11] Even though these comedians may not have attained widespread renown prior to their film careers, the American public certainly was readily familiar with the performing conventions of vaudeville. Since the fledgling film industry sought the largest possible audience for its product, it attempted to duplicate vaudeville's already popular conventions and performing styles.

In films such as *Mabel's Married Life* (1914), *One A.M.* (1916) and *The Cure* (1916) Chaplin employed the drunk act he had perfected in vaudeville. Buster Keaton drew on the fame he earned in vaudeville as part of a comedy acrobat act, 'The Three Keatons', and his films are full of stunts built on his acrobatic skills. There are also references to vaudeville in such Keaton films as *The Playhouse* (1921) and *Steamboat Bill, Jr.* (1928). W.C. Fields was famous in vaudeville for his juggling and also for a pool-hall routine he would use throughout his film career, from as early as *Pool Sharks*. In the sound era, Mae West portrays a vaudeville entertainer in both *She Done Him Wrong* (1933) and *Belle of the Nineties* (1934), while Bob Hope plays a fictional radio personality in *The Cat and the Canary* (1939), *The Ghost Breakers* (1940) and *Where There's Life* as well as a vaudevillian in most of the *Road to . . .* films. In *The Cat and the Canary* Cecily asks Hope if big empty houses frighten him, and he replies: 'Not me, I used to be in vaudeville.' Danny Kaye is a nightclub entertainer in *Wonder Man* (1945) and *On the Riviera* (1951). In *The Inspector General* (1949), which is set in nineteenth-century Russia, Kaye even performs a nightclub routine typical of the kind that made him famous before he entered film. Chaplin portrays an ageing 'tramp comedian' of the turn-of-the-century stage in *Limelight* (1951). Woody Allen's fictional character in *Annie Hall* performs several routines made popular by Allen as a nightclub and television performer.

Instances from other films suggest that comedians referred to vaudeville tradition in general. For example, an aspect of film style could be made to appear like a stage device, as in *The Playhouse* – which ends with a downward vertical wipe, as if a curtain was falling. The main tendency in referring to the vaudeville tradition was the incorporation of certain performing conventions, such as blackface, into individual scenes. Douglas Gilbert points out that: 'a majority of comedy acts in vaudeville wore blackface in the Eighties, but many entertainers in the Eighties and long after appeared in blackface with no attempt at dialect or impersonation.'[12]

These examples point up the transparent relationship between the comedian and a 'like' character. Such transparency is often furthered by the titles of the films. Thus *Go West Young Man* (1936) has nothing to do with going West, but capitalizes on the name of Mae West (as well as her relations with young men in earlier films). *Buck Benny Rides Again* (1940), named after a character played by Jack Benny on his radio programme, is an obvious example of this kind of titling, as are the various *Abbott and Costello Meet* . . . films. Transparency is also foregrounded by those films in which the characters maintain the names of the comedians portraying them – examples include the films of Laurel and The Three Stooges. Harry Langdon and Harold Lloyd also frequently play characters named 'Harry' and 'Harold'. In *Silent Movie* (1976), Mel Brooks, Marty Feldman and Dom De Luise portray characters named Mel Funn, Marty Eggs and Dom Bell, respectively, and are referred to in the film's numerous intertitles as Mel, Marty and Dom.

Enunciation

As well as revealing awareness of the spectator through the inherently theatrical device of camera acknowledgement and by references to the comedian's pre-filmic career, comedian comedy also allows the performer to adopt a knowing stance towards film devices. Comedian comedy cohered into a form built on a system of communication oriented towards the spectator. An examination of how this system functions may be undertaken at the level of enunciation, the manner in which speech acts – including narratives – are communicated to their subjects.

The linguist Emile Benveniste has suggested that in written and spoken communication there are two principal categories of enunciation: *histoire* and *discours*. These categories have been considered in relation to literary narrative by structuralists such as A.J. Greimas, Gérard Genette and Tzvetan Todorov. Film theorists such as Christian Metz and Geoffrey Nowell-Smith have recently appropriated these terms (which I will henceforth refer to as history and discourse) in discussions of film narrative. Both Nowell-Smith and Metz employ the terms to offer a theoretical context for examining communication in 'classical' Hollywood narrative, and Brian Henderson also draws on them in his discussion of romantic comedy. Henderson's use of the categories is in line with the way they have been employed in recent theoretical discussion:

> H*istoire* suppresses or hides all traces of its telling, it refers neither to speaker or to listener, but only to the events it relates. The effect of different modes of enunciation on the receiver is a complex, largely complicated area, but it is clear that *histoire* in general is used to make the events related seem more real, more vivid, present, whereas *discours* modes continually break such illusions, or at least may do so.[13]

In an essay devoted to a more detailed consideration of the general applicability of these categories to film narrative, Nowell-Smith notes that:

> the difference in them |lies| in the fact that in the discursive form the source of the enunciation is present whereas in the historical it is suppressed. History is always 'there'

and 'then,' and its protagonists are 'he,' 'she,' and 'it.' Discourse, however, always also contains as its points of reference, a 'here' and a 'now,' and an 'I' and a 'you'.[14]

Nowell-Smith attributes these qualities of suppressed telling, 'there' and 'then', and third-person pronoun functions to 'classical' Hollywood narrative. Metz aligns the historical register with the way in which the spectator is positioned in 'classical' cinema, contending that this cinema functions to deny the spectator's presence: 'It is this fundamental denial which has channeled all the classic cinema in the "history" mould, which has relentlessly erased its supporting discourse.'[15]

One need not accept Metz's contention that 'all the classic cinema' denies the presence of the spectator, or that this cinema is 'relentlessly historical'. Indeed, certain 'classical' Hollywood films directly acknowledge the spectator, positioning him or her as a subject of address. To take two random examples, Mr. Blandings Builds His Dream House (1948) and Edward, My Son (1949) are essentially in the historical mould but also feature characters who talk directly to the camera. Undoubtedly, other examples of 'classical' narrative that 'break' the mould could be cited. It is preferable, then, to argue for the historical register as being the predominant tendency of 'classical cinema'. The manner in which Metz and Nowell-Smith characterize this register is applicable to the majority of 'classical' Hollywood narratives made between 1929 and 1954 (the years generally cited as the 'classical' period), but not to all of them. These categories are useful only as a means of noting general tendencies, and one can agree that conventionalized genres such as the western, private eye film, the gangster movie and the situation comedy are dominated by certain characteristics of the historical register: suppression of the signs of telling, performers who take on the functions of 'he' and 'she' without acknowledging the spectator and so on.

These two registers of enunciation further necessitate a consideration of who is speaking, that there exists an enunciator who tells a tale to a subject of address in a certain way. In the historical register of film narrative the enunciator's role is inscribed within the tale – as the agency that orders images sequentially while at the same time effacing all signs of that ordering, and without pointing to his or her existence as the teller of the tale. With the fiction-making capabilities I have already mentioned, the comedian in comedian comedy may be seen in the role of enunciator, a usurper of (or at least a stand-in for) the inscribed enunciative privilege of those 'producers' who suppress signs of their presence in the 'classical' narrative film: individual directors, screenwriters, particular studio business practices and so on. Certainly, films with comedians are directed, written and designed as commodities for public consumption. But in comedian comedy both the comedian's awareness of the spectator's presence and the assertion of his own presence are factors which work towards described enunciation, as evidenced by the frequency of revealing the narrative as a contrivance, and exposing the materiality of sound and image. These strategies point to the artificiality of individual films, but in many cases they also underscore the artificiality of filmic construction in general.

Revealing the narrative as a contrivance can take a number of forms in the comedian film. At the end of Ali Baba Goes To Town (1937), for example, when Eddie Cantor goes to the preview of the movie Ali Baba, he is told by a woman from the studio, 'Too bad you didn't get to act in it.' But the film's premise – Cantor's projection of an 'Arabian Nights' fantasy in which he is the hero – is, of course, built on Cantor's talents. Thus, he did get to 'act' in the film and the woman's remark indicates an attempt to deny Cantor's position in the film – which, in turn, underscores the narrative's contrived nature. In *The Gorilla* (1939) The Ritz Brothers portray detectives attempting to solve a mysterious crime; as various of their solutions prove to be incorrect, Harry Ritz exclaims: 'This is liable to turn out to be a mystery!' Similar lines exposing the design of the film's narrative appear even more systematically in *The Cat and The Canary*, which like *The Gorilla* involves solving a mystery in an 'old dark house'. At one point Bob Hope explains the strange occurrences to other members of the family by noting that: 'It reminds me of a lot of melodramas and mystery stories I've played in.' He then remarks, 'All we need is a leading lady', and on this line, the voice of Joyce (portrayed by Paulette Goddard, the film's 'leading lady') is heard off-screen. Hope continually compares the narrative events to mystery plays with which he is familiar, warning Joyce at one point: 'You know how it is in a play. Before the first act is over someone goes up to the heroine and tells her she's in danger' – which Hope then proceeds to do. Hope also tells Joyce that she will get the inheritance because 'In practically every mystery play I've been in the leading lady turns out to be the heir'. Joyce, of course, turns out to be the heir.

Films like *The Gorilla* and *The Cat and the Canary* reveal instances in which the narrative itself reflects upon its own contrived nature, with the comedians commenting upon the tale's significant elements while remaining in character. A different strategy is employed in the *Road to . . .* films, which deconstruct their narrative elements in several ways. These films make use of songs to reflect on the narrative. In *Road to Singapore*, the first of the series, Bing Crosby sings a song containing the lyrics, 'My devastating charm will count – I'm in there pitching for Paramount.' The title song in *Road to Morocco* is even more specific in its references to the artificiality of the fictional situation. While riding a camel, Hope says: 'They could have thought of a better way to get us here.' The two men then break into a song which includes the lyrics: 'I'll lay you 8 to 5 we meet Dorothy Lamour', and 'I hear this is the country where they do the dance of the seven veils. We'd tell you more but we would have the censors on our tails.'

Throughout the *Road to . . .* films Hope or Crosby break character and refer specifically to the artificiality of the fictional situation. At the end of *Road to Morocco* Hope, Crosby and Lamour are adrift on a raft after their ship has blown up. Hope, in tattered clothes, starts to go mad, screaming repeatedly: 'No food, no water, it's all my fault.' But the New York City skyline is then seen in the background, and Crosby tells Hope that they'll be picked up soon. Hope remarks, 'You had to open your big mouth and ruin the only good scene I have in the picture. I might have won an Academy Award.' In *Road to Utopia* the contrived nature of the narrative is revealed continually by Robert Benchley, who explains in a prologue that he was hired by Paramount 'to clarify the plot and other vague portions of the film'. His presence is acknowledged in only one instance, when Crosby repeats a line spoken earlier by Hope, and Benchley remarks, 'Hey, wait a minute. Hope just said that line, didn't he?' Crosby replies, 'Why should he get all the laughs?' Within the narrative itself, both Hope and Crosby expose the narrative as a contrivance. When Crosby makes his first appearance in the film, Hope remarks, 'And I thought this was going to be an "A" picture.' Later, when Hope and Crosby are stoking a furnace in the ship's boiler room, a man enters and asks Crosby for a match. The following exchange ensues:

Hope: Hey, what do you do around here?
Man: Nothing.
Crosby: You in this picture?
Man: No, I'm taking a short cut to stage ten.

I suggested previously that the use of direct address in *Annie Hall* often points up the desirability of breaking fictional bonds. This extends to the way the film underscores its contrived nature as well. For example, Allen, Annie and Rob are able to return to events that transpired in the past. When the trio walk into Allen's childhood home, Allen berates his parents – and Rob is forced to remind him, 'They can't hear you.' Earlier, when Annie recalls her old boyfriends, she and Allen enter a room and watch Annie (wearing different clothes and hairstyle) with one of them. They watch and comment on the scene, but are never acknowledged. Another way in which the film points to itself as a contrivance is by showing Allen walking the streets and discussing his problems randomly with strangers. The strangers often possess knowledge about the narrative, such as the woman who tells Allen that Annie moved to Los Angeles to further her singing career.

Many of these instances point to the comedian's role as an enunciator, one who describes the formation of narrative either by referring to its central elements (*The Cat and the Canary*) or by deconstructing it, both of which expose the narrative's essential falsity. In either case, the comedian articulates the 'somewhere' from which the tale comes. Sometimes the performance of the role as enunciator is 'unsuccessful', as in *Road to Bali* when 'The End' title comes down on Hope before he can attain what he desires. Examples of artificial credit sequences and titling, as in *Kentucky Moonshine* (1938), *The Bellboy* (1960) and *The Errand Boy* (1961), find the comedians starting or ending the film.

The comedian's role as enunciator is also evident in instances where the materiality of sound and image are exposed. This is suggested forcefully in films where the presence of the camera lens is directly confronted. In *One Week* (1920) a fictionally unmotivated hand prevents the spectator from seeing Buster Keaton's wife (Sybil Seeley) as she gets out of the bathtub to retrieve a bar of soap, when it reaches from screen right to cover up the camera lens. The presence of the hand turns upon the spectator's desire to see; this is reinforced when the hand is removed and Keaton's wife, now back in the tub, smiles at the camera. Prior to this scene (and after it) the hand has, in a sense, functioned to propel the narrative, since it also turns the daily calendar pages that demarcate the tale's events. In *The Bellboy* Jerry Lewis enters a room and is at first oblivious to the group of négligé-clad models behind him. When he becomes aware of their presence, he walks to the foreground, does a double-take to the camera, then reaches towards the camera lens and covers it. His gesture produces a fade-out, which leads to another scene. *The Nutty Professor* (1963) ends with Lewis' uncoordinated bow during the 'curtain call'. Lewis virtually assaults the lens in this instance: his falling body covers the lens, the image darkens, and the sound of breaking glass is heard.

Duck Soup (1933), featuring the Marx Brothers, foregrounds its materiality through such 'impossible' visual effects as the close-up of the live dog that 'lives' inside the doghouse tattooed on Harpo's chest. During the film's battle sequence, one of the Brothers announces 'Help is on the way', and a montage shows stock footage of fire-engines, police motorcyclists, marathon runners, monkeys, elephants and a school of dolphins, all moving in the same screen direction.

In *Road to Utopia*, Hope suggests that film materiality is enabling him to play the accordion when he remarks: 'You know, I never knew I could play one of these.' Later in the film, Hope tells Crosby that there's something about Sal that's phoney, 'like she doesn't belong in Alaska'. Crosby replies: 'Look at her. Could you imagine her anyplace else?' Hope then looks off in Sal's direction, and a reverse shot shows her walking in the snow. South Seas music appears suddenly on the sound-track, however, and the fur coat she is wearing dissolves into a sarong, and her hair, now down, has a flower in it. Crosby's off-screen voice finishes his question: '. . . but Alaska?' When the sarong dissolves back into the fur coat, there follows a cut to a bewildered Hope, who admits, 'I guess not.' Later, when Hope and Crosby are riding on a sledge, Hope looks up at the mountainscape and exclaims, 'Get a load of that bread and butter!' Crosby's voice is heard over a shot of the mountainscape, saying: 'Bread and butter? That's a mountain.' Then the mountainscape becomes the familiar Paramount logo: letters form underneath which read 'Paramount Pictures' as a fanfare plays. Hope counters with: 'It may be a mountain to you, but it's bread and butter to me.' In *Road to Hong Kong*, Hope and Crosby invoke 'special effects' whenever they are in danger. While they are fleeing from the villains, for example, they see a group of Chinese peasants. Hope observes, 'If we could only get something like that,' to which Crosby replies, 'Clothes? That's no problem. ' He then looks up off-screen and calls: 'Special effects . . . Us . . . them.' An optical follows, and Hope and Crosby are instantly seen wearing the peasants' clothes.

Recent films with Woody Allen and Mel Brooks also stress the materiality of the image. When Allen is a chain-gang prisoner in *Take the Money and Run* (1969) the work boss has a prisoner beaten so that Allen will know what to expect if he causes trouble. As Allen cringes in fear, a guard is seen whipping a man whose shadow is reflected against the wall, a visual 'quote' from prison scenes in films such as I *Am a Fugitive From a Chain Gang* (1932). But as the beating continues, it is revealed that the guard is really whipping a shadow – there is no victim. While Allen and Annie make love in A*nnie Hall*, he tells her that something is wrong: 'It's like you were removed.' Following his line, a superimposition of Annie steps out of her real body and watches the scene, which causes Allen to remark: 'Now that's what I call removed.' Later, as Allen's relationship with Annie deteriorates further, he explains to a policeman that as a child he fell in love with The Wicked Queen, not Snow White. There follows an animated sequence with Allen and Annie as cartoon figures. Annie is The Wicked Queen, and when Allen asks her if she's having her period, she responds, 'I don't get a period. I'm a cartoon character.'

In *High Anxiety* (1978) a slow tracking shot towards a window ends with the glass being broken by the camera. At one point in the film a doctor fearfully tells the evil Nurse Diesel that 'I feel like I'm caught in a web' as he backs up against a wall where a huge weblike shadow is reflected from a window ornament. At the end of the film, as the camera slowly tracks back from Brooks and Victoria on their honeymoon bed, the off-screen voice of the camera operator is heard exclaiming: 'Jeez, we're moving too fast!' At that point, the motel wall collapses, and another off-screen voice says: 'Keep pulling back. Maybe no one will notice.'

References to the materiality of sound also proliferate in comedian comedy. *Million Dollar Legs* (1932), for example, offers a comment upon the conventional film music track when W.C. Fields, as President of a mythical European country, is introduced. After a guard announces 'His excellency, the President!' a fanfare is heard – seemingly on the sound-track in the manner of films of the period. However, when Fields enters he beats a set of drums strapped to his body and blows a trumpet – he has provided the fanfare. Sound is given an 'impossible' dimension in The Three Stooges short *Men in Black* (1934). When The Stooges finally destroy the loudspeaker that has droned monotonously throughout the film, a close-up of a little tube on the floor shows it still speaking. The Stooges then produce guns and shoot the tube, and as it falls over, it exclaims, 'Ooooh, they got me!'

'Impossible' sound is often evident in Jerry Lewis' films. For example, in *The Delicate Delinquent* (1957) Lewis receives several misplaced phone calls in quick succession from a man asking for Zelda. The frustrated Lewis twists the phone cord, and the man's voice becomes garbled; when Lewis untwists the phone cord, the man's voice gradually becomes normal. Finally, Lewis cuts the cord with a pair of scissors, but the man's voice is still heard. In *The Bellboy* Lewis listens as an off-screen woman talks to her mother in a phone booth. When the 'woman' comes out of the booth, however, it is revealed to be the silent Stan Laurel look-alike whom Lewis has encountered throughout the film.

References to the materiality of sound are often manifested by the presence of un-individuated narrators, who comment on the fiction in which they have no part. For example, in *Road to Zanzibar* as the safari route traced over a map of Africa, the narrator comments: 'No, no. They've been up that river before. I wish I could tell them.' There are also instances where the narration does not match the image track. In *Road to Hong Kong* the narrator talks about life in Hong Kong over a montage of the city's activities, observing at one point that 'people enjoy simple pleasures: smoking, eating etcetera'. There follows a shot of grimacing peasants toiling in the rice paddies.

The comedian's role as enunciator, then, extends to the ways in which he can stop the narrative (covering the lens in *The Bellboy*, 'breaking' it in *The Nutty Professor*), do things he is incapable of doing (Hope playing the accordion or instantly changing into peasant garb; Allen becoming a cartoon character), and see 'impossible' things (Sal in a sarong, the Paramount logo). By manipulating standard visual and aural filmic codes, this role also permits the comedian to point to the status of these codes as codes by revealing their function as narrative signifiers in other films. This further implies a general interrogation of these filmic codes, a suggestion of their essential falsity. Through the questioning of these codes, the spectator's position in a comforting fictional universe is often challenged – at least implicitly. The challenge is occasionally direct, as evidenced by the covering of the lens in *One Week*, which subverts the spectator's desire to see by denying visual pleasure. In *One Week* the presence of the unmotivated hand throughout the film also suggests – as do all of these instances – that there is a 'somewhere' from which the tale is being told. In the case of *One Week*, the hand underscores the power of the 'somewhere', insofar as it allows the spectator to see certain images while denying others.

Self-reference

The extrafictional features of comedian comedy discussed thus far further point to an attitude of self-reference as part of the films. The presence of camera acknowledgement and references to pre-filmic performing traditions may be seen as referents which do not speak of the fictional context, or referents which speak of the fictional context in relation to something outside of it. Similarly, pointing to film materiality and exposing the narrative contrivance divest certain codes of their function as signifiers to speak of that which is apart from, or which mirrors, the fictional context. The 'something else' is the self in these instances, both the self-ness of the comedian as a performer – an extrafictional personality – and the self-ness of the film medium as a vehicle for communicating fictions and illusions.

In an essay on self-reference in film, Stanley Cavell states that this kind of attitude provides 'a further opportunity for exhibiting the self'.[16] The exhibiting of the self may be seen as a vital factor in terms of the comedian's pre-filmic performing career, a mode of self-presentation that emphasizes individual presence and personality. In comedian comedy, self-exhibition is likewise a vital factor. In addition to the extrafictional features already noted, self-exhibition also took the form of references to the comedian's star persona and references to other films in which the comedian had appeared.

References to the comedian's star persona appeared as early as *The Masquerader* (1914), which begins with Chaplin in a dressing-room putting on his Tramp costume. While this short comes early in Chaplin's career, the Tramp character was already well known to filmgoers by this time, and the device of having Chaplin take on characteristics of the Tramp within the film itself refers to both the star and his fictional character. In *The Vagabond* (1916) Chaplin is introduced by a shot which frames the bottom of a swinging door, under which may be seen the tip of Chaplin's cane and his oversized shoes; the recognizable accoutrements of the Tramp costume, then, are the very first things seen in the film.

Buster Keaton also uses accoutrements of his familiar costume to refer to his star persona. Even in *Our Hospitality* (1923), a film set in the eighteenth century, Keaton wears his familiar porkpie hat after the top hat he has been wearing is crushed. In *Steamboat Bill, Jr.* (1928), as Keaton's father gets him to try on numerous hats in a clothing store, Keaton is given a porkpie hat and pulls a distasteful expression before taking it off. It is interesting to note that while Keaton is looking in a mirror as he tries on the hats, the mirror is never seen. It is in the off-screen direction of the camera's position, so when Keaton looks at it he is staring at the camera. The porkpie hat reference is thus directed towards the spectator. In *The Navigator* (1924) Keaton's ultimate mastery of the ship is underscored by his wearing of the porkpie hat, which was not worn during the scenes that pointed up his ineptitude. Moreover, it is never explained how Keaton got the porkpie hat aboard ship in the first place. The lack of explanation points to the hat as a referent of Keaton the star, one who has worn a porkpie hat in a number of previous films.

In *The Pharmacist* (1933) W.C. Fields refers to his star persona by keeping a doll of himself in his store (the doll's presence is never acknowledged). In *The Bank Dick* (1941), Fields talks to a bank teller who wears a straw hat with no top, a part of Fields's costume in his earlier films but not in this one. In *Go West Young Man* Mae West portrays a famous sex siren of the screen named Mavis Arden, obviously modelled on West's persona. Moreover, other characters in the film mimic West's well-known manner of walking and talking.

In The Marx Brothers' films, Chico and Harpo refer frequently to the characters they portray: Chico an Italian and Harpo a mute. In *Animal Crackers*, after learning that Chandler's real name is Abe Fishman, Chico asks, 'How did you get to be Chandler?' – and Chandler counters, 'How did you get to be Italian?' The unspoken answer, of course, is that Chico got that way by the artificial nature of his Italian-ness: overly theatrical accent, organ grinder hat, and so on. In *A Night at the Opera* (1935) Harpo attempts to sing on two different occasions, but no words come out. Harpo's muteness is a condition of his star persona, and his attempts to sing are a reminder of that condition.

Bob Hope's films are permeated by references to his star persona. In both *The Ghost Breakers* and *My Favorite Blonde* (1942) Hope's theme song 'Thanks for the Memory' is often heard on the sound-track. Hope introduced the song in *The Big Broadcast of 1938* (1938), and it became the theme of his radio programme as well. Generally, it was Hope's radio stardom that provided the films with their major source of self-reference. *Caught in the Draft* (1941) and *The Princess and the Pirate* (1944) both contain references to Hope's 'ski-slope' nose, a constant source of humour on his radio programme. Moreover, both films place the nose references on the level of fictional character versus extrafictional personality: in the first film Dorothy Lamour touches Hope's nose to see if it is real, and in the latter film Hope himself tries to remove the nose as if it was made of putty. Hope's 'rivalry' with Bing Crosby was also an element of his radio programme, later given a fictional context in the *Road to . . .* films. That rivalry was also integrated into the non-*Road to . . .* films, as a means of self-reference. In *Monsieur Beaucaire* (1946) the villainous general explains to Hope what is done with impostors: 'We stand them up against the wall, aim our rifles, and . . . bing.' Hope responds, '"Bing?" What a horrible thought.' The self-referential nature of Hope's response is indicated by Hope's being framed in medium close-up by himself, whereas the general's line was spoken in a medium long shot which he shares with Hope. In *Where There's Life* Hope and Trina come upon a poster for *Blue Skies* (1946), a film starring Crosby. When Trina asks who Crosby is, he tells her, 'He's no one. Just a singer before your time.'

In *It's Only Money* (1961), Jerry Lewis refers to his star persona when he is introduced by parts of his familiar costume: white socks and white tennis shoes are seen hanging over a light fixture after an explosion. In *The Patsy* when Lewis' fictional character appears on 'The Ed Sullivan Show', Sullivan precedes his introduction of Lewis by mentioning the stars previously introduced on the programme, including Jerry Lewis. *Three on a Couch* (1966), like *Limelight*, contains veiled references to the career of its star. The film begins with Lewis being awarded a commission to paint in Paris, a reference to his adulation by French film critics. Later, Lewis' friend Ben reads an article about Lewis' award and remarks, 'After all these years of hard work. They finally realize he's a great artist.'

Closely related to these references to star personae are references to other films featuring the same comedian. Chaplin's last films contain many of these references. For example, when in *Monsieur Verdoux* (1947) the police inspector who has been following Chaplin enters the latter's antique shop, Chaplin bumps into a dressing dummy and politely excuses himself to it. Chaplin's confusion of dummies and humans is also a feature of *Mabel's Married Life* (1914) and *The Count* (1916). When the inspector asks, 'What's that?' Chaplin replies, 'That? I don't know where that came from', an ironic comment on the distance between the innocent characters of Chaplin's early films and the bitter murderer Verdoux. *Limelight* contains numerous references to Chaplin's star persona and his earlier film. Towards the end of *Limelight* he is seen as a musician passing the hat in a tavern, as the Tramp had done years before in *The Vagabond*, and he explains to Neville: 'There's something about working the streets I like. It's the tramp in me, I suppose.'

Each entry in the *Road to . . .* series contains references to the films preceding it. In *Road to Zanzibar*, the second in the series, Hope and Crosby try the 'Patty Cake' routine they had used throughout *Road to Singapore* to get the better of their adversaries. In this film, however, the villains do not fall for the trick, which leads Hope to comment, 'Hey, they must have seen the picture!' They try 'Patty Cake' in *Road to Morocco* and a villain knocks their heads together, causing Crosby to remark to Hope, 'Yessir, Junior, that thing sure got around.' At the end of the film Hope tells Crosby that he can't wait to get back to New York because it's been 'three long years we've been waiting to get back', a reference to the gap between the film's production date and that of the first *Road to . . .* film. *Road to Hong Kong* begins with Hope and Crosby seen against a backdrop containing the road signs of all the earlier *Road to . . .* locations. Later in the film the pair are trapped in an alley, where they hear Dorothy Lamour singing 'Personality' – a song she performs in *Road to Utopia*. Although Lamour portrays 'herself' in *Road to Hong Kong* she wears a sarong that signifies her film roles, to which earlier *Road to . . .* films (such as *Utopia*) frequently refer. The pair ask Lamour to help them out of their fictional predicament, with Hope urging her, 'You can't forget all those pictures we made together.'

In *The Family Jewels* (1965) and *The Big Mouth* (1967) Lewis takes on the characteristics of Professor Julius Kelp, one of his dual roles in *The Nutty Professor*: buck teeth, hair combed in bangs, half-lensed glasses, bow tie, tweed coat. Lewis refers to other film roles through advertising posters in the background: a poster for *Cinderfella* (1960) is seen in *The Ladies Man* (1961); *Its Only Money* advertises both *The Errand Boy* and *The Geisha Boy* (1958); a poster for *Who's Minding the Store* (1963) is seen in *The Patsy*. Similarly, during the 'sneak preview' in *Silent Movie*, a poster in the lobby advertises Mel Brooks' earlier comedy *Young Frankenstein* (1974).

Many of the instances of self-reference cited above can be tied to the development of mass media insofar as they draw on both the comedian referring to well-known aspects of his extrafictional self-ness, and the residue of previous film roles. Similarly, mass media enabled a further dimension to self-reference, given film's popularity during the 1930s and 1940s and the assumption in recent years that audiences are film-literate (that is, aware of film styles and traditions of the past and present). That dimension includes: references to film as an outside entity with its own business practices, lore, personalities and history; references to other films and film stars; and the appearance of 'guest stars' in certain films. This dimension provides the films with an intertext, a means of situating themselves within the larger world of film culture, and also suggests that these films are commodities within a larger world of film as products for mass consumption. The spectator is thus implicated as a consumer, one who pays for the pleasure of certain film texts.

References to film as an outside entity appear frequently in *Road to Bali*. When Hope finds a bottle containing a piece of paper reading 'Return to Sam's Supermarket for three cents deposit', Crosby remarks: 'Isn't it a pity? Every movie's got to have a message.' Crosby's response refers to Hollywood's dislike of socially conscious 'message' pictures, an aversion that had broken down during the time of *Bali*'s production (as evidenced, for example, by the early 1950s films of Elia Kazan and Stanley Kramer). Later in the film Crosby bathes in a lavish tub and comments: 'I feel so deliriously De Mille-ish', a reference to the sumptuous bathing scenes in the films of Cecil B. De Mille. When the pair discover that they have been tricked into marrying each other, Crosby says: 'One of us has got to go to Reno', and Hope replies: 'Let's hurry before Louella gets this, huh?' Hope is referring here to Hollywood gossip columnist Louella Parsons.

Intertextuality is also manifested by references to other films and film stars, and by 'quotes' that repeat a particular stylistic device or scene from another film. As Groucho Marx sits in a canoe with Connie in *Horse Feathers*, he quips: 'You know, this is the first time I've been in a canoe since I saw *An American Tragedy*.' This refers to a 1931 film containing a scene in which a woman is murdered in a canoe. In *Pop Goes the Easel* (1935) Curly of The Three Stooges uses his disguise as a woman as an opportunity to walk and talk like Mae West. In *The Ghost Breakers* Bob Hope remarks during a thunderstorm, 'Basil Rathbone must be giving a party' – a reference to Rathbone's role as *The Son of Frankenstein* (1939). In *My Favorite Brunette* (1947) Hope finds a bottle in a chandelier and exclaims, 'A-ha! Ray Milland's been here' – a reference to Milland's role as an alcoholic in *The Lost Weekend* (1945).

Woody Allen 'quotes' a number of film styles in his films. For example, *Take the Money and Run* recalls such Hollywood semi-documentary films of the late 1940s and early 1950s as *The House on 92nd Street* (1945) and *Boomerang* (1947). Allen often 'quotes' specific scenes from other films as well. In *Bananas* (1971) he romantically lights two cigarettes at the same time, as Paul Henreid does in *Now, Voyager* (1942), and during the film's battle sequence a baby carriage careens down the stairs, a 'quote' from the Odessa Steps sequence in Sergei Eisenstein's *Potemkin* (1925). Mel Brooks' *Silent Movie* features a number of 'quotes'. At one point Brooks and Paul Newman engage in a wheelchair race, grimacing at one another as Charlton Heston and Stephen Boyd do in the chariot race from *Ben Hur* (1959). Moreover, *Silent Movie* contains numerous archaic elliptical devices from the early days of Hollywood film-making, such as shaped irises and a montage sequence that superimposes neon signs of various cocktail lounges as Dom, Marty and Vilma 'search' for Brooks. Clearly identified as a homage to the films of Alfred Hitchcock, *High Anxiety* allows Brooks to 'quote' from such Hitchcock scenes as the dream sequence and conclusion of *Vertigo* (1958), the shower murder sequence from *Psycho* (1960) (which is repeated shot for shot), and a bird attack from *The Birds* (1963).

References to the star persona, to the earlier film roles of the comedian, or to film as an industry and a medium all bear a literal relationship to the exhibition of the self – in the sense of individual personality or the role that personality plays within cinema's commercial and cultural operations. Another self-referential device relates to the self-ness of the film as process.

Two of Chaplin's early shorts, *The Masquerader* and *Behind the Screen* (1916), assume a particular stance towards film as a medium. In a study of his acting technique George Lellis suggests that Chaplin's contribution lies 'in the visual language which he uses to express himself, one which successfully synthesizes an instinctive, performance-oriented mime tradition with a new technology, to produce art of both formal excellence and human interest'.[17] Chaplin's earliest shorts, however, reveal less a synthesis of than an opposition between Chaplin and the technology of the new medium. The opposition is clearly fore-grounded in Chaplin's second short *Kid Auto Races at Venice* (1914), in which he continually disrupts a movie crew filming on location. *The Masquerader* brings the opposition inside a studio that is specifically identified as Keystone Studio, the actual place where *The Masquerader* is being made.

The opening shots of Chaplin in the dressing-room putting on his Tramp outfit are cross-cut with shots of a film set in another part of the studio, where a film is being made. Once on the set, Chaplin does not do the scene correctly and spends most of his time flirting with two 'extra girls'. As a result, the director calls Chaplin 'rotten', then asks someone else to play the scene. An angry Chaplin disrupts the filming, and is quickly kicked off the set and into the streets. He returns disguised as a woman and no one is able to recognize him in this disguise. The continual framing of him in long shot is designed to fool the spectator as well. He does not reveal himself until he is back in the dressing-room, where he takes off his wig and smiles briefly at the camera. This momentary acknowledgement of the spectator not only serves to let the spectator in on the 'joke', relaying information that the other characters in the film do not have, but also allows the spectator to see another performance, one that the characters within the fictional world cannot appreciate. Those making the film-within-a-film think Chaplin is 'rotten' but the spectator knows differently, since Chaplin's disguise as a woman is perfect (an intertitle explicitly declares that he fools everyone). Back in his Tramp costume, Chaplin again sabotages the making of the film-within-a-film, at one point even knocking over the camera that is filming the scene. In *The Masquerader* Chaplin is presented as a free-spirited performer who tries to do what he wants but finds certain constraints in the new medium. At the end, those making the film-within-a-film ultimately assert the primacy of the new medium. Their victory is possible because they are able to draw

Chaplin away from the dressing-room – the space where the spectator witnesses his various transformations, and where he enjoys control – to toss him into a well.

Behind the Screen was made during Chaplin's Mutual period, when the traits of his character become more rigorously defined. A significant trait is imagination, manifested most forcefully by Chaplin's ability to give objects a different function than they normally possess through his idiosyncratic powers of perception. Chaplin's imaging power is thus set in opposition to that of the camera apparatus. *Behind the Screen*, like *The Masquerader*, involves the making of a film-within-a-film, which is once more disrupted continually by Chaplin (here playing a stage-hand on the film set). The battle with the camera apparatus is again underscored when he knocks over the camera on the set (the film features an 'actual' battle scene, a pie fight in which Chaplin raises a 'white flag' to surrender). The film establishes a further opposition between comedy and drama (or, as the characters in the film describe it, 'highbrow' and 'lowbrow') through the two film sets that are depicted. The comedy set has echoes of Chaplin's beginnings at Keystone (Keystone Kops, pie-throwing), while the drama set connotes the historical re-enactments typical of early *Film D'Art* costume films (for example, *The Assassination of the Duc De Guis* (1908)). The comedy set eventually wreaks havoc upon the dramatic set, an indication that Chaplin is more securely situated within the new medium than in *Kid Auto Races at Venice* and *The Masquerader*.

Later films such as Harold Lloyd's *Movie Crazy* (1932) and Jerry Lewis' *The Errand Boy* use the presence of movie studios to suggest that the spontaneous clowning of the respective comedians can be nothing more than an unchannelled force until it is captured on the screen. In both films the comedians continually create disturbances on film sets until 'higher-ups' (in *The Errand Boy* it is an 'intellectual') realize the value of their disruptive potential as filmic entertainment. At the end of each film the comedian makes the transformation from clod to star, thus suggesting a more positive stance towards film technology and business.

Chaplin, Lewis and Lloyd use film-making and the movie studio to assume a posture towards their position in the film medium, the way they are exhibited through technology. That posture is also displayed by reducing the film frame to a metaphor that mirrors the larger frame exhibited for the spectator. In *The Playhouse* Buster Keaton runs past a water tank on a vaudeville stage. The tank's rectangular shape suggests a motion picture screen, and Keaton stops in front of it and touches it quizzically, as if he were unsure whether the woman inside the tank were projected or real. In *The General* (1926) Keaton hides under a table in the headquarters of the union army. When a union officer burns a hole in the tablecloth with a cigar, a close-up of Keaton's eye peering through the hole mirrors the iris, a conventional framing device of the silent era. Keaton then sees his girlfriend through the hole, and the shot of her approximates his point of view and frames her within the cigar hole/iris. In *Tramp, Tramp, Tramp* (1926) Harry Langdon's progress in a cross-country race is reported at certain points through a newsreel that is watched by his father on a movie theatre screen. At one point during the film-within-a-film Langdon tries to kiss Betty but she resists, pointing to the movie camera filming the newsreel (though the camera itself is not shown). As Langdon gestures for the camera to move away, the narrative temporarily dislocates itself, with the borders of the theatre screen disappearing to reveal the action that took place during the filming of the newsreel. The borders of the screen are seen again, and the newsreel concludes. The showing of two different temporal actions as transpiring at the same time (the newsreel projected, and the newsreel actually being filmed) mirrors not only Langdon's position as a specular attraction in the larger film but also the way film is able to manipulate time and space.

Mirroring strategy figures prominently in *Take the Money and Run*, since the premise of the film is that it is a newsreel account of Woody Allen's criminal exploits. The presence of the people making the newsreel is indicated towards the end, during one of the film's numerous 'actual' interviews, when an interviewee who witnessed Allen's arrest discusses mundane aspects of his own life instead of the arrest. An off-screen voice asks impatiently: 'Can you get to the point, please?' The mirror construction here functions to give Allen's exploits a sense of verisimilitude that in turn 'validates' his improbable criminal career. Allen employs a frame-within-a-frame in *Sleeper* (1973), when he and Luna argue behind a rectangular screen in a hospital. The two are silhouetted on the wide screen, and gesticulate wildly, suggesting their larger status as images on a screen. The resolution of the argument prefigures the conclusion of the film, insofar as the constantly bickering couple wind-up as a romantic couple – here their silhouettes are seen on opposite sides of the screen until Luna moves to Allen's side.

Narrative

The various extrafictional features of comedian comedy enumerated above may be seen as stylistic tendencies that form a particular approach to narrative. I have implied throughout this chapter that these features run counter to 'classical' Hollywood narrative cinema, which not only denies the presence of the spectator but also any sense of self (actors are not actors but become fictional characters; the movie is not only a movie but a depiction of the 'real'). The narrative approach taken by 'classical' cinema may be termed hermetic: it presents an impression of reality by way of a closed narrative structure and uninterrupted narrative exposition, and displaces itself as a product of consumption. A network of factors that exist at the pro-filmic level is responsible for generating these elements of a hermetic narrative approach: particular studio practices (marketing and distribution policies, for example), individual directors, producers and screenwriters.

The beginnings of 'classical' cinema are often situated around 1908, when D.W. Griffith began to employ various editing strategies (especially parallel editing) to tell a story. Griffith and his contemporaries drew heavily on the nineteenth-century novel and theatre, and were particularly influenced by Charles Dickens (as was Chaplin, with the fundamental difference that Chaplin maintained the performing tradition of music-hall). The hermetic approach was elevated to a position of dominance once the motion picture business became centralized in Hollywood and developed conventionalized genre forms. The final shot of the 1903 film *The Great Train Robbery*, generally considered one of the most important pre-Griffith attempts at narrative, illustrates what was lost when the hermetic approach to narrative became the norm. The film depicts a crude narrative situation that prefigures the standard plot conventions of the western genre: the forces of savagery (an outlaw band that robs a train) are pitted against the forces of order and progress (a town posse), who capture the outlaws through effective action (a gunfight). After the narrative has been resolved, one of the characters aims a gun and shoots directly at the camera before the film ends. Such acknowledgement of the camera, which transcends the narrative's self-containment, was not continued in the development of western film.

Through its various strategies of self-containment the hermetic model further creates a unified sensory environment that situates the spectator within a fixed position of dominant specularity. Dana B. Polan suggests that this environment stems from 'an ensemble of codes which rationalize a particular way of relating to the world and they make this rationalization attractive by not interfering with the fetishistic or voyeuristic perspective of the viewing subject'.[18] The 'attractiveness' of which Polan speaks is contingent upon the manner in which the spectator is 'invited' into a fictional universe through primary identification with the camera. Once the spectator is fixed within this universe, his or her presence is closed off: they are able to watch the universe without being 'seen' since no one within the universe acknowledges the camera's presence.

A non-hermetic approach to narrative comprises a more open and expansive narrative structure that acknowledges the spectator. Narrative exposition is 'spoiled' by actors who 'step out' of character, with a deconstructive foregrounding of the marks of production and the essential artificiality of its signifying practice. The implications of a non-hermetic approach to narrative have been discussed in relation to political and/or personal cinema, generally European. These are said to be subversive in nature – 'radical' texts – insofar as they react to the dominance of Hollywood cinema, and thus ostensibly challenge the spectator to become self-aware of his or her position in relation to the processes of filmic construction. It is further argued that, since a commercial cinema that is ideologically bourgeois and reactionary produces them, these processes subjugate the spectator to a world of fantasy and wish-fulfilment.

Perhaps such non-hermetic Hollywood forms as comedian comedy have not been discussed in the same terms because they, too, are essentially products designed for mass consumption, or because they are assumed to be entertainment (humour, songs, dances), and hence pleasurable. Or because such techniques as direct address and the exposing of film materiality are not so much *anti*-conventional as devices that cohered into conventions of their own. I would agree that these are conventions – indeed, an examination of them as such is the rationale for the study at hand – just as these and other devices have cohered into conventions in the so-called 'radical' cinema. Nevertheless, their recurrence has produced a stylistic counter-tendency to the narrative hermeticism of 'classical' cinema. Many of these conventions – such as performing to the spectator, references to the comedian's star persona, the use of 'guest stars' and movie lore, the exposing of the falsity of certain filmic codes, and the revealing of narrative as a contrivance – are geared towards the production of aware spectators. Whether all spectators who see these films may be so described is highly problematic, just as it is in 'radical' cinema, despite the assumption on the part of many theorists that spectators automatically interact with such cinema.

What comedian comedy does share with other Hollywood genre forms is the repetition of particular character types and formal elements, and the elaboration of certain thematic patterns. In other words, while many films in comedian comedy stress the intrinsic artificiality of fictional presuppositions they are nevertheless about something.

Notes

1 V.I. Pudovkin, *Film Technique and Film Acting*, translated and edited by Ivor Montagu (New York, Grove Press, 1970): 291 (originally published in 1949).
2 André Bazin, 'Theater and Cinema – Part Two', in *What is Cinema?*, Vol. 1, translated by Hugh Gray (Berkeley, University of California Press, 1967): 102.

3 By way of difference, one can point to The Marx Brothers, who moved from vaudeville to legitimate theatre before they embarked on film careers. The plays they appeared in evidenced a marked lack of respect for the fiction, as indicated by their frequent stepping out of character to address the audience, changing lines in the middle of a scene and so on.

4 Douglas Gilbert, *American Vaudeville: Its Life and Times* (New York, Dover Press, 1968): 76 (originally published in 1940).

5 Abel Green and Joe Laurie, Jr., *Show Biz* (New York, Henry Holt, 1951): 40.

6 Bazin 1967: 78.

7 To distinguish other types of Hollywood comedy from comedian comedy in this chapter, I have used the general designation situation comedy, which includes sexual, social and family forms.

8 Green and Laurie 1951: 259.

9 Charles Barr, *Laurel and Hardy* (Berkeley, University of California Press, 1968): 68.

10 It should be mentioned in passing that both Hope and Lewis ultimately attained a cultural recognizability so vast that during the 1950s they were featured as comic book heroes as well.

11 Mack Sennett, the first prolific director of comedy shorts, offered many vaudeville performers a vehicle for performing during vaudeville's off-season. Many of Sennett's films, beginning with 'The Keystone Kops' series in 1911 (the 'Kops' were never individuated by character name or performer name) featured characters who looked at the camera, and though the narratives were slight, they were often interrupted in various other ways.

12 Gilbert 1968: 78.

13 Brian Henderson, 'Romantic Comedy Today: Semi-Tough or Impossible?', *Film Quarterly* 31(4) (summer 1978): 20.

14 Geoffrey Nowell-Smith, 'A Note on History/ Discourse', *Edinburgh Magazine* 1976: 27.

15 Christian Metz, 'History/Discourse: A Note on Two Voyeurisms', translated by Susan Bennett, *Edinburgh Magazine* 1976: 21–6.

16 Stanley Cavell, 'Exhibition and Self-Reference', in *The World Viewed: Reflections on the Ontology of Film* (New York, Viking Press, 1971): 123.

17 George Lellis, 'Chaplin as an Actor: The Iconic and Irrelevant', *The Thousand Eyes Magazine* 6 (January 1976): 17.

18 Dana B. Polan, 'Brecht and the Politics of Self-Reflexive Cinema', *Jump Cut* 17 (April 1978): 29.

2

Derailing the Honeymoon Express

Comicality and narrative closure in Buster Keaton's *The Blacksmith*

PETER KRÄMER

Recently, the consideration of the general features of classical Hollywood cinema has been complicated by an account of genres posing problems for narrative-centered analysis. Two genres which have attracted a great deal of critical discussion are the musical and a particular type of comedy that focuses upon the activities of a specifically marked comic performer.[1] Both the comedian and the singer/dancer are defined more by their specific performance skills than by the character traits and social roles that the film ascribes to them. The emotional appeal of their films relies as much on sequences displaying their skills as it does on their involvement in particular stories.

In these genres, the overall thrust of classical cinema toward the subordination of all filmic elements to the narrative is counterbalanced by a strong emphasis on self-contained and self-validating performance sequences (gag routines, song and dance) and by the foregrounding of the status of the performer as performer. Performers in these films present themselves in moments of intense spectacle as what they are – professional entertainers – rather than representing what they are not – fictional characters. In these moments, the fiction of the films' narratives gives way to the reality of performance; the representation of a diegetic world is replaced by the presentation of filmic spectacle.

Yet scholars are only beginning to develop sustained analysis of how these performance sequences and the larger narrative interact in musicals and comedies and how these films achieve closure; that is, the satisfactory resolution of tensions introduced at their beginning and played out in the course of their progress toward the end. Whereas classical narration is characterized by the almost exclusive concern with psychological and social conflicts of fictional characters, musicals and comedies also have to resolve the more fundamental conflict between fictional representation and spectacular presentation, between narrative and performance.

Steve Seidman has proposed an analysis of what he terms "comedian comedy" (films centering on comic performers) that takes into account the above observations and questions.[2] First of all, he characterizes comedian comedy through its fundamental tension between narrative and comic performance and then proceeds to describe the strategies employed to resolve this tension in the course of each film. Seidman argues that in comedian comedies, the special status of the comic performer is ultimately functionalized for, and

THE LIBRARY
GUILDFORD COLLEGE
of Further and Higher Education

dissolved by, the narrative. This is facilitated by interpreting the comedian's performance as the expression of the character's unresolved personality, which the film's story works to normalize.[3]

Seidman's arguments have been elaborated by Frank Krutnik in "The Clown Prints of Comedy." Yet Seidman's approach has not been applied in a comprehensive analysis of an individual text. Both Seidman and Krutnik develop their generic model on the basis of examples drawn atomistically from a large number of films rather than accounting for the complexities of any individual film. Such an account blinds them to the process by which textual systems resolve the disruptions posed by gags and performance sequences. Moreover, as I will suggest later, the Seidman/Krutnik model displays little interest in the particularities of individual comedians or historical periods, providing no sense of how individuals might inflect or redefine conventions common to the tradition as a whole. All of these limitations suggest a need to return to representative figures and texts within the comedian comedy tradition for a closer consideration of what Seidman and Krutnik's account allows us to discover within these works.

Previous accounts of the early short films of Buster Keaton, one of the key figures in the silent slapstick cinema, have been rare and mostly superficial, especially lacking any sustained analysis of the interaction between, on the one hand, Keaton's performances and gags and, on the other, the film's narratives.[4] Here, Seidman and Krutnik's generic model provides a framework which allows for a more complex account of this relation, particularly of the contribution which Keaton's gags and performances make to the overall meaning structure of his films. Therefore, I have chosen one of Buster Keaton's lesser-known two-reelers, *The Blacksmith* (1922), as a test case for the applicability of Seidman and Krutnik's model for close and comprehensive textual analysis.[5]

While the starting point of this chapter is an account of the disruptive force of the extrafictionally constituted performer personality and the comic incidents he engages in, the following analysis will also focus on the function and meaning this disruptiveness has in the context of the film as a whole. Thus, I will analyze the textual strategies of reintegrating and appropriating comic disruptions within the larger framework of the film's semantic organization for the purpose of playing out a familiar scenario: the formation of the couple, the constitution of the family, the resolution and fixing of an initially ambiguous social and sexual identity.

Significantly, comedian comedies in general, and *The Blacksmith* in particular, foreground the process of narration and thus point to the existence of an authorial agency which is constructing and relaying the narrative sequence of events. Yet the framework provided by Seidman and Krutnik lacks a basis in narrative theory which might account for the departure from "transparent" classical narration and which could allow for the analysis of the strategies by which the "laying bare" of narrative discourses is ultimately dissolved into the story being told.[6] I will argue that in the end, the narrative sequence of events is presented as if it evolved naturally, on its own, rather than being constructed for and relayed to the spectator. Hence, the suppression of the spectators' awareness of narrative discourse must parallel the suppression of their awareness of the comedian's performance.

Comedian comedy

Seidman's analysis of comedian comedy stresses the tension between the audience's extratextual knowledge of the performer and the specific requirements for his personification within a particular filmic text: "Comedian comedy . . . is generated by two seemingly contradictory impulses: (1) the maintenance of the comedian's position as an already recognizable performer with a clearly defined personality . . . ; and (2) the depiction of the comedian as a comic figure who inhabits a fictional universe where certain problems must be confronted and resolved."[7]

As Frank Krutnik indicates, the same tension occurs in all star vehicles, because the star image (i.e., the audience's conception of the actor's personality and appearance in real life and in previous film roles) is always already given when the particular film in question begins. While the star assumes the role of a fictional character within the film's narrative, the audience's interest in the star's screen appearance always goes beyond the engagement with this character's conflicts and goals. This fascination, sparked by the construction of a filmic persona across a number of previous film appearances, is ultimately directed toward revelations of the star's "true" identity (in real life rather than in this particular story) and to the mere fact of his or her "real" presence on the screen (i.e., the reality of the body rather than the nonreality of characterization). All star vehicles are thus characterized by a tension between star image and characterization, between performance and narrative. Typically, these vehicles resolve this tension by matching image and role, rather than playing out the contradictions between the two.

By contrast, Krutnik argues, comedian comedy is characterized precisely by a fundamental mismatch between the identity of the performer (for example, Woody Allen, the neurotic intellectual) and the role he assumes within the fiction (say, the gangster in *Take the Money and Run* [1968, UA]). In comedian comedies, the performer's function is less to create a believable character, to impersonate someone else, than to be himself and thus out of character. In doing so, the performer disrupts not only the coherence of his particular characterization but also that of the fictional world as a whole. Krutnik writes, "The comedian is marked within the text as having a privileged status compared to the other characters/actors: he is less fictionally integrated and has a relatively disruptive function in relation to the fictional world and its code of behavior and action."[8] While realistic fiction defines the screen as a mirror of the real world, the comedian's performance redefines it as a playground, revealing its natural laws as arbitrary conventions that are open to disruption and playful appropriation. Thus, in *Take the Money and Run*, a bank robbery can be halted and even transformed into an extensive discussion of a particular word which Allen has illegibly written on a rather inept hold-up note.

The comedian's disruptive function is already inscribed in his image as a star. The comic star is conceptualized by publicity discourses and consequently by the audience not only in terms of what he really looks and is like, but also in terms of his comic skills, which are to be realized in his performance (for example, Allen's self-depreciating remarks, which are interjected into the text regardless of the narrative situation): "A key expectation the spectator brings to a comedian comedy is to witness/participate in the performance – the 'act' – of the comedian, and this necessitates a certain compromise between the performance mode and the institutional requirements of the individual film."[9] These institutional requirements comprise, on the one hand, the employment of a codified set of filmic devices characteristic of classical cinema (scene dissection, continuity editing, point of view structures) and, on the other, the establishment and resolution of a set of social and romantic conflicts characteristic of the film in question.

In the same way that performance sequences, incorporating, for example, direct looks into and verbal address of the camera and a generally frontal staging of the action, depart from classical scene construction, the personality and behavior of the comedian depart from the classical conception of the protagonist as a well-defined, goal-oriented character. As Krutnik notes, it is this conflict between performer personality and the requirements of the position of the hero, and, in fact, the social norms of proper identity in general, which comedian comedies first state emphatically and then try to resolve:

> Not only is the comedian a misfit-hero, but he is also deviant in regard to more general "rules" of identity and maturity. . . . The comedian, then, is figured forth as a locus of confusion, and the "unresolved personality" comes into conflict with those fictional procedures which are concerned with resolving these aberrations and "fixing" the comedian's persona in terms of the narratively articulated problems and the generic field.[10]

We can see these dynamics at work in *The Blacksmith*. Buster Keaton's film follows specific strategies of situating the performer within the film but outside the fiction and its conventional role ascriptions. Later, the comedian is transformed into a more conventional hero. By such a process, Keaton's fascinating figure becomes increasingly involved in the narrative his performance is both redefined as deviant behavior and gradually replaced by straight acting. At the same time, instances foregrounding the processes of narration are ultimately redefined as actions of the now properly constituted hero.

[. . .]

Performance and narrative

[. . .] There is always a tendency in comedian comedy for the filmic fiction to be disrupted by the performer or an interfering authorial agency in order to produce comic effects. These disruptions do not at all disturb the spectators' relation to the film because they are part of their generic expectations from the start. These transgressions are made enjoyable by provoking laughter rather than producing a critical distance from the operations of the film which would provoke an intellectual and self-conscious reaction.

Furthermore, these disruptions are precisely this: disruptions. They are moments which transgress an otherwise firmly established filmic fiction. The spectators must be engaged with that fiction in order to realize and profit by the disruptive force of the comic incident. Spectators also must return to that fiction after the disruptive force of the gag has been consumed by their laughter. Frank Krutnik has characterized this particular type of spectator positioning as "a dialectic between disruption and (re)ordering," as "a play between engagement and distanciation."[11]

Consequently, the comic incidents which constitute most of *The Blacksmith* cannot be treated as a series of isolated gags but rather must be regarded as contributing actively to the construction of the film's narrative. As these gags generate narrative consequences, they re-establish the filmic fiction and the spectator's engagement with it. The dialectic of "disruption and (re)ordering" operates at the levels of performance and narration as well, with each comic gag creating disruption and the narrative consequences of the gag re-establishing the fiction.

[. . .]

The semantics of gags

In all screen comedy, the filmic discourse creates comic effects in its narration of a story. Not only are most of these effects discernible only when seen in relation to the fictional world of the story, whose conventions they disrupt, but they also gain significance in this context. While comedian comedy is characterized by the disruptive force of the comedian's performance and by the comic incidents he initiates, this force, nevertheless, has to be analyzed as a factor that both subverts the fiction as a whole and contributes to its meaning.

The way Buster as the blacksmith's assistant treats the horse as a woman, with the horse in turn acting as a human, is funny in itself. It further destroys the very coherence of the fictional world in which the assistant's story is supposed to occur. Yet the full force and meaning of this incident can only be realized if it is placed in the context of the assistant's preceding desirous look at the horse's female owner, of the contrast between his present state as an employee and the lady's high class, and of his following maltreatment of the horse, which leads directly (albeit accidentally) to the formation of the couple. In this context, the adoring treatment of the horse arises from the assistant's frustrated desire for the woman and ultimately, though unintentionally, allows him to realize this desire. In this manner, the ongoing narrative invests the gags with meaning, which in turn contribute to its advancement.

Although the comic incidents are, at first sight, disruptive and gratuitous in relation to the fiction, they are integrated in it on a higher level. The formal operation of the comic incident ignores, subverts, transgresses the narrative operations of the classic realist discourse not only to produce laughter, but also to make a semantic contribution to the narrative. Comic incidents are thus both funny and meaningful in terms of narrative issues, with a great deal of their humor deriving precisely from this meaning.

In the comedian comedy, the significance of the comic incidents is centered on the conflicting signs marking the character's identity within the fiction, while on the discursive level these very same incidents are examples of the comedian's performance skills (i.e., of his secure identity as a comedian). The comic incidents/performances place the comedian at the edge of the fictional world; he is in some respects an extrafictional intruder, performing through direct address of the camera/spectator instead of acting only within the fiction.

At the same time, he is at the edge of the social order within the fiction: as a child in a world of adults, comically misplaced in the role of the adult hero. The trajectory of the film is to involve the comic character in a dramatic conflict and with this to educate, stabilize, and integrate him in terms of the fiction and its social order. At the same time, it is necessarily suppressing his extrafictional status as a performer. By the end of the film, the comic character is fully integrated not only into the fiction but also into its social order. He has become an adult by overcoming his unresolved personality; that is, by having found an unambiguous social and sexual identity, and by discontinuing his escapist, nonconformist, transgressive behavior. This is exactly what happens in *The Blacksmith*, and it can best be demonstrated by a comparison between the initial and the final narrative situation and, most specifically, between the gags in which these situations are articulated.

With the disruptive appearance of the blacksmith in shot 8, the stage is set for a dramatic conflict between him and Buster. This conflict between employer and employee is articulated in shots 7–11 with an alternation of shots showing the blacksmith preparing for work and of those showing Buster being engaged in an irregular activity. Both opponents are brought together in the frame in shot 12, which defines their relationship in a climactic and, at the same time, very comic event. Buster has been frying eggs at the fireplace and he has just put them on a plate when the blacksmith enters the frame and disapproves of this unproductive activity of his assistant with an angry look and threatening gestures. Buster reacts to this with a gesture of subordination. Vainly, he attempts to pretend to be working, and in applying the gestures of work to his plate, he smashes it with a hammer.

The comic incongruity of gesture and object in the first comic incident of the story has a very precise effect in terms of the drama that has just started. Buster is forced to refrain from his private activity and return to work. Instead of realizing his self-interest (having a meal), he has to realize the interests of his employer (doing work for him). His subordination under the controlling look and power of someone else has been made blatantly clear.

Furthermore, the comic sequence in its two contrasting parts indicates the basic strategy Buster is going to adopt in the remainder of the film. His ingenuous use of his working place for his own purposes, in the first part of the sequence, contrasts with his sheer destructiveness in the second. His ingenuity later reappears when he is repairing his watch with hammer and anvil, fire and water; when he defeats the blacksmith with a set of pulleys; and also, more indirectly, when he shoes the first customer's horse. His destructiveness, now in the form of incompetence and ignorance, later manifests itself mainly in the demolition of two cars.

The duality of incompetence and ingenuity, failure and success which characterizes the protagonist's actions throughout the film is already present in a condensed form in the first comic sequence of the narrative. This sequence takes on even more significance when compared to the final result of Buster's actions. In the end, they lead him to marriage and family life. In the last segment, he shows all signs of middle-class wealth and familial authority: a pipe and a smoking jacket, expensive toys, a large room, the wife handling the baby, and Buster self-confidently taking a stroll.

The contrast to the first scene in the smithy is even more striking when considered in the light of some peculiar similarities. The clothes Buster is wearing in the smithy already point to the end. His tie and his hat hardly fit into images of work in a smithy, an inappropriateness which is underlined by the far less elegant appearance of the blacksmith. But, even more important is the fact that the irregular activity which he performs, the cooking, is a domestic one and furthermore, one which is firmly rooted in traditional notions of femininity. The apron he is wearing thus not only signifies his being a blacksmith but also takes on feminine connotations. And the physical contrast between him and his boss, together with his subordination under the latter's look and power, expresses not only the authoritarian relationship between employer and employee but also connotes a certain femininity in Buster.

The final scene of the story is already prefigured by its very first one. Consequently, the movement of the narrative can be described as taking Buster out of a pseudo-domestic scene in which he is placed as a female and inserting him into a "real" domestic scene where his masculinity is restored. Simultaneously, the narrative resolves the contradictory signs of his class position (the blacksmith's apron vs. tie and hat) to more fully reveal his essentially middle-class status. Thus, the narrative first states and then resolves the contradictory and "unresolved" sexual and social identity of its protagonist.

Looking even further back beyond the first scene of the narrative to the very beginning of the film, another striking contrast becomes apparent. The comedian who is presented, and presents himself to the camera/spectator in the opening sequence, has been completely reduced to a fictional character by the end of the film. All signs of self-conscious comic performance have been suppressed, and even the pork-pie hat (Buster's trademark, which he was wearing throughout the film) has disappeared. Without any traces of his former identity being left, the comedian has become a petty bourgeois.

Conclusion: toward a history of comedian comedy

At first sight, *The Blacksmith* might appear to be a series of more or less unconnected gags or, more precisely, of comic encounters between the comedian and objects or people. Using the generic model proposed by Steve Seidman and developed further by Frank Krutnik, this analysis has provided an account of the connectedness of these comic incidents, both in terms of their constitution of a causal chain of events (albeit realizing a nonrealistic type of causality) and in terms of their exploration of a number of thematic and narrative issues. The gags focus attention on the social and sexual identity of the performer and his position in relation to the fictional world and to the audience in front of the screen. The overall trajectory of the film is concerned with the integration of the extrafictionally constituted performer personality into the ongoing narrative and, simultaneously, the dissolution of the performer's conflicting signs of class and gender into an unambiguous social and sexual identity. At the same time, the film works to dissolve the interfering authorial agency into the story.

In Seidman and Krutnik's account, this trajectory is seen to be characteristic of comedian comedy in general. Their model allows for only two possible outcomes of a comedian comedy: "The comedian must either become 'adult' by becoming integrated or remain regressively escapist, the latter a 'revolt' which cannot be taken seriously but is excused by the 'special-ness' of the comedian 'putting on his act.'"[12] Both alternatives in this model situate the comedian and his performance within the rules and norms of classical narrative cinema and of "normal" adult behavior. According to this model, the comedian's antics are ultimately perceived and judged by the audience in terms of their deviance, irrespective of the film's specific strategy to achieve closure. The film may proceed to integrate the comedian into the fiction and its social order or, in the end, place him outside these spheres altogether.

In either case, the above model implies that the comedian's performance, which constitutes the film's main attraction, comes across as an aberration. Although comedian comedies and their audiences celebrate this aberration in self-validating sequences which spectacularly display the comedian's skills, these antics ultimately have to be renounced as an untenable, purely imaginary, and temporary departure from the social norms that govern and regulate identity constitution and behavior both in the reality of social interaction and in the realistic fictions which circulate within our culture. In each comedian comedy, the fictional world of the narrative offers "proper" role models and thus develops preferred alternatives to the comedian's antics, which are more in line with the obligations and rewards, the necessities and securities, of what is socially constructed as "normal" identity and behavior. The filmic fiction both in comedian comedy and in other classical films invariably defines this normality through unambiguous identity, stable characterization, and couple formation. Against this background, the comedian's initial antics, pleasurable as they may be, increasingly appear to reflect undesirable shortcomings of his character. According to this argument, then, comedian comedies achieve closure by either correcting these shortcomings and turning the comedian into a respectable member of society or by acknowledging his incurable deviance and placing him as an eternal child in a world of adults which he can never be part of and for which his antics, in the final analysis, have no relevance whatsoever.

Appealing and helpful as it is, Seidman and Krutnik's model of the generic characteristics of comedian comedy needs elaboration, precisely because it so neatly accounts for the common elements and structural features of a wide range of American comedies from the mid-teens up to the present day. In their attempt to provide a generic model for a large body of texts, Seidman and Krutnik have by necessity played down the differences between groups of texts within their corpus. For a historical analysis of the genre, however, these differences are of crucial importance. Within the broad generic characteristics that are shared by all comedian comedies, certain more specific options dominate the work of individual performers or the output of comedian comedies in a particular period and differentiate these bodies of texts from others within the same genre. The first step toward an account of these specific historical manifestations of comedian comedy would be, for example, a modification of Seidman and Krutnik's model along the following lines.

First, a more systematic account of the different ways in which comedian comedies achieve closure, that is, resolution of the initial tension between performance and narrative, performer and character, is needed. Obviously, different types of narratives can be employed to facilitate the engagement of the comedian in a dramatic series of events and eventually resolve his ambiguous sexual and social identity, in the process investing the comedian's performance with narrative meaning. In Keaton's case, an interesting shift from his short films to his features can be observed: Whereas the former generally involve Keaton in a direct confrontation with the authority figure (e.g., the blacksmith) as a precondition for his uniting with the girl, he typically avoids this confrontation in the latter in favor of a battle against less personalized natural or quasi-natural forces (e.g., the storm in *Steamboat Bill Junior* or the Northern army in *The General*). This battle proves his worth in the eyes of the authority figure (here usually more precisely defined as the girl's father) and of the girl and thus brings about the resolution, the formation of the couple. The triangular construction (protagonist–authority figure–object of desire) is the same in both cases, yet the solution is different.

This shift in narrative construction is accompanied by a shift in the articulation of Keaton's performance. The clown's virtuosity is mostly relegated to clearly marked comic sequences that are interspersed with straight dramatic sequences carrying the narrative interests and that culminate in an extended comic action spectacle toward the end of each feature film. This spectacle is only retrospectively motivated by the narrative when it is shown to bring about the father's recognition of the protagonist's worth. This extended spectacle sequence in which Keaton's body is first subjected to and then in turn masters the physical world around him assumes an altogether different meaning from the gag sequences in the shorts. It signifies a retreat from the demands of social life, symbolized within the shorts by the necessity to deal with authority figures in order to realize one's desires, into an asocial realm of mere physical interaction and spectacular display of physical mastery of one's own body and the world around it.

This shift in the types of narratives that Keaton's shorts and his features employ and in their respective articulation of performance is one example of historical developments within the generic framework of the comedian comedy. Other examples have to do with the precise balance between narrative and performance, character and performer. Seidman and Krutnik's distinction between two possible outcomes of a comedian comedy may be more important than they acknowledge. Whereas the integrative solution (the comedian becomes fully integrated into the fiction and its social order) ultimately rejects performance in favor of narrative, the second alternative, that of infantile escapism, is based on a different relation between the terms that form the fundamental opposition of comedian comedy. Performance remains the dominant force throughout the film and can only temporarily be dissolved into narrative. There are certain comedian comedies (e.g., early Marx Brothers) that do without narrative continuity and stability of fictional characterization altogether and instead seem to be concerned mainly with functionalizing ever-shifting narrative situations and possible characterizations for the purposes of comic performance. This type of comedian comedy was most prevalent in the early sound period.[13]

This new form of comedian comedy was one of the major influences on Keaton's early sound films. Keaton moved from independent production to the position of a contract actor in a major studio, MGM, in 1928 and made the transition to talking pictures with *Free and Easy* in 1930. In this new production context, he was first assigned to stories based directly upon particular Broadway plays (for example, *Parlor, Bedroom and Bath* [1931]) or on the general model of the Broadway farce. This meant a retreat from elaborate physical and visual gag sequences into isolated falls and other physical mishaps and into situation comedy articulated mainly through complex narratives of mistaken identity and frustrated sexual desire and through the spoken word.

Already, in *Parlor, Bedroom and Bath*, the appearance of a second comic personality, Charlotte Greenwood, works toward the ultimate dissolution of narrative into comic performance. Toward the film's conclusion, Buster becomes ensnared in an absurd series of formations suggesting potential couplings. Keaton and Greenwood's lovemaking transforms the conventions of popular romantic byplay into a painful and acrobatic exercise in physical combat. In a vain attempt at closure, however, the protagonist suddenly and violently grabs the "proper" (that is, noncomic) love object, who a few shots earlier remarked, "I wouldn't marry him if he was the last man on earth." The abruptness and illogic of this shift in affections is overcome by the sheer force of physical performance when Keaton mechanically goes through the same routine he had exercised with Greenwood. The film's conclusion reduces romance to a strange type of performance, one which belittles the earnest feelings normally associated with couple formation in Hollywood films.

The influence of this new type of comedian comedy became dominant with Keaton's teaming of Jimmy Durante, starting with *The Passionate Plumber* (1932). Keaton's last film as an MGM star, *What No Beer?* (1933), goes even further than *Parlor, Bedroom and Bath* in displacing narrative interests for comic performance. Here, however, it is Durante whose performances become the focus of attention. Durante's incessant talk serves more as a running commentary on rather than as a part of the shifting narrative situations in which he and Keaton become involved. In the movie's final scene, the vamp, who has seduced and betrayed Keaton throughout the film, is suddenly and inexplicably transformed into his romantic lover. With the lifting of Prohibition, Keaton and Durante, petty criminals so far, briefly reappear as rich beer brewers. This conventional, though abruptly realized, happy ending ultimately gives way to a close-up of Durante drinking beer and addressing the camera: "It's your turn, folks! It won't be long now!" Here, the comic performer clearly isn't defined as part of the fiction but as a representative within that fiction of the spectators within the real world, who, at the point the film was released (February 10, 1933), are still prohibited from taking a drink.

In short, Seidman and Krutnik's conception of comedian comedy provides a useful model for the close analysis of individual comic texts as well as providing a framework for constructing a history of the comedian-centered genre. It focuses our attention on the potential disruptiveness of comedian and narrational performance and on the processes by which those disruptions are contained and made to contribute directly to the film's overall narrative and semantic structure.

However, although a powerful analytical tool, this type of abstract generic model cannot fully explain the complex manifestations and inflections of the general performance tradition which occur within a specific film or group of films. The series of shifts in the articulation of narrative and performance in Keaton's films of the 1920s and early 1930s, from shorts to silent features and into talking pictures, reflects historical developments with wider implications: the transition of a major comedian from short to feature production, the conversion of Hollywood to sound, the accompanying decline of independent production, and the influx of Broadway material and performers. Textual analysis, of the sort performed here, necessarily must be coupled with a description that preserves the historical specificity of individual texts or groups of texts and provides an explanation of the historical shifts they represent if it is to avoid collapsing all textual differences in a totalizing generic model.

Notes

I would like to thank Thomas Elsaesser and Henry Jenkins III for their help in revising this essay for publication.

1   For discussions of performance and the musical, see Rick Altman, *The American Film Musical* (Bloomington: Indiana University Press, 1987); Rick Altman, ed., *Genre: The Musical* (Boston: Routledge and Kegan Paul, 1981); Jane Feuer, *The Hollywood Musical* (Bloomington: Indiana University Press, 1982). For discussions of the role of performance in comedian comedy, see Steve Seidman, *Comedian Comedy: A Tradition in Hollywood Film* (Ann Arbor: University of Michigan Research Press, 1981), Frank Krutnik, "The Clown-Prints of Comedy," *Screen* 25, nos. 4–5 (July–October 1984): 50–59; Steve Neale, "Psychoanalysis and Comedy," *Screen* 22, no. 2 (1981): 29–44. Other genres that have attracted a great deal of recent interest for their departure from classical narration, from "deviant" narrative construction and stylistic excess are film noir and the melodrama. See E. Ann Kaplan, ed., *Women in Film Noir* (London: BFI, 1978), Christine Gledhill, ed., *Home Is Where the Heart Is: Studies in Melodrama and the Woman's Film* (London: BFI, 1987).

2   Seidman, *Comedian Comedy*.

3   Seidman employs the masculine pronoun to reflect the fact that there have been few female comedians working within this tradition and that their work has not been

substantially examined to determine if it follows the same formal patterns as male-centered comedian comedies. I have chosen to follow his example here for similar reasons.

4 Full details of the film, including a useful plot summary, can be found in George Wead and George Lellis, *The Film Career of Buster Keaton* (Boston: G. K. Hall, 1977), pp. 37–39.

5 There have been relatively few texts concerning Keaton's shorts as opposed to the wealth of essays and book-length studies concentrating on his silent features. See Daniel Moews, *Keaton: The Silent Features Close Up* (Berkeley: University of California Press, 1977) for the most useful of these discussions. The more extensive analyses of Keaton's shorts can be found in Sylvain du Pasquier, "Buster Keaton's Gags," *Journal of Modern Literature* 3 (1973): 269–291, and Peter F. Parshall, "Demonic Farce, Saturnalia, and Buster Keaton's *The Cops*," *Perspectives on Contemporary Literature* 7 (1981): 18–26. Margaret Gabriella Oldham's Ph.D. dissertation on the topic, "The Nineteen Independent Short Silent Comedies of Buster Keaton" (Columbia University Teacher's College, 1981) is mainly descriptive, giving plot summaries and describing individual gags.

6 Seymour Chatman, *Story and Discourse: Narrative Structure in Fiction and Film* (Ithaca: Ithaca University Press, 1978), amongst others, has proposed a model for the type of communication that is realized by narrative texts, using the following concepts:

> Each narrative has two parts: a story (*histoire*), the content or chain of events (actions, happenings), plus what may be called the existents (characters, items of setting); and the discourse (*discours*), that is, the expression, the means by which the content is communicated. (p. 19)

> Narratives are communications. . . . But we must distinguish between real and implied authors and audiences; only implied authors and audiences are immanent to the work, constructs of the narrative-transaction-as-text. The real author and audience of course communicate, but only through their implied counterparts. What is communicated is story . . . ; and it is communicated by discourse. (p. 31)

7 Seidman, *Comedian Comedy*, p. 3.

8 Krutnik, "Clown-Prints", p. 51.

9 Ibid., p. 52.

10 Ibid., pp. 54–55.

11 Ibid., pp. 51, 58.

12 Ibid., p. 55.

13 See Henry Jenkins III, "What Made Pistachio Nuts?: *Diplomaniacs*, Anarchistic Comedy and the Vaudeville Aesthetic," *Velvet Light Trap*, no. 26 (Fall 1990), pp. 3–27.

PART TWO

APPROACHES TO SILENT COMEDY

Introduction

As the General Introduction outlines, James Agee's hugely influential (1949) article 'Comedy's Greatest Era' commemorated the silent films of Charlie Chaplin, Buster Keaton, Harold Lloyd and Harry Langdon as the artistic high point of Hollywood screen comedy. More recent critics and historians have interrogated Agee's canonical presumptions, not only by revising his dismissal of sound comedy but also by examining the formal and institutional contexts within which silent comedy was produced. The approaches to silent film comedy presented here move beyond Agee's golden age thesis to suggest more dynamic modes of historical and theoretical analysis.

In an extract from the book *Popular Film and Television Comedy* (1990) Steve Neale considers how developments in silent comedy relate to the broader aesthetic and institutional changes within American cinema through the 1910s and 1920s. Neale posits that the yoking together of gag-oriented slapstick and genteel narrative comedy makes the feature films of Chaplin, Lloyd and Keaton more unstable hybrids than Agee acknowledges. The pressures of product standardization intensified with the relative stabilization of the vertically integrated studio system in the late 1910s. With Hollywood having established the feature-length narrative film as the dominant cinematic format, comedian comedy faced potential problems because of its association with the short format. To secure more favourable distribution and exhibition conditions, the star comedians thus found themselves having to extend the length of their screen vehicles. A further incentive was provided by adverse criticism of slapstick comedy in the trade press, which suggested that old-style physical comedy conflicted with classical Hollywood's gentrified aspirations.

As a consequence of such factors, the premier silent comedians needed to pay more heed to fictional protocols without sacrificing the comic specialities that were their stock in trade. Focusing upon three films, Neale considers the different strategies that Lloyd, Keaton and Chaplin adopted as a means of accommodating their physical comedy both to genteel comedy and to the discipline of feature-length narration.

Tom Gunning's contribution to this Reader provides a refreshingly nuanced take on the well-worn comparison between Chaplin and Keaton. In this lucid short chapter, which initially reviewed a videotape collection of Keaton's films, Gunning explores the historical specificity of the two comedians in regard to their roles as observers of contemporary US society. Gunning outlines the contrasting responses of Chaplin and Keaton to capitalist modernity, and to the quintessentially modern medium of cinema. While they both addressed the consequences of an ever more rationalized machine age, Chaplin sought to humanize the machine while Keaton 'seemed determined to push its unnerving mechanical possibilities'. Identifying in Keaton's work an ambivalence towards mechanical rationality that was shared by many contemporary observers of the American scene, Gunning explores how this impacts upon his handling of narrative, gags and performance.

Where Neale and Gunning both deal with the historical determination of the silent comedian comedy, William Paul's chapter (adapted from work conducted for his book *Laughing, Screaming: Modern Hollywood Horror and Comedy* (1994) has an explicitly theoretical agenda. Paul argues that critics who approach Chaplin's feature films as masterpieces of cinematic sensibility do so at the cost of their invigorating vulgar comedy. Starting his screen career at Sennett's studio, where he made thirty-five films in 1914, Chaplin left after a year because he was not comfortable with 'the hectic, broad Keystone style' (Maland 1991: 4). Agee praises Chaplin for introducing greater sophistication to slapstick comedy, both in his handling of gags and in the emotional resonances he brought to his predicament as comic misfit (Agee 1974: 445–6). When James Agee proclaims Chaplin to be 'the first man to give silent comedy a soul' (Agee 1974: 445), he advocates transcendence of the 'vulgar' body as a criterion of art. As Charles Maland considers, Chaplin himself deliberately courted the approval of genteel critics who had a low opinion of cinema's cultural influence, and attempted to convince them that he could extend his comedy beyond the crude template of the Keystone films (Maland 1989: 14–20). After leaving Keystone, he aimed to 'upscale' the appeal of his films by incorporating romance, pathos and social issues, and by adapting 'myself to a more subtle and finer shade of acting' (Maland 1991: 17).

Paul's deliberately provocative analysis seeks to rescue *City Lights* from its 'official' reputation as a genteel masterpiece, by uncovering the film's persistent strain of anal and sexual imagery. In wresting the film from the singularity of an artist's vision, Paul aims to restore its significance within centuries'-old traditions of 'unofficial' popular cultural expression. As Paul argues, only with the coming of film was it possible to capture the vivacious performative attractions of a clown such as Chaplin, whose art was rooted in the cultural experiences of 'lower' social bodies. Chaplin should be celebrated, he suggests, not for transcending the vulgar sources of his material but for renewing them.

The Case of Silent Slapstick

3

STEVE NEALE and FRANK KRUTNIK

[. . .]

One of the reasons for the emergence, and rapid dominance, of the feature film, in America as elsewhere, was its cultural prestige, and hence its ability to generate profit and income. It was felt that feature films could attract middle-class audiences, audiences with a high disposable income, and that more could be charged to see them than the average programme of shorts. *The Birth of a Nation* (1915), for which the hitherto unheard-of price of a $1 was charged for admission, and which earned the hitherto unheard-of sum of $5 million on its initial release alone, was to prove them right.[1] For Hollywood, feature-length films meant extensive and carefully organized narratives. Both on this count, and because of its low cultural standing among the classes Hollywood was seeking to attract and maintain as a regular audience, there was a great deal of adverse criticism of slapstick comedy in the trade press during the late 1910s and early 1920s, and concomitant demands for a type of comedy with greater capacities for narrative organization and feature-length development. The *Moving Picture World*, for example, argued in September 1919 that:

> Slapstick must be taboo. The public has gone beyond the rough-and-tumble perfor-mances that used to be classed as humorous. Instead, a more subtle, clean-cut production, with at least some semblance of a story, is the current demand in the comedy line.[2]

Three years later, Frederick Palmer, in his *Photoplay Plot Encyclopaedia*, wrote that:

> Burlesque and farce are becoming less and less popular, and there is no real demand for stories of this type. The comedy producers are desirous of polite, plausible situation comedies, preferably founded upon an amusing situation that might very naturally occur in the life of almost any spectator.[3]

A tradition of 'plausible situation comedies' of what Tom Dardis, Kalton Lahue, and Donald McCaffrey have all loosely called 'polite' or 'genteel' comedy, already existed within the field of the single-reeler. According to Dardis, it was indeed precisely this tradition that provided the basis for most feature-length comedies in the late 1910s and early 1920s:

> while many feature-length comedy films were being made in 1919–22, they were nearly all 'story' films, usually based on popular novels and plays and *Saturday Evening Post* serials. They would star performers like Constance Talmadge, Will Rogers, and Mabel Normand. The story was always the main thing.[4]

Thus what is significant about the comments of Frederick Palmer and the *Moving Picture World* (and others) is not that they sought the invention of a new kind of comedy, but that they represented a threat to the old kind, one which hitherto had clearly been important (important enough, at any rate, to be singled out for attack). For the producers of slapstick comedy this threat carried with it, as we shall see, very particular financial implications. More than that, though, it marked a final shift away from a form and conception of cinema in which slapstick was not just important, but central, a shift away from a period in which, prior to 1906, at least, slapstick was fundamental, not just to film comedy, but to the aesthetic nature, cultural function, and institutional location of films as a whole.

As Tom Gunning has pointed out, the cinema prior to 1906–7 was a 'cinema of attractions', its films, both individually and collectively, a series of effects and points of interest and astonishment aimed, often directly, at the viewer.[5] In fact during this period, as Gunning goes on to argue, 'the cinema' as we know it, an industry and institution with its own specific product, its own internal organization, its own ancillary activities, did not exist. There were no sites or buildings dedicated solely, or even primarily, to the showing of films before the advent of the nickelodeon in 1905. And there was no distinct and interlocking system of film production, distribution, and exhibition. Hence there was no concept of 'going to the cinema', nor any concept of 'cinema' itself. Films – moving photographic pictures – were produced for exhibition and consumption within frameworks, sites, and contexts that existed already, and that had been developed for the presentation of magic lantern shows, scientific novelties, magical displays, theatrical entertainments, and so on. In addition to the limitations and characteristics of contemporary film technology, these contexts greatly determined the forms and modes of the films that were made. They account, in particular, for the characteristics that follow from the status of the films as attractions, and for the forms of internal organization used to display the attractions they contained.

Among these contexts were the forms and institutions of variety entertainment. Some, like fairs and circuses, involved travelling from place to place. Others, like vaudeville and music hall, were located in fixed sites and specialized buildings. Whether permanently sited or itinerant, though, the hallmark of these forms and institutions was the range of very different types of entertainment they each provided, and the way these entertainments were presented and programmed. All of them, in one way or another, adopted a modular format in which a variety of acts, and a variety of *types* of act, each unrelated to the others, would appear before an audience for a fixed and limited period of time.[6] Usually, the mode of presentation was sequential, but occasionally, as in circuses and fairs, it could be simultaneous as well. Each form or institution had its own particularities, either specializing in a certain array of acts, or having its own unique, individual structure. However, all of them aimed, in the words of Garff Wilson, 'to satisfy the tastes of a polyglot audience by providing novel and varied entertainment', entertainment which would be both diverting, and 'easily understood'.[7]

Given this structure, and given these aims, every act within each of these forms and institutions tended to be highly self-contained, to build rapidly towards a powerfully marked climax, and to strive for novelty, immediacy of impact, and instant appeal. Since films and programmes of films were initially nearly always shown as acts within one kind of variety format or another, they, too, were subject to these aims and concerns. They, too, were marked by these formal characteristics. Not surprisingly, comedy was a key generic component, both in live acts and films.[8] Not surprisingly either, the predominant kinds of comedy were slapstick and gag-based: instantly intelligible, full of powerfully marked effects designed to produce an instant (and audible) audience response, and internally structured so as to build across a series points to a climax without the aid of a plot. In the words of one contemporary commentator:

> The great demand . . . is for low comedy with plenty of action. Broad sweeping effects without too much detail are wanted. The artistic 'legitimate' actor wastes too much time in working up to his points, but the skilled vaudevillist strikes them with a single blow and scores. A successful vaudeville sketch usually concentrates in one act as many laughs and as much action as are usually distributed over a three-act comedy.[9]

Many of the earliest – and therefore shortest – film comedies consisted simply of gags, with more or less time devoted to the stage, and the task, of preparation. In order to constitute a ten- or fifteen-minute 'act', a number of films would be shown, each of them individually providing some kind of 'point'. In an English film, *The Miller and the Sweep* (1897), a miller, dressed in white, and carrying a bag of flour, approaches the foreground space of the frame from a mill located at the back. A sweep, dressed in black, and carrying a bag of soot, enters the frame from the left. There is virtually no preparation at all. The two men simply collide with one another and begin to fight. The gag is a visual one: the miller gets covered in soot and turns black, while the sweep gets covered in flour and turns white. (Significantly, given the importance of nineteenth-century variety to early comedy, the origins of this gag seem to lie in the circus.)[10] In *The Treacherous Folding Bed*, a French film of 1897, there is more preparation. A group of soldiers enters a room, makes adjustments to a bed, and leaves. Another soldier comes in, sits on the bed, and the bed, of course, collapses. There is a minimal narrative here. Two distinct events are presented in sequence, linked by a logic of cause and effect. There is even a degree of characterization. The group of soldiers are pranksters. The individual soldier is an unwitting dupe. But, again, the 'point' is the gag. Any narrative there may be exists solely to set up the pratfall. Any characterization there may be is simply an effect of the structure of the gag.

From this earliest period to the mid-1910s, films, and the institutional context in which they were made, shown, and viewed, underwent a number of significant changes. The cinema itself began to emerge as a distinct cultural entity, a distinct nexus of socially recognized characteristics, features, and practices. Cinemas were built. Audiences increased in size. A large-scale industry devoted almost exclusively to the production, distribution, and exhibition of films now existed. As a result, the films themselves changed, both in nature and in function. First, they increased in length. By 1908, the standard length of a film had increased from one or two minutes to ten or twelve minutes (the length of a single reel). Secondly, films were no longer just 'attractions' in theatrical variety. Cinemas now existed, devoted either solely or primarily to the showing of programmes of films. Thirdly, films were made increasingly and specifically to attract 'respectable' (and relatively wealthy) middle-class audiences, and hence to cater to middle-class tastes, and to embody middle-class aesthetic values.

The consequence of all these developments was an increasing abandonment of the aesthetic of attraction, an increasing attention to the values of narrative, and an increasing narrativization of the films themselves. Just as one reform group in America in the early 1910s attacked the aesthetics of variety on the grounds that it was dependent upon 'an artificial rather than a natural human . . . interest',[11] so the trade press and contemporary commentators on the cinema began to demand 'art' and coherent narration:

> To secure art in a motion picture, there must be an end to be attained, a thought to be given, a truth to be set forth, a story to be told, and the story must be told by a skillful and systematic arrangement or adaptation of the means at hand subject to the author's use.[12]

One of the consequences of *this* was the development of a new kind of comedy in the cinema, the genteel tradition mentioned earlier. Another was an increasing uncertainty, on the part of commentators and critics, as to the value (and values) of slapstick, and an increasing attention to what came to be perceived as its exceptional and anachronistic characteristics.

One of the earliest genteel comedies is D. W. Griffith's *The Peach Basket Hat* (1909). According to Tom Gunning, Griffith had been largely responsible for shifting the emphasis at Biograph, the studio for which he worked at this time, away from slapstick comedy and towards what he calls 'domestic' modes and forms.[13] *The Peach Basket Hat* is one of a series of films Griffith made about a fictional couple called Mr and Mrs Jones. Like the others in the series, it exemplifies a commitment to the representation, within the field of comedy, of 'respectable' middle-class characters and 'respectable' middle-class institutions like the family and marriage. Significantly, in using a name like 'Jones' it marks the characters, their values, and their settings as ordinary, unexceptional, and familiar – in direct contrast to the emphasis in slapstick on the extraordinary and the grotesque. More than that, though, *The Peach Basket Hat* exemplifies a commitment to the values of narration. As Gunning points out, the extent of this commitment can be measured by comparing it with *The Lost Child* (1904), an earlier Biograph prototype.[14] Both films concern the apparent disappearance of a baby. In *The Lost Child*, a man with a large basket is suspected of stealing the child. In *The Peach Basket Hat*, the suspects are gypsies. In *The Lost Child*, the baby has been hidden from view by a dog kennel. In *The Peach Basket Hat*, its disappearance is due to a large cardboard box. Although there are similarities, then, the films are different. But the difference between them lies not so much in their respective narrative detail, nor even in the number of shots they involve (eleven in *The Lost Child*, thirty-four in *The Peach Basket Hat*). It lies rather, as Gunning points out, in the relative attention they accord to spectacular comic action on the one hand, and to narrative exposition and motivation on the other, something the distribution of the shots serves to measure:

> In *The Lost Child*, the first shot set up [*sic*] the basic narrative situation: the baby's disappearance and the beginnings of the search for him. The following 8 shots are devoted to the chase and capture of the supposed culprit (the last two shots revealing where the child really is). In Griffith's film, 22 shots are spent setting up the situation: Mr. Jones reading the newspaper about a kidnapping; the arrival of Mrs. Jones' new hat; the box falling over the baby. Only the last 11 shots are devoted to the chase.[15]

The chase was a key device in the cinema at the time *The Lost Child* was produced. It marked the increasing length of films at this time, and allowed them to move in the direction of edited narration, articulating one particular kind of narrative action across a variety of shots, locations, and spaces. It also functioned, within comedy in particular, as a new kind of slapstick attraction. Of particular significance, then, is the way that *The Peach Basket Hat* both absorbs its chase into an elaborated narrative context, and uses editing to construct a distinct and consistent narrative voice:

> In 1904, the chase was the narrative form *par excellence*. By 1909, filmmakers felt the need to embed it in a story that provided some characterization and motivation (Mr. Jones has read in the newspapers about a kidnapping and is anxious . . . however, the superstitious nurse invites some gypsies in to tell her fortune, and therefore . . .).
>
> The filmic expression of the chase sequences in the two films also involves some important differences. The earlier film followed the usual format, including pursuers and pursued in the same shot and linking shots together on the movement of characters from one location to the next. Griffith introduces parallel editing into the chase sequence, but in a curious fashion. The gypsies and the group of pursuers led by Mr. Jones both appear in each shot; there is no parallel editing between them. Rather, Griffith interpolates 4 shots of the baby-concealing box back at home into the chase sequence. The effect is clearly ironic. The omniscient *narrator-system* reminds the audience of the babby's [sic] actual situation, still unknown to the characters. . . . Even in this simple comedy a sense of *voice* is revealed in the ironic contrast of frenzied pursuit with baby safely at home.[16]

Having made these points, it is important to stress that 'genteel' comedy and the values of well-made narration did not displace silent slapstick during the early 1910s. It rather grew up alongside it. The single-reel format could be used either to produce self-contained, internally developed, consistently motivated, and coherently narrated narratives. Or it could be used to pile gag upon gag, chase upon chase, in an escalating frenzy of movement. Griffith himself made a number of slapstick chase films, including *The Curtain Pole* (1908) and *The French Duel* (1909), both of them more or less contemporary with *The Peach Basket Hat*. And the continuing viability of slapstick, both aesthetically and economically, was still to be marked by the advent of Mack Sennett's Keystone comedies in 1912. Critical comment, however, drew increasing attention to the aberrant and old-fashioned nature of slapstick. Referring to the basis of a great deal of slapstick in French comedy, *The Moving Picture World*, for instance, criticized *The Curtain Pole* in the following terms:

> One is disposed to wonder why the Biograph company with its splendid organization has felt forced to adopt the worn-out scheme of foreign producers and introduce these long chases and destruction of property as part of their amusement films. No fault can be found with the picture technically, but the plan under which it is worked is not quite so satisfactory.[17]

More neutrally, the same paper some two years later merely noted the general difference between slapstick and other forms in matters of characterization and narrative: 'In farce-comedy alone', it declared, 'can characterization be *subordinated* to incident and action'.[18] But other commentaries usually sought, in marking differences such as these, to imply disapproval or contempt. Thus *Photoplay* in 1912:

> The moving picture play has altogether outgrown themes of single individuals in a series of incidents that have no relation to one another except for the presence of the main character. For instance, the mischievous small boy in a series of pranks; the victim of sneezing powder in various mishaps, the near-sighted man, etc. They are all passé.[19]

And thus film director, James Kirkwood, writing in 1916:

> I believe that the most desirable sort of play today is modern and American, whether a swift-moving drama with strong, human characterization, or a comedy devoid of extravagance, its incidents growing out of the foibles of human nature rather than produced by one of the characters smiting another with what is commonly called a slapstick.[20]

With Kirkwood's criticisms, and the year in which they were made, we are back again in the era of the feature film, and the kinds of criticisms quoted earlier in the chapter.

As already mentioned, Sennett's Keystone Studios had, in the interim, played a major part in sustaining the slapstick tradition. A new wave of comic performers from vaudeville, the circus, pantomime, and English music hall, among them Ford Sterling, Chester Conklin, Charlie Chaplin, and, a little later, Ben Turpin, all featured in Sennett's films. Their success led other variety comics, like Stan Laurel and Buster Keaton, to make films too, thus helping to establish a second phase of comedian comedy in the cinema (following a first phase dominated much more by French performers like 'Rigadin', 'Boireau', and Max Linder).[21]

By the early 1920s, therefore, despite criticism throughout the 1910s, slapstick seemed still to flourish, and slapstick shorts continued to be made. Now, though, they were made against prevailing trends, in very different, and increasingly circumscribed, industrial and economic conditions. The feature film had arrived, marking the ascendancy of narrative values. It was now the industry's principal product. Thus whereas in the early to mid-1910s, slapstick's format, the single-reel short, was at one and the same time the format best suited to its aesthetic characteristics, and the format to which the industry as a whole was geared as its standard commodity, there was now a discrepancy. The industry was geared to one form, slapstick to another. Slapstick's form was secondary. Its industrial position was weaker, much more marginal. So, too, was its financial position. Hitherto, because its form was standard, slapstick comedy was able to make as much money at the box office as any other kind of film. Now, although slapstick tended to be made as much in double-reel as single-reel formats, and although the films of Chaplin, Lloyd, and Keaton, in particular, made a great deal of money, its earning capacity in any short form was simply not as great as feature-based genres and modes.

It is therefore significant that the renewed demands in the late 1910s and early 1920s for 'genteel' comedy and narrative values – the values of the feature film – were now not just ignored. They could not afford to be. And it is even more significant that two of the most popular slapstick performers, Keaton and Lloyd, were among those who publicly acknowledged these demands, in articles they wrote for a book called *The Truth About The Movies*, first published in 1924. Keaton, for instance, expressed the view that 'explosives, cops, stock situations, flivvers, pie throwing and bathing girls' were *passé*: 'A comedian today no longer finds his dressing room filled with slapstick, property bricks, stuffed clubs and exploding cigars. Comic situations have taken the place of these veteran laugh getters.'[22] Lloyd's view is similar: 'We have noticed . . . that audiences are drawing closer to an appreciation of comedy wherein gags are mingled with story than in [sic] just straight gag comedies – pictures built entirely for laughs.'[23]

Lloyd and Keaton, of course, along with Chaplin, were among the first of the slapstick comedians to move into features. Chaplin made *The Kid* in 1921, Lloyd the four-reel *A Sailor Made Man* in 1921 and the five-reel *Grandma's Boy* in 1922, and Keaton *The Three Ages* and *Our Hospitality* in 1923. The financial stakes involved can be gauged by comparing some figures. In 1920, Lloyd made a two-reel short called *Bumping Into Broadway* for $17,274. The film was a success. Within three years of its initial release it had grossed over $150,000 at the box office.[24] However, three years later Lloyd made a feature called *Safety Last*. It cost $120,963. But it grossed more than $1,580,000.[25]

A move into features could clearly be profitable. But it could also be problematic, for it entailed a dilution of the characteristics of slapstick and an accommodation to genteel values and the demands of well-made narration. Buster Keaton has pointed to some of the aesthetic issues involved:

> In one or two of my later two-reelers I tried putting in a story-line. But this had not always proved feasible, and the faster the gags came in most short comedies, the better. In the features I soon found out that one had to present believable characters in situations that the audience accepted. . . .
>
> One of the first decisions I made was to cut out custard-pie throwing. It seemed to me that the public by that time – it was 1923 – had had enough of that. . . .
>
> We also discontinued using what we called impossible or cartoon gags. These can be very funny in a cartoon short, and sometimes in a two-reeler. . . .
>
> But that sort of gag I would never use in a full-length picture – because it could not happen in real life, it was an impossible gag.[26]

We would like to conclude this chapter by taking a more detailed look at some of the issues Keaton has identified here, together with a number of others raised by the encounter between slapstick, genteel comedy, and well-made, feature-length narration. We take as examples for discussion Harold Lloyd's *Grandma's Boy*, Buster Keaton's *Our Hospitality*, and Chaplin's first sound feature, *City Lights* (1931).

Slapstick and narrative cinema

It is Donald McCaffrey's thesis that Harold Lloyd's work is, from 1917 onwards, increasingly marked by a combination of genteel and slapstick elements.[27] Abandoning his earlier slapstick style and 'Lonesome Luke' persona, and influenced in particular, according to McCaffrey, by contemporary genteel performers like Charles Ray, Douglas McLean, and Johnny Hines, Lloyd now develops what he called his 'glass' character, and turns much more to plausibility, plot, and the humour of situations. Lloyd himself discussed the changes in his style and persona in precisely such terms in his autobiography, *An American Comedy*, first published in 1928.

> The glasses would serve as my trademark and at the same time suggest the character – quiet, normal, boyish, clean, sympathetic, not impossible to romance. I would need no eccentric make-up, 'mo' or funny clothes. I would be an average recognizable American youth and let the situation take care of the comedy.[28]

McCaffrey suggests that Lloyd rather overstates the extent to which he abandoned slapstick elements. While his 1920s films *are* marked by a more genteel persona, and while they are marked also by plots and situations which provide motivation for the gags, the pratfalls, and the chases, are still there.

McCaffrey discusses *Grandma's Boy*, along with *Safety Last* and *The Freshman* (1925), in order to pinpoint both the nature of its genteel and slapstick components, and the way these components are used. *Grandma's Boy* tells the story of a young man whose timidity and cowardice lead him firstly to be beaten up and thrown into a well by a rival for his girl (Mildred Davis), then intimidated by a brutal-looking tramp. He goes to visit the girl, but suffers further humiliation on account of his old-fashioned clothes. He is asked to join a posse in search of the tramp, but separated from the others he runs home in terror. Grandma hears of his cowardice, and tells him about his grandpa. Grandpa, too, was a coward. However, inspired by a voodoo talisman, he conquered singlehandedly a group of Union officers during the civil war. Now in possession of this selfsame talisman, the young man finds the tramp and finally captures him in hand-to-hand combat. Finally, congratulated by grandma and the girl, he learns the truth: grandma's story was only a story, and the talisman only an ornately carved umbrella handle. But the young man then realizes that courage is only a state of mind. With his newfound knowledge and self-confidence he convinces the girl that they must get married at once.

Grandma's Boy contains a number of slapstick elements: several comic fights, a lengthy chase, eccentric costume, and numerous gags and pratfalls. However, they are all related either to the nature (and transformation) of the central protagonist, or to the development of the narrative, or both. Thus the chase is embedded in a story; indeed it marks the culmination of a narrative thread concerning the pursuit and the capture of the tramp. It features characters introduced much earlier in the film. And it marks the transformation undergone by one of these characters – the young man – and hence a reversal in the relations between them. One of the gags in the film, meanwhile, occurs during the course of the young man's visit to the girl's house. He gets his finger stuck in a vase and frantically tries to remove it while keeping it hidden from the girl and, therefore, avoiding impropriety and social embarrassment. Here there are direct links to the genteel tradition. The visit itself constitutes an episode in the romance plot that provides the film with its basic narrative frame. It is the location of the gag with the vase within this frame, and the consequent production of humour not just from a physical incident but also from its social and situational context, that marks the way the film consistently integrates slapstick material into both genteel and narrative contexts. A similar strategy is at work early in *Grandma's Boy* when the young man is embarrassed by having to walk past a group of children wearing wet and shrunken clothes. There are clear echoes here of the way the slapstick tradition uses ill-fitting clothes and bodily exposure for laughs. But in this case, ill-fitting clothes are the consequence of a previous narrative incident – the ducking in the well – an incident itself related both to a consistent character trait (the young man's cowardice) and to the romance plot (the young man is dumped in the well by his rival). The stress, moreover, in the presentation of this sequence is as much on the way the young man suffers humiliation as a consequence of wearing the clothes as it is on their ludicrous nature.

McCaffrey sums up many of the differences between earlier slapstick films and the way slapstick is used in Lloyd's films of the 1920s as follows: 'The difference between Lloyd's works and the early works can be explained in one word – motivation.'[29] Motivation – of various kinds – is also a feature of Keaton's Our Hospitality. It is a feature stressed, in particular, by Bordwell and Thompson, in their discussion of the film in Film Art.[30]

Our Hospitality concerns a young man, Willie McKay (Buster Keaton), who journeys to the South from New York to inherit what turns out to be a derelict mansion. On the journey he meets a young woman, and is invited to her home. She is a member of the Canfield family, and, unknown to either of them, the Canfields are sworn enemies of the McKays. Willie visits the Canfield home, where, ironically, the rules of southern hospitality mean that he is safe from attack. He stays the night, but is forced to leave in the morning. During a chase through the countryside and down to the river Willie eludes his pursuers, then, spectacularly, rescues the daughter from drowning. The Canfield men return home disappointed, but determined to continue the feud. They are surprised to discover, however, not only that Willie is there in the house, but that he and the daughter are now being married by a local minister. Confronted with a fait accompli, the elder Canfield eventually relents, and decides that the feud should now end.

As Bordwell and Thompson have noted, nearly all the elements in Our Hospitality – including the gags – are multiply motivated: used to advance the narrative, used to delineate character, and, often, presented in such a way as to ensure a high degree of narrative economy. Thus

> virtually every bit of behavior of the figures functions to support and advance the cause–effect chain of the narrative. The way Canfield sips and savors his julep establishes his Southern ways; his Southern hospitality in turn will not allow him to shoot a guest in the house. Similarly, Willie's every move expresses his diffidence or resourcefulness. Even more concise is the way the film uses the arrangement of figures and settings in depth to present two narrative events simultaneously . . . the Canfield boys in the foreground make plans to shoot Willie, while in the background Willie overhears them and starts to flee. . . . Thanks to depth in spatial arrangement, Keaton is able to pack together and connect two story events, resulting in tight narrative construction, and in a relatively unrestricted narration.[31]

Multiple motivation, and this particular kind of narrative economy, helps give the film compositional coherence. Such coherence is also provided by the way in which elements of mise en scène, and actions and gags, are interlinked as recurring motifs. One example would be what Bordwell and Thompson call 'the fish on the line motif':

> Early on in Our Hospitality Willie is angling and hauls up a miniscule fish. Shortly afterward, a huge fish yanks him into the water. . . . Later in the film, through a series of mishaps, Willie becomes tied by a rope to one of the Canfield sons. A great many gags arise from this umbilical-cord linkage, especially one that results in Canfield's being pulled into the water as Willie was earlier.

Perhaps the single funniest moment in the film occurs when Willie realizes that since the Canfield boy has fallen off the rocks, so must he. . . . But even after Willie gets free of Canfield, the rope remains tied around him. So in the film's climax, Willie is dangling from a log over the waterfall like a fish on the end of the line.[32]

One particular point worth noting about 'the fish on the line motif' is that its development serves progressively to narrativize a type of action – a figure – which begins as an incidental gag. The catching of a miniscule fish early on in the film serves no plot purpose whatsoever. In the climax, however, the figure is crucial to the outcome of the story. For it is by swinging on the rope – like a fish on the end of a line – that Willie is able to rescue the daughter from the waterfall.

In all these ways, *Our Hospitality* exemplifies all the virtues and characteristics demanded of the well-made narrative feature film. But what of the genteel tradition? As Bordwell and Thompson have noted, one of the film's recurrent elements is a sampler bearing the homily 'Love Thy Neighbor':

> It appears initially in the prologue of the film, when seeing it motivates Canfield's attempt to stop the feud. It then plays a significant role in linking the ending back to the beginning; it reappears at the end when Canfield, enraged that Willie has married his daughter, glances at the wall, reads the inscription, and resolves to end the years of feuding.[33]

The sampler here not only plays a significant role in the provision of compositional and narrative unity. It also plays a role in the way the film uses its genteel components. It helps to cement the romance, and thus provide a happy ending, while it is also used ironically, to mark the differences between two incompatible sets of southern values: the values of genteel propriety (which mean among other things that a guest must be treated hospitably) and the values of 'chivalry' and 'honour' (which mean that Willie is in mortal danger as soon as he steps out of the Canfield house). The film takes a distance from those who hypocritically espouse both at once. But it finds in the outsider, Willie, both someone who acts in a truly chivalrous manner (he rescues the daughter) and someone who, almost literally, loves his neighbour (so much so, of course, that he marries her). In this way, Keaton, the slapstick comedian, finds himself playing the part of a character who incarnates all the genuine genteel virtues.

Before turning, lastly, to *City Lights*, it is worth recalling the extent to which Chaplin and his films were criticized during the 1910s and the early 1920s for their slapstick values, and for the vulgarity of much of their humour. Writing in *Variety* in 1915, for instance, Sime Silverman described Chaplin's films and persona as 'mussy, messy and dirty': 'never anything dirtier was placed upon the screen than Chaplin's Tramp'.[34] Even those who liked Chaplin felt compelled to acknowledge, and to deprecate, these qualities. This is from *The Little Review*, again in 1915:

> the stuffy, maddening 'bathos' that clings to the mob like a stink is dispelled, wiped off the air. Charlie Chaplin is before them, Charles Chaplin with the wit of a vulgar buffoon and the soul of a world artist. . . . He is absurd; unmanly; tawdry; cheap; artificial. And yet behind his crudities, his obscenities, his inartistic and outrageous contortions, his 'divinity' shines.[35]

Photoplay, meanwhile, considered that Chaplin was facing a choice:

> What is to become of Charlie Chaplin? Will the little genius of laughter relegate himself
> to comic history, or will he, changing his medium of expression, pass to a higher and
> more legitimate comedy? He must do one or the other.[36]

A year later, following criticism of films like A Woman (1915), in which Chaplin not only dresses
in drag, but creates jokes around his pincushion bosom and flirts with a number of men, the
Motion Picture Magazine reported that an announcement had been made by the National Board
of Censorship:

> the old Charlie Chaplin has seen that the very methods by which his personality achieved
> success now imperil his unprecedented reputation by alienating a great part of the
> American public.[37]

The result would be 'a new fame based on a more delicate art'.[38]

At first glance, it may seem as though Chaplin did, indeed, capitulate to the criticisms and
demands with which he was faced. Already, in *The Tramp* (1915), he had introduced pathos,
romance, and an ambiguous, bittersweet ending. And in 1916 he made *The Vagabond*, a film
which, as described by David Robinson, is replete with genteel and narrative values:

> Charlie is a street musician. . . . Out in the country, he rescues a little blonde drudge
> from villainous gypsies. Their life together in a stolen caravan is a (very chaste) idyll
> until a handsome young artist chances along and wins the heart of the girl. The artist's
> portrait of her is exhibited and recognized (thanks to the inevitable birthmark) by
> her long-lost mother. The girl is whisked off to a new life, leaving Charlie alone and
> disconsolate, unable even to manage the usual recuperative flip of the heels.[39]

As Robinson himself points out, *The Vagabond*, as 'a well-turned miniature drama' in which
Charlie adopts a friendless girl, 'anticipates *The Circus, Modern Times, City Lights* and *Limelight*'.[40]
But in the meantime, Chaplin continued to make slapstick shorts, like *The Floorwalker* (1916)
and *Pay Day* (1922), and he continued to get into trouble with 'respectable' opinion (notably
over *The Pilgrim* (1923) and *Monsieur Verdoux* (1947), but also over scenes like the one in *The Kid*
in which he improvises a toilet, for the boy he has befriended, from a chair with a hole in the
seat and a cuspidor placed underneath). Even in the most apparently genteel and sentimental
of the story films, and 'well-turned' dramas, neither the gags nor the vulgarity were ever fully
abandoned – *City Lights*, for instance, contains a gag about shit, in the sequence in which the
tramp is trying to earn some money as a road-sweeper: he cleans up the droppings left by a
string of donkeys, but walks off in the opposite direction when a group of elephants pass by.
Thus if Chaplin did indeed find 'new fame based on a more delicate art', its delicacy did not
lie in the unequivocal adoption of genteel and story-based values. But nor, on the other hand,
did it lie in any of the strategies of combination, motivation, and integration adopted by
Lloyd and by Keaton.

Chaplin's solution was very much his own. It consisted not of blending, or seeking to
blend, genteel and slapstick components, but of playing the one off against the other in order
to highlight their differences. As David Robinson has pointed out, one of the commonest

forms this strategy takes is that of using slapstick elements to undermine, or cut across, the genteel ones. This form is evident as early as *The Vagabond* itself (almost as early, in other words, as genteel components begin to appear):

> Chaplin's sentiment is invariably saved from mawkishness by comedy and the belligerence that always underlies his despair. His jealousy as he watches the girl dancing with the artist is not entirely impotent: he maliciously flicks a fly in the man's direction, and later manages to drop an egg in his shoes. After the girl's elegant mother condescendingly shakes hands with him, he suspiciously sniffs the perfume left on his fingers. He uses his favourite trick of deflating his own dramatic despair with farce: in *The Vagabond* the anguish of a lover rejected is quite eclipsed by the agonies of the same man accidentally sitting on a stove.[41]

Similar moments occur in *City Lights*, as for instance when the Tramp first meets the blind Flower Girl with whom he instantly falls in love. He stops to gaze at her adoringly; she – unwittingly – throws a container of water over him. But *City Lights* illustrates particularly well that moments like this are part of a wider strategy.

Having met the Flower Girl, the Tramp is determined to help her. He makes the acquaintance of a millionaire by saving him from suicide in a moment of drunken depression. When drunk, the millionaire is friendly to the Tramp – he pays for flowers which the Tramp gives to the Girl, and allows him to borrow a limousine, thus enabling the Tramp to present himself to the Girl as a rich and eligible benefactor. When sober, however, the millionaire has no recollection of the Tramp. He leaves for a holiday just at the point when the Tramp discovers that the Girl's sight may be cured if he can find the money to pay for an operation. He tries various methods – including street-cleaning and prize-fighting – all without success. But then he meets the millionaire again. The millionaire gives him the money in another moment of drunken generosity. But the gift coincides with a burglary at his home. Now sober, he can remember neither his gift nor his friend. Having given the money to the Girl, the Tramp is arrested and jailed.

Up to this point, *City Lights* is marked by a number of divisions. Apart from setting up thematic oppositions (rich versus poor, blindness versus sight, powerlessness versus power, and so on), it has also established a principle of alternation, moving between sequences which feature the Tramp and the Girl, on the one hand, and sequences which feature the Tramp and the millionaire, or the Tramp trying unsuccessfully to earn some money, on the other. This alternation serves to articulate the double plot structure required of a classical feature film. There is a romance plot involving the Tramp and the Girl, which is predominant, and a plot whose goal is the gaining of money, which is subsidiary. The two plots are structurally interlinked, as is conventional. But the principle of alternation serves to stress the extent to which they are different. Moreover, if the plot about money is conditional upon the romance, the romance is conditional upon the Girl's ignorance of, and separation from, the scenes of which the plot about money consists.

The romance, of course, is the film's major genteel component. However, although most of the slapstick sequences occur in scenes which feature work or the millionaire, there is no clear-cut structural division here corresponding to the two kinds of plot. Indeed, as in the gag with the water referred to above, slapstick constantly interrupts and cuts across the sequences of genteel romance, thus displacing their sentimental tone. Inasmuch as this is the case, however, a further opposition is constructed, an opposition involving Chaplin's performance, persona, and role. Slapstick occurs in the romance scenes because the romance involves the figures of the Tramp, and because the Tramp is played by Chaplin. The romance itself, however, is sustained only because the Girl is unaware of the identity of her benefactor (and of the gags that go on around her), and because the Tramp is able to pose as somebody else.

Having thus constructed, indeed insisted upon, this opposition between genteel and slapstick components, and having thus both acknowledged and marked the extent to which the Chaplin persona is linked to the latter, the problem, for this film as for all Chaplin's features, is how to provide a suitable ending. In *The Circus* (1928), the Tramp retains his identity, but at the cost of losing his love. In *The Gold Rush*, he refinds his love, but at the cost of losing his identity and becoming a millionaire. Both endings acknowledge that the opposition cannot be resolved. The ending of *City Lights* is a variation on the ending of *The Gold Rush*. The Tramp, released from jail, is now a shabby vagrant. While disconsolately wandering the streets he catches sight of the Girl, her vision now restored, working in a flower shop. She laughs at him initially, not knowing who he is, but finally recognizes him when she touches his hand while giving him a flower and some money. This ending is by no means unequivocal. There is no way of knowing whether the romance will be conventionally fulfilled. What is important, though, of course, is the act of recognition. It is this act that rounds off the story and its themes, and it is of a kind entirely consonant with genteel values. It takes place, however, at a cost. For the figure now recognized by the Girl is no longer the spirited, mischievous centre of all the gags. Just as the condition of existence of the romance plot itself is that the Tramp is a rich young man, so the condition of the plot's resolution is that the Tramp is simply a tramp.

All three of the films discussed above show the extent to which slapstick no longer existed in anything like its original form or context by the mid-1920s (except in shorts and cartoons). They also, therefore, show the extent to which the feature films made by Chaplin, Keaton, and Lloyd represent not so much the final flowering of an authentic slapstick tradition as the point at which it came either to be hybridized, combined with other components, or else industrially and institutionally marginalized.

Notes

1 David Pirie (ed.), *Anatomy of the Movies*, Windward, London, 1981, p. 284.
2 Quoted in Tom Dardis, *Harold Lloyd: The Man on the Clock*, Viking, New York, 1983, p. 86.
3 Quoted in Donald McCaffrey, *Four Great Comedians: Chaplin, Lloyd, Keaton, Langdon*, Zwemmer, London, 1968, p. 92.
4 Dardis, op. cit., pp. 96–9; Kalton C. Lahue, *World of Laughter*, *The Motion Picture Comedy Short, 1910–1930*, University of Oklahoma Press, Norman, 1966, op. cit., *passim*; Donald McCaffrey, *Three Classic Silent Screen Comedies Starring Harold Lloyd*, Associated University Presses, Cranbury and London, 1976, pp. 30–4 and 41–4.
5 Tom Gunning, 'The cinema of attraction: early film, its spectator and the avant-garde', *Wide Angle*, vol. 8, no 3–4, 1986.
6 See Robert C. Allen, *Vaudeville and Film, 1895–1915*, Arno Press, New York, 1980, pp. 46–7.
7 Quoted in Brooks McNamara (ed.), *American Popular Entertainments*, Performing Arts Journal Publications, New York, 1983, p. 17.

THE LIBRARY
GUILDFORD COLLEGE
of Further and Higher Education

8 On p. 29 of his book, *Movie-Made America: A Cultural History of American Movies* (Random House, New York, 1975), Robert Sklar claims that 'by 1904, comedies had become the staple of motion-picture production'. However, he offers no evidence, and precise facts and figures regarding this period of the cinema are hard to come by, in part because so many of the films have been lost.

9 Hartley Davis, 'In vaudeville' (1905) in Charles W. Stein (ed.), *American Vaudeville as Seen by its Contemporaries*, Da Capo, New York, 1984, p. 104.

10 George Speaight in *The Book of Clowns*, Sidgwick & Jackson, London, 1982, provides a description of a nineteenth-century circus routine involving a miller and chimney sweep very similar to that represented in the film:

> The miller dressed in a white smock, entered with a sack of flour, and the black-coated chimney sweep carried a sack of soot. They started to argue and the chimney sweep laid a hand on the miller, leaving a black mark on the white smock. The miller retaliated, leaving a white mark on the black coat. They eventually came to blows and the white smock and the black coat were soon covered in soot and flour respectively. The climax of the fight was when the combatants emptied their sacks over each other so that the miller ended up all black, and the chimney sweep all white! (p. 50)

Owing to technical limitations on length, the film has clearly condensed an elaborate slapstick routine into a single, simple gag.

11 Michael David, *The Exploit of Pleasure*, Russell Sage Foundation, New York, 1911, quoted in Gunning, op. cit., p. 68.

12 David S. Hulfish, *The Motion Picture, Its Making and Its Theater*, Electricity Magazine Corporation, 1909, quoted in David Bordwell, Janet Staiger, and Kristen Thompson, *The Classical Hollywood Cinema*, Routledge & Kegan Paul, London, 1985, p. 174.

13 Thomas Gunning, D. W. *Griffith and the Narrator System: Narrative Structure and Industry Organization in Biograph Films, 1908–1909*, 2 vols, UMI, Ann Arbor, 1988, p. 404.

14 Ibid, pp. 407–9.

15 Ibid., p. 408.

16 Ibid., pp. 408–9.

17 Cit., ibid., p. 191.

18 Quoted in Bordwell, Staiger, and Thompson, op. cit., p. 178.

19 Cit. ibid., p. 175.

20 Cit. ibid., p. 178.

21 See David Robinson, *The Great Funnies: A History of Film Comedy*, Studio Vista, London, 1969, pp. 11–27.

22 Quoted in McCaffrey, *Four Great Comedians*, p. 38.

23 Cit. ibid., pp. 38–9.

24 Dardis, op. cit., p. 88.

25 Ibid., p. 142.

26 Buster Keaton (with Charles Samuels), *My Wonderful World of Slapstick*, Da Capo, New York, 1982 edn, pp. 173–4.

27 McCaffrey, *Four Great Comedians*.

28 Cit. ibid., p. 31.

29 Ibid., p. 206.

30 David Bordwell and Kristin Thompson, *Film Art: An Introduction*, Knopf, New York, 1986 edn,
    pp. 142–6.
31 Ibid., pp. 141–2.
32 Ibid., p. 146.
33 Ibid., p. 145.
34 Quoted in Raoul Sobel and David Francis, *Chaplin: Genesis of a Clown*, Quartet, London,
    1977, p. 146.
35 Cit. ibid., p. 146.
36 Cit. ibid., p. 147.
37 Ibid.
38 Cit. ibid., p. 148.
39 David Robinson, *Chaplin: His Life and Art*, Paladin, London, 1986, p. 171.
40 Ibid., p. 171.
41 Ibid., p. 172.

Buster Keaton,

or the work of comedy in the age of mechanical reproduction

TOM GUNNING

[...]

The debates over Keaton's art are now decades old. The 1970s saw the first major and nearly complete revivals of his films, and critics were nearly unanimous in pronouncing Keaton a master of filmmaking. Almost invariably this took the form of a comparison with Chaplin, a comparison almost as potentially misleading as it is inevitable. The general consensus that Keaton is a more interesting filmmaker than Chaplin certainly holds – but only if one ignores the extremely cinematic aspect of Chaplin's performance and restricts one's sense of film to editing, composition, and special effects. There is no question that Chaplin's unique sense of performance and gags defined the rich field of silent comedy. There is also no question that Keaton redefined that field in an eccentric and breathtakingly brilliant manner.

While stylistic comparisons between these two masters are endlessly intriguing, I want to speculate on the different social attitudes contained in their films. Chaplin's social commentary has always been almost too legible. His tramp character was founded on his exclusion from society and his ironic attitudes towards social norms. Increasingly his 'little fellow' was placed in opposition to the values of modern society, the regimentation of work, and the conventions of class status. Chaplin's personal support for left-wing causes, especially during the 1940s (and his unconventional sexuality), led ultimately to the horrendous campaign of vilification and red-baiting so well chronicled in Charles Maland's *Chaplin and American Culture*. Chaplin ended up literally denied access to the US in the 1950s, one of the emblems of the paranoid, antiesthetic, inhumane hysteria of the period.

Keaton never possessed such a recognizable political profile. In the 1940s and 1950s, rather than standing as a target for demagogic attacks, he suffered near eclipse, emblematically playing a featured extra role in Billy Wilder's *Sunset Boulevard* as one of the 'waxworks,' the forgotten, cadaverlike corps of actors stranded from the silent era. Working on the outskirts of the Hollywood studio system, according to his biographer Rudi Blesh, he constructed in his bungalow on the Metro lot an elaborate Rube Goldberg contraption called "The Nutcracker" in which a nut was moved through a maze of mechanics before being smashed by a pile driver. Blesh's reading of the device was simple: "The Nutcracker equaled MGM, the nut equaled Buster Keaton."

A great deal of truth undoubtedly lurks within this equation. Unlike Chaplin, Keaton's tragedy did not end with exile and defiant independence, but with oblivion and gradual absorption into the impersonal meshes of the Hollywood system. A careful viewing of

Keaton's films, however, reveals that from the beginning he had a peculiarly modern insight about individuality and systems which contrasts rather sharply with Chaplin's romantic vagabond. While both these masters of silent comedy devised a style of physical performance in which the human body seemed possessed by the machine-like rhythms and manic tempo of modern life, Keaton's whole world and visual style reflected an intricate Taylorized and Fordian environment. Keaton's character was caught in impersonal systems long before he had surrendered artistic control. The fascination of Keaton's universe, the absurdist aspect of its vast, recessive spaces and oversized props, lies in adapting a vaudeville humor of non sequiturs to a truly modern, environmental art form. Keaton's reputedly 'blank-faced' expression actually reflects the deadly concentration of someone trying to find his place within a system too large and too intricate for him to control. Keaton projects not the freedom of the open road but the plight of modern man trying to find, within a chaos of fast-moving traffic and demonic machinery, a spot where he won't get hurt.

Like Chaplin, Keaton emerged from the performance idiom of turn-of-the-century popular entertainments. But even though both began as child performers, Chaplin's English Music Hall training and Keaton's role within his family's American vaudeville act define fundamentally different attitudes. Billed as "the human mop," Keaton as a child formed part of a knockabout farce of Irish family life. Made up as a miniature stage Irishman complete with sideburn whiskers, Keaton served mainly as a projectile hurled about the stage by his irascible father. The child's deadpan reaction to this treatment set the pattern for Keaton's later characterization. Keaton learned the value of speed and precision from this acrobatic tradition as opposed to the more character-based English pantomime of Chaplin. Keaton became less an expressive character than a master of physical comedy, a ricocheting, impassive body within a larger comic scheme.

When Keaton moved into films under the ample wing of Fatty Arbuckle, he understood how to attract attention by underplaying in contrast to the fat man's buoyant hilarity. According to legend he also immediately investigated the camera mechanism itself and the craft of filmmaking, recognizing it as more than a simple means of self-reflection and reproduction of performance. For Keaton, film through the technology of the camera and the process of editing figured as another complex system in which he had to find his place and plot out a vector of action. Whereas Chaplin used film to create a startling intimacy with his audience, allowing them insight into his most private moments of romantic longing and disappointment (as in the final shot of *City Lights*), Keaton's relation to the audience remained distanced. Only occasionally did he risk a sidelong furtive glance towards the camera at a moment of panic, as if it were a stern parent forcing him to accomplish a difficult task. Keaton's technological control of the cinema undermined the intimacy of performance which Chaplin's English Music Hall experience had nurtured. His short film masterpiece, *The Playhouse*, is fashioned like a demonstration of cinema as an art of mechanical reproduction, multiplying Keaton's images beyond anything even Méliès might have imagined, as Keaton plays all the roles on a vaudeville bill, and every member of the audience as well. Instead of humanizing the cinema as Chaplin had, Keaton seemed determined to push its unnerving mechanical possibilities.

If Chaplin's performance style incorporated a new understanding of the mechanical nature of man's modern behavior, Keaton's films extended this insight into a view of the world itself as machine-like, an alien and alienating system in which only lightning reactions and an identification with the mechanical might aid the all too vulnerable human body. Although Chaplin provides one of the most enduring images of Taylorist Scientific Management and

Fordian assembly-line production in his late feature, *Modern Times*, Keaton's films from the beginning portrayed characters trying to make sense of a rationalized system based on irrational principles. If Chaplin's reaction to industrial production was one of Luddite destruction or anarchic hysteria, Keaton tried constantly to adjust his body to the new demands of systematic environments. These adjustments unmasked the absurdity of the system itself, its anxiety-causing, infantilizing power.

Keaton's characters contend with a modern world in which nothing is stable and in which the rhythms of large machines (particularly the emblem of the industrialization of America's garden, the locomotive) seem to rule. A number of Keaton's early shorts begin with his impassive character on trains, such as *The Goat*, which begins with Keaton falling into the first shot from a passing freight train, while later in the same film Keaton enters a shot seated on the train's cowcatcher and seeming to stare down the camera lens as he approaches it implacably. This identification with the emblems of industrial might places Keaton in a more modern world than the Little Tramp's bucolic wanderings. Keaton's truce with these forces, however, remains an uneasy one.

Keaton's individual gags (and often even the structure of entire films) depend not only on a perfection of performance but also on an encounter and interaction with physical properties. This appears most obviously in the features where the huge ocean liner of *The Navigator*, the trains of *The General* and *Our Hospitality*, or even the movie theatre of *Sherlock Jr.*, provide the antagonists against which Keaton must match his wits. Keaton's anthropomorphizing of the inanimate was widely admired by the Soviet formalists and filmmakers of the 1920s, who proclaimed it a new modern dramaturgy in which objects and machines could play leading roles.

A Keaton gag, as earlier critics have pointed out, plots a sort of comic geometry in which Keaton himself is only one point within a confluence of intricate angles and intersections. Numerous Keaton gags involve his ability to occupy a mathematically precise point within a dangerous process, allowing buildings to collapse around him while he remains unscathed within the tightly circumscribed safety zone of a window, or lowering himself on a crossing barrier in order to land nonchalantly in the back seat of a moving car. Unlike the highly emotional Chaplin, Keaton achieved within his gags a sort of automatism that was widely admired by avant-garde performers of the era, and which reflected the nonconsciousness of the machine. This conception of the performer's strangely inert role within a gag also involved a new conception of the modern environment as a space criss-crossed by physical forces, appearing almost like a physical grid along whose vectors the human protagonist must plot his action with the deftness of a machine or the grace of an angel. Not the least of Keaton's modernity lay in the way he blurred the distinction between these two categories.

Keaton alternates between victimization and mastery of this inhumanely ordered environment. This oscillation between a childish position of apparent impotence before the might of machinery and an athlete's applied knowledge of the laws of physics (which makes him operate like a sublime machine himself) constitutes the narrative structure of most of Keaton's features, as David Moews insightfully pointed out some decades ago. Moews saw this scenario of accomplishments, however, as a Horatio Alger story of acquired maturity and achievement, a pattern found as well in the most popular of the silent comedians of the 1920s, Harold Lloyd. Keaton's subversive role within this narrative of the triumphant overcoming of all odds derives from an essential ambivalence about the nature of this success, an ambivalence due largely to the character's progressive identification with the mechanical.

In this ambivalence Keaton reflects an essential paradox of the 1920s' romance with modernity, both esthetically and politically. It was during this period that utopian visions of a modern mechanical world as a liberating influence contended most forcefully with a growing sense of modern industrial production's dehumanizing potential. While this ambivalence can be traced through philosophers and political theorists as diverse as Joseph Stalin, Antonio Gramsci, and Martin Heidegger, and artists such as Diego Rivera, Vsevolod Meyerhold, Bertolt Brecht, and Fritz Lang, no one blends the promise and the threat of the modern production environment as well as Keaton.

Keaton's victories are hardly the result of an energetic, All-American go-getter's spirit like that of Harold Lloyd. Rather, Keaton's performance introduces to the cinema an uneasy biomechanics which teeters between the utopian possibilities of the machine man so celebrated by the Russian Constructivists and the pliant automaton desired by Henry Ford and Frederick W. Taylor. At this point in history, we may look back at these two alternatives and wonder how different they ever really were. But, watching Keaton, we certainly see not only the dehumanized worker on the assembly line eternally emblematized by Chaplin's Modern Times, but also the lightning reflexes of cinema's Electric Young Man prophesied by Dziga Vertov.

The inherent contradiction between romantic heroism and adaptation to the machine age may explain why the most heroic of Keaton's characters in the feature films look back to a point in the nineteenth century where a few highly skilled professionals gained social status and an aura of romance through their mastery of titanic machines. Keaton in The General or at the climax of Steamboat Bill Jr. reflects the image of the heroic nineteenth-century locomotive engineers and steamboat pilots who seemed to meld with their machines. This sort of romantic union is nevertheless always portrayed in Keaton's films as anachronistically nostalgic (a time that is clearly over) and as somehow already bearing the threat of dehumanization. The end of The General, as Keaton takes over the rhythm of his locomotive to repetitively salute while simultaneously making love to his girl, shows the uneasy nature of Keaton's adaptation to the machine. As Peter Wollen has shown in his important essay on Americanism and the romance with mechanization, "Modern Times: Cinema/Americanism/ The Robot,"[1] the blending of the sexual with the mechanical was a recurrent fantasy and occasional anxiety behind Taylorist-Fordian speculations. Indeed, the overcoming of a sort of immature sexual panic through an identification with the machine seems to drive a number of Keaton's films, most obviously in Sherlock Jr., in which Keaton's film projectionist character watches the screen for step-by-step advice on how to kiss his girl, and ends scratching his head in bewilderment as the screen image cuts to show his model couple surrounded with children.

Keaton's stiff-limbed gestures and his widely expressive eyes conflicting with his frozen mouth invoke a bewildered child astray in an adult world. His astonishing moments of sudden action, control, and physical grace present a contrast to his previous awkwardness, but at the price of becoming machine-like, a billiard ball in thrall to the laws of physics, a cog in a wheel. Keaton's films balance a sense of fatal control with moments of breathless liberation, but both extremes are simply points within an all-embracing mechanics. Keaton may never have articulated these intuitions into a political position, but his films stand as one of the great insights of twentieth-century art into a world in which man had to learn not only to work in a new way, but also to move, fall, and make love in a new rhythm in order to keep pace with systems no longer measured to human demands.

Note

1 Peter Wollen, *Raiding the Icebox: Reflections on Twentieth Century Culture* (Bloomington: Indiana University Press, 1993), pp. 35–71.

Charlie Chaplin and the Annals of Anality

WILLIAM PAUL

[. . .]

The general critical reception of Charlie Chaplin has always recognized the vulgar sources of his material, although usually to point out how much he transcends them. As with Aristophanes, the vulgarity is often acknowledged in order to be dismissed. Chaplin is most often praised for his abilities as a mime, his pathos, his subtlety of expression, his humanism, and, whenever the comedy is addressed specifically, most especially in his later films, his satire. As far as I know, no one has ever thought to praise him for the anality of his humor. A point that touches on this might be mentioned in passing but always in a way that ends up containing it; this aspect of Chaplin's humor is simply not regarded as fit for praise, certainly not to be made central to his art. In effect, there's a kind of censoring here of the lower bodily stratum. This censoring represents an astonishing distortion of his films.

Consider the following scene from *City Lights*: the Tramp is visiting for the first time the home of a poor blind girl, whom he has met on the city streets where she was selling flowers, her meager means of earning a living. Because she has mistaken him for a handsome millionaire, the Tramp tries to live up to the image she's formed of him by demonstrating his largesse with the gift of groceries, including, among other things, a naked, fleshy goose that he tries to describe to her. One oddity I should mention in passing: because this is a silent film, the Tramp inevitably describes things for the blind girl by means of mime, so there is paradoxically a suggestion that the girl has some power of sight. Here it comes up around the plucked goose, which anticipates the denuding of the Tramp that is soon to follow. I'm not sure how much I would want to ascribe this to conscious intent on Chaplin's part, but the use of mime here is not a minor flaw. Rather, it nicely serves to underscore much of the tension in the scene between the Tramp and the blind girl, the danger that she will be able to see him for the tramp he actually is rather than the millionaire she pictures him to be.

Appropriately, then, the central action in the scene revolves around an uncovering. As they sit down to talk, the blind girl asks the Tramp if he will help her roll up a skein of yarn. As the Tramp obligingly holds the wool, she mistakenly takes hold of a thread from his underclothes and winds that up instead. The Tramp is indirectly responsible for what takes place because he had pulled this thread loose from inside his vest and was nervously toying with it while talking to the blind girl. Happy to be with her, the Tramp nonetheless experiences some anxiety in her presence, an anxiety centered on exposure, an act he both desires – he inadvertently initiates it – yet dreads. Too embarrassed to point out that the blind girl has taken hold of the wrong thread, the Tramp allows the accidental unraveling to take place. Wiggling his hips back and forth to allow free movement of the thread and glancing down in dismay at his crotch, the Tramp makes clear as can be, short of actual nudity, exactly what is being exposed.[1] Nonetheless, one critic who has written quite extensively and with great admiration on Chaplin has the blind girl unraveling the Tramp's *undershirt*, thereby neatly censoring out the lower bodily stratum and most of the comic force of this scene.[2] Much as there is a fear of exposure in all of the Tramp's scenes with the girl, finally culminating in the actual exposure in the last scene when the girl with restored sight finally sees the Tramp for what he is, this is the one scene that specifies the nature of the exposure by casting it in terms of the lower body.

This is not an incidental detail any more than the obscenity in Aristophanes is incidental detail. The sexual innuendo in the comedy that I'm foregrounding deserves as much to be foregrounded as it has generally been ignored in the past. Without the foregrounding in this particular instance, the film would be incoherent because Charlie in this film, in fact all his films, rarely doubts himself in *social* terms: indeed, the chief point of his ragged but upper-class costume complete with the dandy affectation of cane is that he sees himself as superior to all other society and for the most part also makes the audience accept that superiority. For the fear of exposure to make sense here, it must be presented in sexual terms, for it is only in sexual terms that Charlie can be made to feel inferior. The sexual imagery in the scene's emphatic pointing to the lower body is something far more important to the film than a simple bit of titillation thrown to the *vulgus* to ensure Chaplin's popularity. In fact, this "vulgar" humor both informs and forms the entire film through a richly articulated complex of sexual imagery.

The misunderstanding of this particular scene might appropriately be a blind spot, a lack of local insight that overlooks the connection between sight and sexuality the film is making here. Nevertheless, there are other ways in which the comedy of *City Lights* is distorted, turned to "reduced forms of laughter," to make it more acceptable to dominant critical standards and take it out of the realm of vulgar comedy. I want to look briefly at the opening scene – the public dedication of a grotesquely monumental statue on which the Tramp is discovered to be asleep – because it is one of the funniest set pieces in all Chaplin and, as such, one of the most frequently commented on. The commentary generally honors the scene for its satire, but if one comes to the film from reading texts on it, the most striking aspect of the scene is in fact the slightness of the satire.[3] Not that the scene isn't satirical, but next to, say, Jonathan Swift, George Bernard Shaw, or Bertolt Brecht, it's all pretty weak stuff, hardly the basis for any claims for Chaplin's art. And in any case, I'm not sure that even the sharpest satire can ever produce the kind of belly laughs we have here, rumbling forth from the lower body into convulsions that go far beyond the more intellectual appeal of satire. *Belly* laughs are the appropriate response here because what *is* very powerful about the scene, hilariously so, is the raucously insistent lower body imagery.

In a large public square, a statue to "peace and prosperity" is about to be unveiled. After a couple of pompous speeches by public figures, the film's first image of uncovering occurs: the great gray cloth is raised to display a grouping of figures in the early 1930s monumentalist style – a seated woman in the center (is she peace or prosperity?) surrounded by reclining male figures.[4] But more is revealed than the statue, for the Tramp has apparently taken refuge here for the night: he is discovered asleep in fetal position in the lap of the seated female. Whether peace or prosperity, she is clearly beneficent, although once revealed, she can no longer protect the Tramp. Awakened by the uproar of the respected gathering, he must emerge from this womb, and the climb down sets his troubles in motion because another figure in the grouping, a reclining male with an upended sword, interferes with the Tramp's progress. There is unfortunately – or is it functionally? – a hole in the Tramp's trousers directly over his anus, and through this hole he is impaled on the erect sword. At one point during his struggles to free himself the national anthem is played, which compels him to stand rigidly at attention until he can resume his struggle.

When he finally gets down from his impalement, he briefly sits on the head of the reclining male so that his anus fits directly onto the man's nose, a nice echo of the sword but also appropriate, albeit unconscious, revenge for it. Leaving this figure, he accidentally, although perhaps again with some unconscious intent, steps in the marble man's crotch. He tips his hat as if to excuse himself, but then as he leaves, he looks at his foot with a grimace, like someone who has just stepped in dog shit, seemingly concerned that something might have rubbed off on his shoe. There is in fact a confusion around this action that is typical of the Tramp: he had actually stepped in the crotch with his left foot, but then looked at his right as if that were the offending foot. Because the revenge against the phallic penetration of the statue must seem accidental, the Tramp distances himself from the agent of his own aggression, suspecting that the passive foot is the one that was contaminated by what the active foot stepped in. One last accidental aggression occurs while he talks to a public official about how to get down: he places his face against an outstretched marble hand that brings about an unexpected "Kiss my ass" gesture. If all this anal and genital imagery represents satire, it's hard to see exactly what's being satirized. It's clear something else is going on.

It might be enough for my purposes to limit my discussion to this scene alone because it is so insistent about something that has just as insistently been ignored in writings on Chaplin. And this limitation would be easy enough to bring off because Chaplin's dramatic structures often seem to break down into a series of set pieces. Nonetheless, the raucous lower body imagery that informs all the comedy of this scene takes on a retrospective resonance from the rest of the film. What I want to stress is some concern for why the scene with its emphasis on womb, anus, and genitals should open the film. This seems to me an especially problematic matter for criticism that sees the scene primarily as satire: usually some attempt is made to relate it to the scenes with the millionaire because some social satire can be read into those sections of the film, but this effectively weakens the force of the opening. If, instead, the sexual imagery is fully recognized, if the vulgar humor is embraced as central to Chaplin's vision, the scene has great importance for the rest of the film.

I can get at this most fully by looking at something else that has been generally ignored in City Lights: the homosexual theme that runs so pronouncedly throughout the film. Even the couple of critics who have mentioned this at all end up dismissing it.[5] Yet at the least, any homosexual theme in the body of the film should relate to the head of the narrative where there is an explicit invocation of homosexual intercourse in the Tramp's troubles with an erect sword. If it were to recognize the homosexuality at all, the satiric view of the film might see an anticipation of the Tramp's getting shafted by the millionaire, who throughout the film wavers between extremes of a lavishly bestowed affection and a cold denial of recognition. This might in fact be an appropriate way of looking at some of the byplay between the Tramp and his inconstant patron. At one point, for example, a gun accidentally goes off as the Tramp is trying to prevent the millionaire from committing suicide. At the sound of the shot, the Tramp dives head first into a couch and immediately begins a protective probing of his backside as if this were the one area most vulnerable to the millionaire's aggression. There *is* satire here, and it has something to do with harm coming from the Tramp's attempt to do good, but why the satirical thrust should be cast in sexual terms still requires explaining.

Beyond that, satire could not account for the one other scene in which the homosexual theme is explicit: finding himself about to fight a boxer who towers over him, the Tramp, to curry favor, simpers, minces, and even makes flirting gestures toward his powerful opponent. The guy is so unnerved by this outrageous behavior that he hides behind a curtain to change into his boxing shorts, even though he has them on under his street pants. His sudden shyness is odd to the extent that he is clearly the Tramp's superior physically, yet he feels genuinely threatened by this display of feminized behavior. The scene, then, suggests that eroticizing a same-sex context endows the Tramp with a surprisingly aggressive power. The homosexual theme generally invokes an issue of power in the film, and as the confrontation with the boxer makes clear, this issue is something more than the opposition of social classes that the satiric view would suggest. In fact, this is an issue that could extend beyond *City Lights* because Chaplin's films are always filled with men who are bigger and stronger than he, men against whom he always measures himself and generally finds some inadequacy that expresses itself in something like coquettish behavior.

To get at what is going on with all these lower body issues in *City Lights* involves me in some speculation that I suspect will be resisted by those who admire the "beauty" and pathos of the ending. Let me state the proposition directly: the Tramp loves the blind girl precisely because she's blind. If you look at the scene where they first meet, you can see him being flirtatious with her as the Tramp would be with any pretty girl, but the point at which she becomes special for him is when he recognizes her defect. Suddenly his whole manner and bearing change; his face takes on an expression of deep concern and solicitousness that signal how much he feels her defect. But I question how much we in fact feel that defect; it seems to me one of the most important strategies of the film, both dramatically and thematically, that we never take the blindness seriously as an actual physical condition. The use of mime in conversation with her that I mentioned earlier suggests the metaphorical status of the blindness. The ease with which the condition is cured drives the point home.

If this is metaphor, then, and the metaphor can be interpreted psychoanalytically, which the insistent sexual imagery in the rest of the film should incline us to, it is not too much of a leap to see that the Tramp loves her for what she lacks, which is to say that the Tramp loves her because he sees her as castrated. This is one way of making sense of the homosexual theme that has puzzled other writers, but also of the very structure of the film, which alternates between night-time scenes with the millionaire whom the Tramp is dependent on and daytime scenes with the blind girl, who is dependent on the Tramp. The two plot lines parallel each other, with each plot presenting one character who acts as the benefactor for the other, but in the nighttime plot the Tramp takes over the role occupied by the woman in the daytime plot. In the nighttime world of men, then, the Tramp becomes a woman, but in the daytime world of women, he at least has the possibility of asserting himself as a man.

In the film's rich sexual imagery, this problematic opposition of masculine–feminine relates to central issues of sight and voyeurism, which might be seen as a kind of phallic privileging.[6] Again, once the sexual imagery is understood, what might seem like an un-integrated set piece becomes central to the film's concerns. What I have in mind is the scene that immediately follows the opening, well before the main narrative lines of the film become clear. The Tramp is passing by an art gallery that has two objects in its window; a rather small figure of a horse on the left and a large statue of a naked woman at the right. The Tramp is immediately arrested by the sight of the naked woman but doesn't want this to be apparent to the passing crowds, so he looks instead at the horse, every now and then stealing a glance at the larger statue. Finally, to indulge his gaze more fully, he adopts the pose of art connoisseur, hand under chin, stepping back to take the measure of the aesthetic experience. Unbeknown to him, a sidewalk elevator has opened up, leaving a gaping hole behind him, but every time he steps back, the elevator returns to street level. The power of the Tramp's gaze is of course dependent on a blindness – the fact that the statue cannot look back – but it is also placed in the context of a danger to which he himself is blind.[7]

Much as the joke here revolves around the privileging of masculine vision, the power of that vision is itself placed in a potentially disempowering context: the capper to the scene foreshadows the homosexual theme that always places Chaplin in subservient position to larger and stronger men. Stepping back one last time, the Tramp finds himself on the elevator as it descends. Scampering back on the sidewalk for safety, he begins to yell and shake his fist at a workman who is riding back up on the elevator. When the elevator fully reaches sidewalk level, it turns out that the workman is another one of Chaplin's imposing giants. Facing this greater physical power, the Tramp immediately loses his belligerent stance: he turns tail and runs. Facing the naked woman who cannot look back, the Tramp possesses power but must express it surreptitiously because he is constrained by propriety. Facing another man, he sees himself as powerless and openly displays his lack of courage.

The ending of *City Lights* presents the culmination of these interlocking themes of sight and power. And however consciously we might be aware of it, the insistent sexual imagery throughout the rest of the film is responsible for the devastating emotional force of the film's ending. The blind girl, having regained her sight, has clearly become empowered by the physical transformation: she moves up the social scale right into the bourgeois classes by becoming a shopkeeper. When the two of them finally see each other the *mise-en-scène* specifically invokes the scene of the Tramp looking at the statue. As in the earlier scene, the camera is inside a store looking through a display window toward sidewalk and street; once again the Tramp has his attention arrested by the female object in the window. This time, however, the woman can look back, and when the Tramp recognizes this he defensively starts to move away from her gaze. The power of sight granted to the woman is a power the Tramp feels he must protect himself from.

To set up this final meeting, Chaplin has deliberately introduced the two characters separately to define a new life for each. In contrast to the blind girl's rise in fortune, the Tramp is seen just after his release from prison, where he had been sent because of the money he had gotten for the blind girl's operation. The sequencing of events is important to our understanding of the Tramp in the final scene because we see him in such an uncharacteristic fashion: for the first time in his screen life, the Tramp really looks like a bum – his clothes now ragged, his entire body bent over in a posture of defeat. Most important of all, he is now missing his cane, the most phallic-aggressive part of his costume.[8] Precisely because we have just seen the blind girl transformed into an independent woman, we must interpret the Tramp's unusual appearance as a loss of power. Clearly, the power has gone elsewhere.

Just before the Tramp meets this newly empowered woman, there is a gag, no longer funny, that deliberately echoes two earlier gags. Two newsboys who had teased the Tramp previously in the film, but to whom he displayed all his self-respect and dignity, again tease him, but now the Tramp can no longer defend himself. This loss of dignity is the greatest defeat for

Chaplin because it represents a loss of the self-image that had always sustained him in all other films against the expectations of conventional social structures. The defeat is specifically tied in to the lower body imagery: as the Tramp bends over, one of the newsboys pulls a rag of torn underwear through the anus hole in the Tramp's pants.[9] The Tramp grabs the rag back from the boy, wipes his nose with it, neatly folds it, and places it in his jacket pocket. The Tramp's response is congruent with other attempts to assert his dignified view of himself, but for once it doesn't work; in effect he defiles himself as he rubs his nose with wipings from his anus. The whole routine recalls both the sword impalement from the opening sequence with its similar anal–nasal progression and the blind girl's inadvertent baring of the Tramp's privates. It is in this context, then, that their final meeting and her recognition of him must be understood as the film moves through an odd play of anal aggression, which the opening makes something passive by always assigning to accident, set against phallic aggression, which is understood as sight.

At its simplest, the cross-cut close-ups that end the film – alternating shots of the once-blind woman looking at the Tramp, slowly recognizing him, and the Tramp tremulously accepting the consequences of her recognition – serve to focus the central questions of the film: can the Tramp allow the woman to see him as he really is, and commensurately can Chaplin allow us in the audience such a privileged view without becoming emasculated? There is a fascinating stylistic figure in this final sequence in a jump cut that effectively isolates the two shots that bring the film to a close.[10] The shot that's angled toward the seeing woman is an over-the-shoulder two-shot, with the Tramp's profile on the left side of the screen; the shot angled toward the Tramp is effectively a single, although there is a slight indication of the woman's presence at the extreme right edge of the image. The sense of opposition gained by the two-shot/single contrast is extended by a mismatched action across the cut. In the single of the Tramp, he holds the flower he had picked up from the sweepings of the shop directly in front of his mouth, defensively covering the bottom of his face; in the two-shot, his hand has dropped to expose his face fully to her view. This opposition, this play between wanting to expose and wanting to cover up, can never be resolved as the jump cut fully separates the two conflicting desires.

Furthermore, there is an issue explored in this scene that ties into some of the central questions in Chaplin's art as I've outlined them here: the scene boldly articulates an opposition between the vulgarity of the grossly material world and the elevated quality of the more spiritual, at times sentimental, impulses implicit in Chaplin's treatment of character. As the now-seeing woman confronts the flesh-and-blood reality of the man she could previously see only in her imagination, as she must confront the apparent disparity between the material and the spiritual, the following questions emerge: How can upper and lower body be made whole? How can the spiritual grace we accord the eyes be made commensurate with the other organs that bring us into contact with the outside world and with other people? There is no full embrace, no assurance of a future together. The film must end on a kind of suspension, a rift the jump cut will not allow to mend, because this is a question that for Chaplin cannot be answered: the demands of upper and lower body remain apart, and yet they also remain within the same body.

The Tramp is most at home in the world of material values; he is a character most fully defined by appetites, which accounts for the great emphasis on hunger in most of his films and the countless gags about eating.[11] Yet the Tramp's appetite also extends to a hunger for the spiritual, which has enabled critical appreciation of Chaplin to emphasize the spiritual over the material, a clear distortion of much of the impact of Chaplin's comedy. The vulgar humor is not merely decoration necessary for an artist who sought widespread appeal; in fact vulgar humor is close to the essence of his work. The kind of material–spiritual opposition that can be found in Chaplin has made it possible for critics to excuse his vulgarity. In focusing on the vulgar roots of Chaplin's art, the delight it takes in exploring the lower body, I have tried to establish that there are values inherent in the vulgarity itself.

Notes

1 In reviewing Chaplin's notes for the film in its early stage of composition, David Robinson locates what seems to be the source for this scene: "There might be a complex variation on the shame gag-nightmares: Charlie could lose his trousers, but then realize that there is no cause for shame since the girl cannot see" (394).
2 The scene is so described by Gerald Mast: "Charlie holds up hands to help her. She, however, mistakenly grabs a strand from Charlie's undershirt, not from the package of yarn she has just bought" (108). It would be most appropriate to identify the garment as a union suit.
3 In a book-length analysis of the film, Gerard Molyneaux, drawing strongly on Bergson's theory of laughter, provides extended analyses of the opening scene that concentrate on the satire and "social comment" (124–138, 212–218).
4 David Robinson identifies the male figure on the right as peace, although there is nothing in the statue that specifically indicates this. It is perhaps the presumption of satiric intent here that leads Robinson to assume Chaplin wants the figure with the sword to represent peace (400).
5 In "some notes on a recent viewing," Stanley Kauffmann observes "a surprising amount of homosexual joking" in the film but more or less throws up his hands in the face of it: "I can't remember this element in another Chaplin picture. I can't explain it here, but the hints are inescapable" (18). Kauffmann at least raises the possibility of an interpretation, but Gerald Weales mentions the homosexuality chiefly to deny it: "[Charlie's] flirtatious attempts to show how harmless he is, which his opponent (Hank Mann) takes as a homosexual advance, suggests nothing so much as the placating behavior with which animals assure the pack leader that they are not challenging his position" (26).
6 Although I think the ending of the film raises real questions about phallic privileging, the connection of sight with phallic aggression is congruent with Laura Mulvey's argument about the masculine gaze (305–315).
7 Julian Smith notes two "blind" statues, lumping the nude together with "Peace and Prosperity" and seeing both solely as foreshadowing (92). Weales also notes the statue's "blindness" and regards its purpose similarly (17).
8 Weales raises this point as well, again to dismiss the sexual meaning: "We do not need to play sexual symbology with the poor man's walking stick to recognize in his pathetic figure a loss of manhood" (27). The capacity for denial when dealing with the more vulgar aspects of Chaplin's art seems limitless.
9 Smith refers to this action as an "unveiling" to relate it to other scenes of exposure in the film, but he is curiously unconcerned with what is being unveiled. Once again, the sexual aspects of the action are ignored.

10 Walter Kerr terms the mismatch a fault, which expresses a narrow notion of film style (351). Given the amount of time Chaplin spent on production and the endless retakes he indulged in, it's unlikely the jump cuts were unintentional. Robinson provides some information on the shooting of this scene, which included seventeen retakes (409–410).

11 This is an issue I have explored more fully in an article on *The Gold Rush*.

References

Robinson, David (1985): *Chaplin: His Life and Art*, New York: McGraw Hill.

Mast, Gerald (1973): *The Comic Mind*, Indianapolis: Bobbs-Merrill.

Molyneaux, Gerard (1983): *Charles Chaplin's "City Lights": Its Production and Dialectical Structure*, New York: Garland Press.

Kauffman, Stanley (1972): "*City Lights*", *Film Comment* (September–October).

Mulvey, Laura (1975): "Visual Pleasure and Narrative Cinema", *Screen*, vol. 16 no. 3 (autumn 1975), reprinted in Bill Nichols (ed.) (1985): *Movies and Methods, Vol. 2*, Berkeley: University of California Press: 305–15.

Smith, Julian (1984): *Chaplin*, Boston: Twayne.

Weales, Gerald (1985): *Canned Goods as Caviar*, Chicago: University of Chicago Press.

Kerr, Walter (1979): *The Silent Clowns*, New York: Knopf.

Paul, William (1972): "*The Gold Rush*", *Film Comment*, vol. 8 no. 3 (September–October): 16–18.

PART THREE

SOUND COMEDY, THE VAUDEVILLE AESTHETIC AND ETHNICITY

Introduction

James Agee and his fellow advocates of the silent screen offer little scope for exploring the new possibilities brought to the comedian film by synchronized and pre-recorded sound. Instead of provoking an irreparable decline in the artistry of film comedy, as Agee would have it, the introduction of sound may be seen to have enriched the cinema's comic potential by allowing it to showcase a broader range of entertainment attractions. After some three decades of muteness, comic performers were now able for the first time to deploy onscreen the verbal and musical specialities they had plied on the stages of vaudeville and Broadway. The two chapters in this section of the Reader take contrasting approaches to considering how the transition to sound impacted upon screen comedy. Henry Jenkins provides an insightful overview of the formal consequences of the vaudeville aesthetic upon the comedies of the period, while Mark Winokur focuses upon the opportunities that sound comedy afforded for the articulation of ethnic identities. Both chapters suggest how the films of this era embody formal and ideological alternatives to the feature comedies of the canonical silent stars.

Jenkins argues that the reputation the Marx brothers have attained as exceptional comedians has tended to dislodge them from the broader context of early sound comedy. The late 1920s and early 1930s witnessed an intensive renewal of the vaudeville aesthetic as Hollywood sought to exploit the potential of the sound film by recruiting legions of entertainers from the stages of Broadway and big-time vaudeville. One consequence was a cycle of what Jenkins terms 'anarchistic comedies', which were wild and crazy entertainment packages that subordinated narrative coherence and character consistency to the demands of performative virtuosity. For Jenkins these films are of interest because they reveal the last gasp of a once vital popular entertainment tradition that came into being with the birth of mass publics' through industrialization, urbanization and immigration. Hollywood comedies of the early sound era reveal the selective assimilation of an entertainment paradigm that operated in a very different way from the classical narrative model embraced by the 1920s feature comedies. Instead of aspiring towards genteel elements, narrative integration or characterization, anarchistic comedies sought to approximate the attraction-oriented mode of the vaudeville aesthetic by emphasizing affective immediacy, performance and interaction with an audience.

Jenkins' chapter concerns itself largey with the formal aspects of anarchistic comedy, dealing with the ways in which these films are shaped by the competition between the distinct aesthetic logics of classical narrative and vaudeville-inspired entertainment spectacle. To emphasize that the Marx Brothers were not alone in exemplifying the anarchistic style during the early sound era, he focuses on the less remembered duo of Bert Wheeler and Robert Woolsey. Jenkins' extended case study of their 1933 vehicle *Diplomaniacs* has been eliminated from this selection to focus upon his more general mapping of the anarchistic comedies, but it is worth noting here some of the conclusions he comes to in his examination of this film. Like other Wheeler and Woolsey vehicles, *Diplomaniacs* positions its comic sequences within a narrative that has two major plotlines: the first concerns the attempt by the Wheeler and Woolsey characters, who are barbers turned diplomats, to secure a peace mission; the second involves a conventional romance between a young couple who unite in the face of social opposition. However, these conventional narrative intrigues are treated in a highly cavalier fashion as the film 'often works to systematically dismantle the causal logic that structures' them (Jenkins 1990b: 12). For example, rather than aiming for the careful braiding of cause and effect that typifies classical Hollywood fiction-making, *Diplomaniacs* delivers its exposition in compressed chunks that serve to set up opportunities for 'assertively independent units of performance and spectacle' (Jenkins 1990b: 13) as the two comedians display the various skills they honed in vaudeville.

The film show-cases a range of performance attractions that includes 'crossfire comedy, Busby Berkeley-style choreography, tearful Irish ballads, knockabout romantic duets, parodic operetta, comic acrobatics, and minstrel cakewalk' (Jenkins 1990b: 14). This emphasis upon performance overrules traditional expectations of character consistency, as 'characters become simply vehicles for moving performers from place to place, creating opportunities for the narrative to give way to the pure spectacle of performative virtuosity' (Jenkins 1990b: 21). The comic protagonists are explicitly stereotypical and, as is commonplace in Hollywood comedy of the early sound era, the film indulges in frequent play with motifs of impersonation and masquerade that serve to mock the very concept of unified identity (for further discussion of such strategies, see Musser 1991: 39–81). Much of what Jenkins has to say about *Diplomaniacs* may be applied to the Marx Brothers' Paramount vehicles, but his focus upon Wheeler and Woolsey does succeed in making the point that such techniques far outweigh the contribution of any particular set of performers.

Where Jenkins challenges the canonical status accorded the Marx Brothers, Mark Winokur's chapter provides a fruitful reinterpretation of their film comedy. In this intriguing selection from his ambitious and provocative book *American Laughter: Immigrants, Ethnicity, and 1930s Hollywood Film Comedy*, Winokur explores the ethnic dynamics of the Marx Brothers' comic style. The introduction of sound, he suggests, 'enabled a Bakhtinian dialogism in which a multiplicity of voices compete for attention and primacy' (Winokur 1996: 137). This not only increased possibilities for direct communication between comic performers, whereas the silent comedian had generally worked alone, but also allowed for the vernacular profiling of ethnically marked voices, accents, dialects and identities. Winokur situates the Marx Brothers within an extended history of negotiation in American cinema (and the broader culture) between ethnic identity and the mainstream. Rather than conceiving of relations between ethnic and dominant cultures as a one-way process in which ethnicity is sacrificed on the altar of mainstream acceptance, he suggests that we should acknowledge the degree to which ethnic dynamics make a revitalizing contribution to the official host culture. Winokur explores the interplay (and simultaneity) of processes of cultural accommodation and resistance in the Marx Brothers' comedy, investigating the manner in which they use hostility to forge a *landsmannschaft* (an unofficial communal alliance of resistant identities) both within the films and between film and audience. This is achieved, he posits, through a variety of techniques: for example, by exposing cultural identity as a multiplicity of potentialities; by satirizing desires for upward mobility; and by disrupting the self-sufficiency of language and fiction.

Anarchistic Comedy and the Vaudeville Aesthetic

HENRY JENKINS III

Writing in 1932, Antonin Artaud characterized the Marx Brothers' *Animal Crackers* as a "hymn to anarchy and whole hearted revolt" against the constraints of narrative, morality, psychic and social repression, everyday logic, and rational thought.[1] Artaud's contemporaries proposed a variety of other metaphors by which to understand the peculiar qualities of the Marx Brothers. They were variously described as "irrepressible clowns," "wild men," "mad and aimless," children at play, hysterics and lunatics, fools, "surrealists," and "nihilists."[2] Yet, of this range of possible metaphors, Artaud's conception of comic "anarchy" has endured, dominating subsequent accounts of early 1930s comedian comedy.[3]

This metaphor survives, I suspect, because it conforms so well to the way that progressive-minded academics like to remember 1930s American culture – as a period of tremendous political upheaval and, at least initially, of a succession of radical alternatives to a capitalist order that seemed to be teetering on the edge of collapse. Politically charged metaphors ("anarchists," "guerilla warriors," "Marxists," "revolutionaries") allow us to claim for the Marx Brothers and their contemporaries a kind of progressive voice. This fantasy of a radically informed comedy finds vivid expression in Robert Warshow's treatment of the team: The Marx Brothers display "an uncompromising nihilism that is particularly characteristic of the submerged and the dispossessed. . . . The Marx Brothers are lumpen, they spit on culture, and express a blind and destructive disgust with society."[4] These writers often see the formal disruption and fragmentation of the Marx Brothers' comedy as expressive of this same type of political "disgust," sliding easily between form and content in their interpretation of the comedy.[5]

We must not become seduced, however, by the power of our own metaphors. Inviting as it is to imagine an American comedy of radical discontent, it is not clear in what meaningful sense the Marx Brothers' films and other early sound comedies may be read as a political reaction against any particular social system or as reflecting any coherent ideological position (anarchistic or otherwise).[6] A film like *Duck Soup* certainly sought to exploit contemporary interest in political and governmental practices; it was part of a large cycle of comedies produced in 1933 and 1934 which evoked a political setting as a basis for broad gags and bizarre comic performances, a cycle which also included *Million Dollar Legs*, *Cracked Nuts*, *Phantom President*, *Stand Up and Cheer*, and *Diplomaniacs*. No doubt this cycle of films can be read in relationship to the heated campaign between Herbert Hoover and Franklin Roosevelt and to the first years of the New Deal, political developments which dominated newspaper headlines during those years. This topicality, however, was offered as simply one audience appeal among many within a polysemous text designed to attract a number of different types of spectators – children as well as adults, city dwellers as well as rural and small-town residents, women as well as men, working-class as well as middle-class viewers, etc. – and we probably should not privilege it in our interpretation of such a mutivalent work.

The film's topical content was submitted to the same aesthetic logic which governed the production of all comedian comedies and took its characteristic shape because this particular conception of the political order best served the formal requirements of the genre and best met audience expectations. The immediate political content of these films, which can be understood as readily as a response to the popularity of Lubitsch's operetta films as to any real-world political crisis, is finally less important as an explanation for this process than the larger comic logic by which that content was transformed into suitable material for comic performers.

Unlike later writers, contemporary critics paid little attention to the political content of these films, regarding them primarily as conventional vehicles for their star comedians and judging them according to how well they conformed to the aesthetic demands of that generic tradition. For example, the *Motion Picture Herald* critic noted the "timeliness" of *Phantom President* but treated its satirical aspects as simply one audience appeal among many in a film that promised "the farcical comedy of an old-time burlesque show, some of the thrills of a circus, and a lot of that surprise that seemed to pass out of existence with the deaths of the old fashioned carnival and medicine show."[7]

These analogies to older types of popular amusements may hold a key to understanding the generic conventions which gave early sound comedy its particular character. Anarchistic comedy emerged from an attempt in the early sound era to assimilate into the classical Hollywood cinema certain aspects of the vaudeville aesthetic, an alternative set of artistic norms which enjoyed an uneasy relationship with dominant filmic practice in the early 1930s. Neither fully contained within the classical cinema nor fully free of its norms, these films represent a succession of uneasy compromises, painstakingly negotiated during the production process, between two competing aesthetic systems, one governed by a demand for character consistency, causal logic, and narrative coherence, the other by an emphasis upon performance, affective immediacy, and atomistic spectacle. Probably no two films resolved these formal problems in precisely the same way. During this transitional period, a variety of different strategies for the creation of comic texts was tested; some embraced classical conventions, while others rejected those conventions in favor of a more faithful reproduction of vaudeville performance traditions, but most texts fell somewhere between these two extremes. Spatial metaphors – attempts to describe these films as "inside" or "outside" the classical cinema – confuse what is essentially a process of negotiation between competing aesthetic logics, logics which can overlap and coexist in ways which spatial categories cannot. What is clear is that these films cannot be fully explained through reference either to classical Hollywood norms or the vaudeville aesthetic but represent some type of overlapping or interplay of the two formal systems.

The history of anarchistic comedy is the history of Hollywood's attempts to absorb those aspects of the vaudeville tradition most compatible with its dominant set of norms, to make its devices functional within the pre-existing logic of the narrative film, and to jettison those elements which proved irreconcilable with classical conventions. Such an approach builds upon the model of the American cinema advanced by David Bordwell, Janet Staiger, and Kristin Thompson, who have persuasively documented the ways that the classical norms responded both to technological changes – the coming of sound, the development of wide-screen, deep focus, and color cinematography – and to outside aesthetic systems – Soviet montage, German Expressionism, European art film – without radically altering its underlying aesthetic logic.[8] While agreeing with their general claim for a high degree of stability within the classical Hollywood norms, I want to emphasize some of the hesitations and localized transgressions which necessarily occurred in the process of adapting an alternative set of formal practices into the mainstream of the American cinema. However successful in the long run in containing disruptions to its normal operations, Hollywood's attempt to assimilate this alien aesthetic was initially marked by tentativeness and experimentation, resulting in far more artistic and popular failures than successes. Yet this creative tension also gave rise to a number of remarkable works which gain their vitality and fascination from their ability to break free, if only momentarily, from the conventional structures of the classical cinema.

Focusing primarily upon the formal rather than the political aspects of "anarchistic comedy," this chapter will sketch some central characteristics of this alternative aesthetic tradition and then show how a greater understanding of the vaudeville aesthetic sheds light on the "anarchic" qualities of [. . .] early sound [comedies such as] the 1934 Wheeler and Woolsey vehicle *Diplomaniacs*. My selection of this somewhat obscure example reflects not simply a desire to bring about greater critical awareness of the neglected talents of Wheeler and Woolsey. My hope, rather, is that by shifting the focus from the Marx Brothers on to a competing comedy team of the same period, we may begin to distinguish between what is idiosyncratic and original and what reflects a commitment to a broader set of performance practices and aesthetic assumptions, between those aspects of anarchistic comedy which fit within a much older performance tradition and those aspects which can be read as responsive to more immediate sociopolitical concerns.

"Built for entertainment purposes only"

The dawn of the twentieth century witnessed an explosion of comic materials of all types into the marketplace, a development which delighted mass audiences and proved highly profitable for entertainment entrepreneurs, a development witnessed with horror by literary critics and progressive reformers who felt that it would contribute to a collapse of the existing social and cultural order.[9] Increased leisure time and expanded family budgets had greatly broadened the potential market for commercial entertainment; shifts in technology and corporate organization had created conditions which allowed for a large-scale exploitation of this market. The result was a large-scale commodification of the joke. According to one study, the number of joke books published in the USA had grown from eleven in 1890 to 104 in 1907 and continued to expand throughout the first two decades of the new century.[10] More than thirty-five different humor magazines, many of them weeklies, were added to the market between 1883 and 1920, providing a key base of support for would-be gag writers.[11] Amateur humor magazines, such as the *Harvard Lampoon*, appeared on the campuses of many universities. Comic strips invaded the newspapers, often expanding dramatically their circulation. Comedy constituted a sizable percentage of the acts on vaudeville, the films in the nickelodeons, and, later, the programs on radio. Each of these new forms of mass amusement tended to emphasize fragmentation and intensification over more classical concerns of character consistency, thematic ambitiousness, or narrative coherence as criteria for evaluating the quality of their product.

The clash of these two paradigms can be seen in sharp relief in the contrast between two statements, the first by a literary critic for *Blackwood's Magazine* which reflects the norms of nineteenth-century elite culture; the second from Brett Page's guidebook for would-be vaudeville writers which suggests the craftsmanlike orientation of this new discourse about comedy:

> The great men who dared to laugh in an earlier age than ours laughed in moderation. . . . They held folly up to ridicule, not to amuse the groundlings, but to reveal, in a sudden blaze of light, the eternal truths of wisdom and justice . . . They did not at every turn slap their reader on the back and assure him that there is nothing congruous in the visible world. . . . They kept their humor in its proper place; they used it for a wise purpose; they did not degrade it for an easy round of applause.[12]

> The purpose of the sketch is not to leave a single impression of a single story. It points no moral, draws no conclusion, and sometimes it might end quite as effectively anywhere before the place in the action at which it does terminate. It is built for entertainment purposes only and furthermore, for entertainment purposes that end the moment the sketch ends.[13]

For the *Blackwood's* critic, comedy must "instruct"; for Page, it need only "entertain." For one, the outward display of emotion is to be distrusted, laughter is to be restrained; for the other, outward affective response is a measure of success in a craft which ruthlessly exploited any and all means of producing a laugh. The moral certainty of bourgeois Victorian comic sensibility, which was governed by a pursuit of a restrained and thoughtful laughter and a distrust of all overt efforts at laugh-making, was called into question by these brash new merchants of mirth for whom it was perfectly acceptable to say of their comic material that it was "built for entertainment purposes only."

While the traditional aesthetic saw the ability to perceive comic incongruity as a mark of social distinction, the new aesthetic sought to level the classes, to appeal to the types of visceral responses its advocates saw as basic to all humans.[14] George M. Cohen and George Jean Nathan wrote in 1913: "If we are normal, we all cry at the same things, laugh at the same things, and are thrilled by the same things."[15] Spectators, they argue, are drawn to the theater to have their "emotions played upon," to be pulled away from the humdrum reality of their workaday experience and thrust into a situation where they may experience affect without consequences. Making explicit references to the developing science of reflexology, Cohen and Nathan suggest that humans possess certain "emotional reflexes" which are manipulated by the playwright and performer into a predictable audience response. A mastery of a vocabulary of basic mechanical devices, calculated to produce certain affective responses, may ensure success in gratifying audience demands for stimulation and release of intense emotions.

Consider, for example, how burlesque clowns Joe Weber and Lew Fields characterize the devices which produce the best response from their audience:

An audience will laugh loudest at these episodes:

a)   when a man sticks one finger into another man's eyes,
b)   when a man sticks two fingers into another man's eyes,
c)   when a man chokes another man and shakes his head from side to side,
d)   when a man kicks another man;
e)   when a man bumps up suddenly against another man and knocks him off his feet;
f)   when a man steps on another man's foot.

Human nature . . . will laugh louder and oftener at these spectacles, in the respective order we have chronicled them, than at anything else one might name.[16]

The audience's response to such gags did not involve the quick perception of subtle incongruity or any specialized knowledge and background; it required merely a visceral reaction to crude shock, intense stimulation, and immediate sensation.

The vaudeville aesthetic

Vaudeville embraced this new style of humor more fully than any other form of commercial entertainment, though these practices and norms could also be found elsewhere in turn-of-the-century commercial culture. A reconstruction of the aesthetic practices of vaudeville will suggest the ways that the principle of affective immediacy could be translated into particular performance techniques calculated to win audience approval and to ensure the commercial viability of mass entertainment.

The underlying logic of the variety show rested on the assumption that heterogeneous entertainment was essential to attract and satisfy a heterogeneous mass audience.[17] The vaudeville program was constructed from modular units of diverse material, no more than twenty minutes in length each, juxtaposed together with an eye toward the creation of the highest possible degree of novelty and variety. The program as a whole offered no consistent message; the individual acts might very well offer conflicting or competing messages. A melodramatic playlet might exist alongside a comic sketch parodying those same conventions; Shakespeare and opera shared the stage with Salome dancers, trained dogs, and acrobats who strapped hammers to their feet and danced atop giant xylophones. What mattered was the quality of the individual performances rather than their logical relationship to the overall bill.

The vaudevillian, as master of the act from conception to execution, sought material tailored to particular performance skills. The performers were never subservient to the script; rather, the narrative, where it existed at all, simply served as a vehicle to showcase their familiar tricks. Theater critic Vadim Uraneff wrote, "The actor is always in the foreground, the literary form is calculated with a view to the individual possibilities of the actor. The interest of the act never depends upon the plot, for it is the actor that counts."[18]

The merits of the program were determined by the performer's ability to manipulate the audience to the point that they suspend conscious thought and simply felt. Robert Littell told *New Republic* readers in 1925 what he saw as characteristic of the best vaudeville performers:

Human horsepower, size, electricity, energy, zingo. . . . These people have a fire in their belly which makes you sit up and listen whether you want to or not, which silences

> criticism until their act is over and you can begin thinking again. . . . They seize you and
> do pretty nearly anything they want with you and while it is going on, you sit with your
> mouth open and laugh and laugh again.[19]

This intense style of performance evolved in response to theater managers who looked
toward audience response as a tangible measure of quality and as a determinent of future
bookings.[20] To achieve this impact, the clowns shoved their gags, literally and figuratively, into
their patron's faces, demanding that they laugh, refusing to accept a complacent response.
No other aspect of the performance was more important than establishing and maintaining
an intense bond which bridged the gap between stage and seats. Most commentators
suggested that sets should minimize details which might distract attention away from the
foregrounded performer.[21] Monologists and comic teams whose appeal was primarily verbal
frequently played in front of the olio curtain with no sets or props whatsoever. The absence
of these other types of stage effects simply intensified the focus upon the performer as a
primary source of audience fascination.

Performers were expected to execute their specialties with a consistently high level of
speed and precision. Frequently, the nature of the act focused attention precisely upon the
display of their performance skills, having little or no other justification or interest. Such
was certainly the case with the protean or quick-change acts, where the star might perform
an entire one-act play, alone on the stage, shifting gestures, vocal patterns, and costumes
to convey as many as forty or fifty different characters. Impressionists, quick sketch artists,
male and female impersonators, whistlers, rag-folders, cloth-drapers, eccentric dancers,
impersonators of animals or babies appealed to a desire to be impressed by the skill of the
performer rather than absorbed within the development of a narrative.

This fierce competition for the spotlight often pushed performers toward adopting more
and more different specialties into a single act. Jugglers like Fred Allen and W. C. Fields,
acrobats like Mitchell and Durant, rope artists like Will Rogers incorporated comic material
into their acts as a means of giving them a creative edge over other acts which utilized
the same basic tricks. The consummate performer was one who could do the broadest range
of different types of specialties within the shortest period of time. The Siamese Twins, a 1925
act, showcased a pair of circus "freaks" who engaged in saxophone and clarinet duets,
impersonated other sister acts, sang sentimental love songs, cracked jokes, and performed
ballroom and tap dancing, all within a fifteen-minute appearance. A jaded *Variety* critic
remarked that they were "not bad for an act of this type."[22]

The demand for immediacy also pushed the variety artist toward the utmost economy of
means. Eddie Cantor told an *American Magazine* interviewer in 1924: "A comedian in vaudeville
. . . is like a salesman who has only fifteen minutes in which to make a sale. You go on the
stage, knowing that every minute counts. You've got to get your audience the instant you
appear."[23] This brutal economy weighed against the types of exposition necessary to develop
particularized characters or to place them within particularized situations. Instead, characters
and situations needed to be immediately recognizable. An elaborate system of typage
developed through which exaggerated costumes, facial characteristics, phrases, and accents
were meant to reflect general personality traits viewed as characteristic of a particular class,
region, ethnic group, or gender. Such characters made few claims toward complex personalities or motivations nor even much attempt toward particularity or individuality. Indeed,
Brett Page warned would-be sketch writers that they did "not [have] much chance of making

new characters" but their contributions came from employing the prefabricated types in a novel fashion.[24] Performers won praise not for their ability to assume the "cloak" of a character but rather from their ability to rise above characters, to project a unique personality that transcended stock roles.

Vaudeville's push toward the intensification of affective experience also meant that concern with narrative development often fell by the wayside. The comic sketch or monologue depended more upon the comic "bits" than upon the sense of the whole. Vaudevillian Wilfred Clarke told Variety readers in 1906 that an ideal sketch "must be full of business and situations, not one but many; no time for plot; no time for scenic effects."[25] Each segment within the sketch was expected not to contribute to the overall development of a narrative but to assist in the gradual intensification of audience response. Clarke continued, "Each sentence should create a laugh, so as to never allow the ball to stop rolling. To obtain such continuous laughter, a sketch must border on the ridiculous, but if played seriously by the actors engaged . . . the audience forgets the lack of plot and story and laughs!" What mattered was "the impression of the time being," not the larger context within which a particular comic "bit" might be placed.[26]

The vaudeville sketch, monologue, or crossfire routine was to be built up from component parts much as the vaudeville program was constructed from the modular units of the various acts. Brett Page's instructions about how to write a vaudeville monologue point to just such a conception of the performance text:

> Have as many cards or slips of paper as you have points or gags. Write only one point or gag on one card or slip of paper. On the first card, write "Introduction" and always keep that card first in your hand. Then take up a card and read the point or gag on it as following the introduction, the second card as the second point or gag, and so on until you have arranged your monologue in an effective manner. . . . By shuffling the cards you may make as many arrangements as you wish and eventually arrive at the ideal routine.[27]

These "bits" of comic business or patter could be drawn from a number of different sources, only to be yoked together by the performer into some loose structure. Certain moments in the performance were more or less fixed and inflexible. The introduction needed to quickly establish the characters and their immediate situation or perhaps to define the theme from which other variations would be derived. The act should build toward a "wow finish" which tops all preceding gags and ends on a note of peak emotional intensity. Closure was of little importance to the vaudeville performer, but climax was, since the audience's final response to the act would be the major determinant of the house manager's report. Other elements could be added, subtracted, or rearranged with far greater flexibility, shuffled about like Page's index cards. The sequencing of the various comic bits had less to do with their logical relationship or narrative function than with their emotional impact; the laughter was to grow with each point until it reached a crescendo, then a few throw-away lines allowed the audience to catch its breath before the onslaught began again.

The commercial logic underlying the vaudeville aesthetic pushed performers toward the intensification of audience response, the milking of laughter and applause. The performer's need to ensure future bookings within a mode of production which granted aesthetic independence at the expense of economic vulnerability similarly pushed desperate performers to cast themselves as the focus for that response, as a kind of lightning rod which could attract and direct emotional energies. Writing in 1923, theater critic and playwright Vadim Uraneff suggested that the rest of the vaudeville aesthetic evolved from this fundamental need to generate outwardly recognizable spectator reactions to performer virtuosity: "The actor works with the idea of an immediate response from the audience; and with regard to its demands. By cutting out everything – every line, gesture, movement – to which the audience does not react and by improvising new things, he establishes unusual unity between the audience and himself. . . . Stylization in gesture, pose, *mise-en-scène* and make-up follows as a result of long experimentation before the primitive spectator whose power as judge is absolute."[28]

Vaudeville and the classical Hollywood cinema

The importance of vaudeville both as an early exhibition outlet and as a model for early film-making practice has been well documented.[29] What Tom Gunning has labeled the "cinema of attractions" was at least partially a response to the insertion of early films into existing forms of variety entertainment and the need to appeal to audiences schooled in the conventions of vaudeville practice.[30] Historically, Hollywood's construction of a system of classical norms and its push toward middle-class acceptance meant a conscious rejection of vaudeville norms in favor of those of theatrical realism or, at the very least, a marginalization of texts produced in response to the vaudeville aesthetic into specific classes of films or specific moments safely contained within larger film narratives.[31] While the comic film tended to lag behind the rest of the American cinema in its acceptance of classical Hollywood norms, remaining one of the places where marginal film practices enjoyed the greatest acceptability, the genre nevertheless experienced and ultimately capitulated to the same pressures which shaped all of classical cinema.

The recruitment of vaudeville and revue performers in the early sound period and the effort to construct appropriate vehicles for their talents represented a conscious return to an aesthetic previously rejected, a new effort to appropriate devices from vaudeville and to integrate them into the system of classical codes and conventions. Initially, Hollywood sought to establish a solid urban base for talking pictures through presenting recorded versions of pre-existing stage productions, hoping to preserve the qualities which made those shows popular with their audiences.[32] The stage recruits brought with them only a limited supply of previous theatrical material which was quickly exhausted by the studio system's demand for a rapid turnover of star vehicles; this depletion necessitated the creation of original screenplays which fell within this same performance tradition, preserving those aspects of the star's image which had generated their initial popularity, but which were perhaps more compatible with the standard plot formulas of the classical film and the more conservative taste of rural and small-town spectators. Pressures toward standardization of product and normalization of star image would eventually result in the formal and thematic conservatism of the late 1930s comedian comedy. In the short run, however, the studios were prepared to tolerate a certain degree of experimentation, even experimentation which pushed against (and perhaps beyond) the limits of what might legitimately be labeled classical narrative, provided these experiments found a receptive audience at the box office.

The vaudeville aesthetic contrasts sharply with the formal norms which Bordwell, Staiger, and Thompson have found to be characteristic of Hollywood studio practice during this same period:

We find that the Hollywood cinema sees itself as bound by rules that set stringent limits on individual innovations that telling a story is the basic formal concern . . . ; that unity is a basic attribute of film form, that the Hollywood film purports to be "realistic" in both an Aristotelian sense (truth to the probable) and a naturalistic one (truth to historical fact); that the Hollywood film strives to conceal its artifice through techniques of continuity and "invisible storytelling."[33]

A comedy which sought to integrate some central aspects of the vaudeville aesthetic into dominant studio practice would be a strange-looking film indeed. It would be a text shaped by competing if not directly contradictory aesthetic impulses, one that asserted the centrality of narrative only to puncture that narrative with a series of self-contained performance sequences that are often far more memorable than any story the film might tell, one that ruptured character consistency to allow for a constant display of performer virtuosity.
[. . .]

Conclusion

This highly fragmented and disruptive style of comedy in *Diplomaniacs* may be understood in at least two ways: either as a failure to successfully construct a classical Hollywood narrative, a noisy but static decline from the brilliance of "comedy's greatest era," or as a successful attempt to complete a narrative film which nevertheless satisfies the criteria of the vaudeville aesthetic. Both evaluations were in circulation at the time of *Diplomaniacs'* release. Contemporary critics of early sound comedy frequently characterized the films' narratives as "flimsy," "incidental," "inconsequential," "sloppy," "scattered and shapeless," "just thrown together without rhyme or reason," or "so much padding."[34] More favorable commentators suggest that their stories are "wild nonsense," "pleasantly irrational," "giddy goofiness and aimless goings-on," and "senseless but clever."[35] All of these phrases represent different responses to similar aspects of the films' formal organization – a sense of fragmentation, heterogeneity, and disunity, an excessive concentration on comic performance at the expense of story and character development, a fundamental deviation from the norms of classical Hollywood cinema. One group of critics finds these breaks with standard film practice an obvious source of pleasure while the other just as obviously finds them displeasurable and distracting; one reads them as a necessary component of the films' overall style while the other treats them as reflecting an inability to conform to acceptable craft standards.

If later commentators have championed the Marx Brothers' particular inflection of this generic tradition as a radical break with the ideological and formal norms of Hollywood, the genre's detractors increasingly came to dominate the contemporary debate surrounding this style of comedy. By late 1934, box office revenues for these comedies began to decline sharply, a decline which the trade press attributed to the overexposure of their comic stars and their failure to produce a consistently high quality product. *Diplomaniacs* was Wheeler and Woolsey's twelfth film together in four years, the fourth vehicle they had made under the direction of William A. Seiter.[36] The stars had begun to exhaust the repertoire of "tried and true" material they had developed through their years in vaudeville and the New York revues. As the appeal of individual performers declined, the absence of a solid story or particularized characters became harder to tolerate; the number of moments of "astonishment" and virtuosity dwindled beyond the threshold of audience enthusiasm. Local exhibitors, especially those in outlying areas who had initially been the most enthusiastic about this style of broad comedy, now complained of their incomprehensibility and "slap-dash" construction. While *Diplomaniacs* stands with *Peach O'Reno*, *Hips Hips Hooray*, and *Cockeyed Cavaliers* among the team's most accomplished films, this opinion was apparently not shared by its contemporary audience. Theater owner A. E. Hancock (Columbia City, Indiana) told *Motion Picture Herald* readers that it was "the poorest they have had," complaining that "the same people that made *The Cuckoos* and *Rio Rita* [the team's first successes, both based on Broadway musicals] . . . evidently have lost what it takes to make a picture with this pair."[37] J. J. Hoffman (Plainview, Nebraska) agreed: "Not as good as their others; seemed to have missed a cog somewhere but couldn't figure out where. We expected a big laugh but only got a few chuckles."[38]

Wheeler and Woolsey faced additional resistance because of their heavy reliance upon scatological humor. Their previous film, *So This Is Africa*, had been the subject of heated controversy because of the alleged vulgarity of its treatment of sexual themes, especially the issue of homosexuality, which eventually provoked an official response from the Production Code Administration. PCA executives sat down with the Ohio and New York censor boards and substantially re-edited the film to conform to their far-reaching complaints. The Ohio board alone requested sixty-six cuts including the omission of twelve entire scenes.[39] Individual exhibitors expressed considerably more ambiguity about the degree to which the film violated acceptable standards, noting that it shocked many of their patrons ("When college boys think a film vulgar, nothing more can be said about it"), yet acknowledging that the controversy attracted considerable trade: "If you can get it by the 'blue-noses,' grab this one. One of the best nights we've had in a long time."[40] *Diplomaniacs* faced an uphill struggle to overcome perceptions both by the Production Code Administration and by the general public that Wheeler and Woolsey were "dirty comics," a perception which cut deep into their box office returns and may account for why they are remembered less favorably today than the Marx Brothers, who somehow escaped similar labeling.

Responding to declining box office, exhibitor dissatisfaction, and public outrage, the studios either jettisoned declining comic stars or brought their vehicles into greater conformity with classical storytelling conventions and established social standards. The shift in the Marx Brothers' comedies from their Paramount vehicles to those produced for MGM was mirrored by all the other comic teams who weathered this difficult transitional period. By the fall of 1934, the "bounds of difference," the possibilities for formal experimentation and aesthetic deviation within the classical Hollywood cinema, were narrowing; anarchistic comedy would soon be replaced by a style of comedy which was far more conservative both formally and ideologically, a style of comedy best exemplified by the films of Joe E. Brown, Joe Penner, Abbott and Costello, and Danny Kaye. RKO continued to feature Wheeler and Woolsey in a string of progressively less satisfying vehicles until 1937, when their career was ended by Robert Woolsey's death, yet most of their subsequent films lack the anarchic energy, comic inventiveness, and performance virtuosity of *Diplomaniacs*.

If these anarchistic comedies deserve reconsideration today, it is not because they offer a vivid expression of Depression era anxiety and discontent but rather because they represent the last gasp of a once lively theatrical tradition and because they suggest possibilities for alternative aesthetic systems to function within the mainstream of classical Hollywood cinema. That formal disruptiveness cannot be reduced to a mere symptom of some deeper political disruptiveness, as might be suggested by much of the critical discourse surrounding the Marx Brothers, but can be read in the context of a series of complex negotiations between competing aesthetics, a series of stylistic shifts made in response to the changing composition of the audience for talking pictures, and an increasing standardization of studio product following the experimentation of the early sound period. Understood in that light, the comedians' consistent challenge to the hegemony of cinematic classicism tells us as much or more about the limits of innovation within standardized film production as their passing topical references or even their underlying comic vision suggest about the dominant ideological structures of their times.

Notes

I am indebted to Tino Balio, David Bordwell, Donald Crafton, John Fiske, Kristine Karnick, Peter Krämer, James Moy, Murray Smith, and Lynn Spigel for suggestive comments or careful readings of one or more segments of this manuscript.

1 Antonin Artaud, "The Marx Brothers," in *The Theatre and Its Double* (New York: Grove, 1968), pp. 142–44.
2 Otis Ferguson, "The Marxian Epileptic," in Alistair Cooke, ed., *Garbo and the Night Watchmen* (New York: McGraw-Hill, 1971); John Grierson, "The Logic of Comedy," in Forsyth Hardy, ed., *Grierson on Documentary* (New York: Harcourt, Brace and Company, 1947), p. 34; "The Marx Brothers Abroad," *Living Age* (September 1932): 371–72; Meyer Levin, "Duck Soup," *Esquire* (February 1934); William Troy, "Films," *Nation*, December 13, 1933, p. 688, Clifford Fadiman, "A New High in Low Comedy," *Stage* (January 1936): 322–28; Arthur Knight, *The Liveliest Art* (New York: New American Library, 1959), pp. 163–65.
3 See, for example, Raymond Durgnat, *The Crazy Mirror: Hollywood Comedy and the American Image* (New York: Dell, 1969), pp. 150–58; Andrew Bergman, *We're in the Money: Depression America and Its Films* (New York: Harper and Row, 1971), pp. 30–48; Gerald Mast, *The Comic Mind: Comedy and the Movies* (New York: Random House, 1976), p. 281; Gerald Weales, *Canned Goods as Caviar: American Film Comedy of the 1930s* (Chicago: University of Chicago Press, 1985), pp. 55–83.
4 Robert Warshow, *The Immediate Experience: Movies, Comics, Theatre and Other Aspects of Popular Culture* (New York: Atheneum, 1975), p. 50.
5 Bergman characterizes the formal fragmentation and zany performances of the Marx Brothers' comedies as "a wild response to an unprecedented shattering of confidence" in the national leadership and capitalist economic system (*We're in the Money*, pp. 30–48).
6 I have retained the term *anarchistic comedy* to maintain consistency with my other writings on this topic, even though I am not directly concerned with the thematic construction of the films here. The ideological implications of this particular type of comedy are discussed at greater length in Henry Jenkins, "What Made Pistachio Nuts?: Anarchistic Comedy and the Vaudeville Aesthetic," Ph.D. Dissertation, University of Wisconsin, 1989. I prefer the term *anarchistic comedy* to the alternative form, *anarchic comedy*, for two reasons: First, anarchistic comedy preserves a sense of process in the texts, a movement from order to disorder, while anarchic comedy might suggest a consistent state of anarchy throughout the narrative, second, anarchistic comedy foregrounds the active and central role of the central clowns as bringers of anarchy in a way that anarchic comedy does not.
7 "Showmen's Reviews," *Motion Picture Herald*, September 24, 1932, p. 30.

8 David Bordwell, Janet Staiger, and Kristin Thompson, *The Classical Hollywood Cinema: Film Style and Mode of Production to 1960* (New York: Columbia University Press, 1985). For a historiographical discussion of this project, see David Bordwell, "Historical Poetics of the Cinema," in R. Barton Palmer, ed., *The Cinematic Text: Methods and Approaches* (New York: AMS Press, 1989), pp. 369–98.

9 What had changed was not so much the style and content of American "low" comedy but rather the degree to which it was able to penetrate the marketplace and to gain a broader circulation than previously. Many of the traits I will link in this paper to vaudeville can be traced back to earlier traditions in burlesque, showboats, circuses, and minstrel shows. What provoked heated response from progressive era reformers and literary magazine intellectuals was a threat to their own ability to police culture and to define the boundaries of cultural respectability. The expanding power of entrepreneurs and the increasing diversity of audiences meant more and more people were embracing an aesthetic tradition fundamentally at odds with contemporary bourgeois taste and a traditional comic aesthetic. There is an ever-expanding literature on the subject of the origins of American mass culture. For representative works, see Kathy Peiss, *Cheap Amusements: Working Women and Leisure in Turn-of-the-Century New York* (Philadelphia: Temple University Press, 1986); John Kasson, *Amusing the Millions: Coney Island at the Turn of the Century* (New York: Hill and Wang, 1981); Shirley Staples, *Male–Female Comedy Teams in American Vaudeville, 1865–1932* (Ann Arbor: UMI Press, 1984); Lewis A. Erenberg, *Steppin' Out: New York Nightlife and the Transformation of American Culture, 1890–1930* (Westport: Scarecrow, 1981); Roy Rosenzweig, *Eight Hours for What We Will: Workers and Leisure in an Industrial City, 1870–1920* (Cambridge: Cambridge University Press, 1983).

10 Harry B. Weiss, *A Brief History of American Joke Books* (New York: New York Public Library, 1943); Albert McClean, Jr., *American Vaudeville as Ritual* (Louisville: University of Kentucky, 1965), Albert McClean, Jr., "U.S. Vaudeville and the Urban Comics," *Theatre Quarterly* (October–December 1971): 50–57.

11 Stanley Trachtenberg, ed., *American Humorists, 1800–1950* (Detroit: Gale Research, 1982).

12 *Blackwood's Magazine*, "The Limitations of Humor," *Living Age*, August 31, 1907, pp. 485–95.

13 Brett Page, *Writing for Vaudeville* (Springfield: Home Correspondence School, 1913), p. 147.

14 James Sully, *An Essay on Laughter: Its Forms, Its Causes, Its Development and Its Value* (New York: Longmans, Green, 1902), p. 283.

15 George M. Cohan and George Jean Nathan, "The Mechanics of Emotion," *McClure* (November 1913): 95–96.

16 Joe Weber and Lew Fields, "Adventures in Human Nature," *Associated Sunday Magazine*, June 23, 1912, as cited in Page, *Writing for Vaudeville*, pp. 103–04.

17 For the sake of parsimony, this chapter intentionally ignores a set of distinctions which are traditionally in place within historical discussions of variety entertainment – both the hierarchical distinction between burlesque, vaudeville, and New York revue and the historical one between variety and vaudeville. While space does not allow me to develop this position here, I would contend that the high degree of continuity between these various types of variety entertainment makes such distinctions somewhat arbitrary. Many performers moved in the course of their careers from burlesque to vaudeville, from vaudeville to revue, from revue to musical comedy, and from Broadway to Hollywood with relative ease and only limited shifts in the style and content of their performances. Like

the distinction between variety and "refined vaudeville," these categories are really the product of entrepreneurial discourse, the push toward product differentiation and audience expansion which characterizes all of commercial entertainment. Reviews of city recreational surveys and other middle-class response to vaudeville during this period suggests that variety entertainment never achieved the degree of universal middle-class acceptability claimed for it by Pastor, Albee, Keith, and others but rather remained a site of cultural struggle between an emergent style of entertainment and traditional aesthetics and canons of good taste. While attention to these aesthetic distinctions may tell us much about the politics of taste and the process of creating and maintaining cultural distinctions, a topic which my dissertation addresses at some length, they do not prove as useful in discussing a set of aesthetic practices which crosses over the boundaries the entrepreneurs and intellectuals sought to erect.

18 Vadim Uraneff, "Commedia Dell'Arte and American Vaudeville," *Theatre Arts* (October 1923): 326.

19 Robert Littell, "Vaudeville Old and Young," *New Republic*, July 1, 1925, p. 156.

20 Walter De Leon, "The Wow Finish," *Saturday Evening Post*, February 14, 1925, pp. 16ff.

21 "Settings must not overshadow the performance . . . if the essentials of movement and active diversion are to be kept" (Constance Mayfield Rourke, "Vaudeville," *New Republic*, August 27, 1919, pp. 115–16). See also Marsden Hartley, "Vaudeville," *Dial* (March 1920): 335–42. We must not overlook, however, the economic imperative which restricted the complexity of settings in vaudeville. Performers were responsible for the purchase, upkeep, and transportation of their own scenery. To save money, they minimized stage effects and worked with the limited range of backdrops which could typically be found at most variety houses.

22 "New Acts: The Siamese Twins," *Variety*, February 25, 1925, p. 8.

23 Mary. B. Mullett, "We All Like the Medicine 'Doctor' Eddie Cantor Gives," *American Magazine* (Jul 1924): 34ff.

24 Page, *Writing for Vaudeville*, p. 118.

25 Wilifred Clarke, "The Vaudeville Novelty," *Variety*, December 12, 1908, p. 43.

26 Cohan and Nathan, "Mechanics of Emotion."

27 Page, *Writing for Vaudeville*, p. 86.

28 Uraneff, "Commedia Dell'Arte."

29 See, for example, Robert C. Allen, *Vaudeville and Film, 1895–1915: A Study of Media Interaction* (New York: Arno, 1980); Bordwell, Staiger, and Thompson, *Classical Hollywood Cinema*.

30 Tom Gunning, "The Cinema of Attraction: Early Film, Its Spectator and the Avant Garde," *Wide Angle* 8, nos. 3/4 (1986): 63–72.

31 For a similar argument, see Peter Krämer, "Vitagraph, Slapstick and Early Cinema," *Screen* (Spring 1988): 99–104.

32 These issues are discussed more fully in Henry Jenkins, "'Shall We Make It for New York or for Distribution?': Eddie Cantor, *Whoopee* and Regional Resistance to the Talkies," *Cinema Journal* (forthcoming).

33 Bordwell, Staiger, and Thompson, *Classical Hollywood Cinema*, pp. 19–20.

34 SHAN, "Fifty Million Frenchmen," *Variety*, April 1, 1931, p. 16; Mordaunt Hall, "Maybe It's Love Shown," *New York Times*, October 18, 1930, p. 23; SID, "Flying High," *Variety*, December 22, 1931, p. 17; "What the Picture Did for Me," *Motion Picture Herald*, February 24, 1934, p. 52; HOBE, "High Flyers," *Variety*, November 10, 1937, p. 19; A. E. Hancock, "What the Picture

Did for Me," *Motion Picture Herald*, July 15, 1933, p. 84; WAIG, "Cracked Nuts," *Variety*, April 8, 1931, p. 18.

35 Mordaunt Hall, "Putting a King on the Spot" (*Cracked Nuts*), *New York Times*, April 6, 1931, p. 24; Mordaunt Hall, "*The Cuckoos* Is Riotous," *New York Times*, April 20, 1930, p. 11, "A *Day at the Races*," unidentified magazine clipping, Marx Brothers File, Herbert Blum Collection, Wisconsin Center for Film and Theater Research; "*Monkey Business*," unidentified fan magazine clipping, Marx Brothers File, Herbert Blum Collection, Wisconsin Center for Film and Theater Research.

36 For background on the team and their films, see Leonard Maltin, *Movie Comedy Teams* (New York: New American Library, 1970), pp. 85–104; Anthony Slide, *The Vaudevillians: A Dictionary of Vaudeville Performers* (Westport: Arlington House, 1981), pp. 167–68, Joe Franklin, *Encyclopedia of Comedians* (Secaucus, N.J.: Citadel, 1979), pp. 332–34.

37 "What the Picture Did for Me," *Motion Picture Herald*, July 15, 1933, p. 84.

38 "What the Picture Did for Me," *Motion Picture Herald*, July 22, 1933, p. 71.

39 *Diplomaniacs* file, MPPDA collection, Margaret Herrick Library, Academy of Motion Picture Arts and Sciences, Los Angeles.

40 H. A. Griswold, Sewanee Union Theater, Sewanee, Tennessee, in "What the Picture Did for Me," *Motion Picture Herald*, April 29, 1933, p. 37, Joe Hewitt, Lincoln Theatre, Robinson, Illinois, in "What the Picture Did for Me," *Motion Picture Herald*, June 17, 1933, p. 45.

The Marx Brothers and the
Search for the Landsman

7

MARK WINOKUR

Duck Soup (1933), so the critical narrative asserts, is the last in a series of Marx Brothers films made at Paramount Studios in which the protagonists' actions grow increasingly outrageous and antisocial. Afterwards, under the tutelage of Irving Thalberg at MGM, the Brothers become more gentrified, or are at least placed in a more empathetic position in relation to the already genteel heroes and heroines of their films. While the Paramount films offered no characters with whom one would want to identify one's passional life, the later films find the Brothers less inclined to satirize the romantic leads. In the post-Paramount films the Brothers are eccentric characters given top billing as the feature attractions of the films, while in fact they move further and further from center stage until, by Copacabana (1947), and Love Happy (1950) they are mere sideshows meant to elicit more nostalgia than astonishment. In short, they are no longer the subjects of their own histories. Like the ethnic and immigrant, they are paid homage and then excluded from their own films.

Critics tend to perceive this movement as a degeneration in ethnic presence. Marx Brothers comedy, like [that of Chaplin's Tramp], gradually becomes more genteel, a move critics perceive as a falling away from their more characteristically detached and antisympathetic lampoons of all value. This critical sensibility, however, is itself both anarchic and reactionary: it enjoys the Brothers' destruction of society, but it desires only safely infinite repetitions of that destruction in a sort of nostalgia for nihilism. Joe Adamson gives a classic, even generous, assessment: "A Night at the Opera is the Marx Brothers decked out in refinery like a Christmas shopping window, going through some very funny motions against a stops-out backdrop of posh set design, realistically reacting extras. . . . This keeps them from being the figures of fantasy that Mankiewicz allowed them to be: Harpo can never step outside the bounds of reality any more."[1] Henry Jenkins especially, in a chapter on Eddie Cantor, argues that Hollywood comedy becomes "desemitized" in the early 1930s, becoming more Anglo-Saxon for a greater reception in the hinterlands.[2] But Adamson's and Jenkins's assessment describes only one half of a dialectical process in which overt ethnicity disappears at the expense of critiques of and changes in the host culture. In the process Hollywood culture, and mainstream culture, internalize certain ethnic dynamics as well. For example, while the principal sign of the Marx Brothers MGM gentility in the 1930s is a kind of deference to the romantic couple, that romantic couple is, in another genre, destabilized through a kind of humor more characteristic of the Marx Brothers and other ethnic comics: screwball comedy. Because the newer gentility of the MGM Brothers includes taking the romantic couple seriously in a way they had not before, they may be seen as one of the last instances of pure new-immigrant ethnic comedy and one of the first attempts in the 1930s to evolve from team comedy into a comedy more congenial to a middle-class and intellectual audience. They attempt, in other words, to evolve a middle-class romantic comedy of assimilation. But because theirs is a comedy of social dissolution, a synthesis is difficult to achieve, which is why critics complain about the MGM films.[3] Though harbingers of screwball comedy, the Marx Brothers cannot become screwball comedians themselves.

By the time of the MGM films, the Great Depression, and the activation of the production code and other attempts at social control, ethnic codes dominated the Hollywood sound film even if ethnic images did not. Assimilation, accommodation, and acculturation became obsessive topics in American film for the next sixty years, from A Star is Born (1937) to The Addams Family (1991), and not just for a moment in the early 1930s, as Henry Jenkins implies. What critics call "desemitization" is in fact a representation – across-a number of personae, films, genres, and decades – of various strategies of incorporation and resistance. Critics who notice one ethnic dynamic within a particular set of films then assume that any opposing dynamic across a number of films must as a consequence not be ethnic. This critical judgment, for example, fails to perceive that assimilation is itself an immigrant phenomenon that recurs in several careers before and after the Second World War. Chaplin moves from the savagery of The Pawnshop (1916) to the sentimentality of City Lights (1931). Jerry Lewis moves from the idiot-savant adolescent of his early career to the more thoughtfully urbane, if still inept, representative of the middle class. (The transition films for him are The Nutty Professor [1963], in which he plays both parts, and The Family Jewels [1965], in which he plays all parts.) Even the perennially disgruntled W. C. Fields makes motions towards respectability: Never Give a Sucker an Even Break (1941) begins with Fields playing a successful Hollywood star. Contemporary comics retain one voice for their nightclub show, and a more sanitized version for their films. It is as if comic ontogeny recapitulates comedic phylogeny; each artist, no matter his aesthetic ethos, begins as cultural critique and ends as an object of nostalgia for the critiqued culture.

This chapter will consider some dynamics that Henry Jenkins and other critics omit: the Marxian critiques that make "accommodation" and "resistance" simultaneous phenomena. [. . .] Through the Jewish institution of the landsmannschaft, the chapter will examine the Marx Brothers' attempt to build a community based on one of the few roads to authenticity: hostility. After the first section, which outlines the theme of the landsman in the films, the second section will contain a discussion of the attempt to find a landsman in the audience. [. . .]

The landsman and the crypto-ethnic

Every Marx Brothers film contains a doppelgänger of Groucho, someone Groucho might be were his gestures toward upward mobility in earnest. In Duck Soup Ambassador Trentino, though no arriviste, is the foreigner – the Sylvanian – in the Freedonian court. Like Rufus T. Firefly (Groucho), he wants control of Freedonia; like Firefly, he pursues Mrs. Teasdale as a stratagem based in realpolitik. In The Cocoanuts (1929) Groucho is just as invested in real estate fraud as the ostensible villain, Harvey Yates, is invested in jewel theft. This dynamic gets carried over to the MGM films, with Sig Rumann vying as Mrs. Teasdale's lover and the lead tenor's manager in A *Night at the Opera* (1935) and as the alter-ego hotel manager in *A Night in Casablanca* (1946). In *Animal Crackers* (1930) that character is Roscoe Chandler, a financier and patron of the arts: "I am just a lover of art, that is all. What people have given to me, I give back to them, in the form of beautiful things."[4] But Chandler is really Abie Kabibble, an arriviste with an assumed voice, a wealthy art patron eager to hide his origins, a fish peddler in the old neighborhood. Like Groucho, Abie is crashing a party to which he does not belong. Like Groucho, he convinces the guests that he is who he represents himself as being. Ravelli and the Professor (Chico and Harpo) question the authenticity of the art authenticator, revealing his real identity as the arriviste Abie the fish man, a fellow ex-denizen of the old neighborhood, by finding his birthmark. They blackmail him; then, after having stolen Abie's tie, 500 dollars, his garters (and, in the stage version, his teeth), the Professor steals the birthmark. Playing the traditional double's role of scapegoat, the ritual humiliation of this doppelgänger is explained as a deflation of social pretension.

The Marx Brothers' satire of the wealthy is always a satire of the pretensions of upward mobility and a denial of the existence of authentic gentility. Culture is always only veneer, the attempt to escape the consequences of a self that is neither genteel nor refined. The treatment of the arriviste cannot be easily dismissed as merely a xenophobic treatment of upwardly mobile ethnics because it appears in a film in which *everyone* becomes the object of similar criticism.

[. . .]

In the Brothers' Paramount films the truest subversion lies in the fact that *all* the roles are satirized, not just those of the ethnics. More important, almost all the people in the films are depicted as arrivistes, in the sense that they all have something in their identities they wish to hide, something that does not harmonize with the conventional decor. In *Animal Crackers* the unveiling of a painting is spoiled because of its theft by different, respectable attendees of the party: once by the representatives of old money (they believe even Mrs. Rittenhouse [Margaret Dumont] is a social climber), once through the offices of the butler, and once by the romantic couple. Rittenhouse's genteel weekend party is over-populated by amateur thieves with hidden agendas. The romantic lead wants to sell his paintings. Rittenhouse's daughter, Mary, wants to marry a penniless male artist. Even Mrs. Rittenhouse like Abie, wants to enhance her prestige by featuring social lions and works of art. The only characters who seem to have no "hidden agendas" are the Brothers. (Hence, they have less desire to stay: "Hello, I must be going.") Their manifest agenda, though, involves an "outing" of guests like Abie through ritual torture and humiliation. And as with Abie, they always hope to find a common origin, or way of being, in the other whom they torture.

It is as if the Brothers are attempting to found a *landsmannschaft*, an organization consisting of "individuals from the same village (*shtetl*) or region in the Pale."[5] The *landsmannschaft* was an attempt to maintain a recognizable bond apart from sanctioned identities; as an attempt to help the immigrant fit in, it emphasized a memory and history separate from American memory and history.[6] *Landsmannschaften* were forums for conducting business with people – landsmen – one might not otherwise meet, with an air of familiarity one might not otherwise assume. They allowed, for however brief a time, the fiction that identity was familial, independent of one's present economic and class definitions. In a world of tight collars and constricting belts, it was an ephemeral return to the more comfortable, if rougher, robes and tunics of the shtetl.

This *landsmannschaft* is, of course, not merely a Jewish phenomenon, but rather characterizes virtually every ethnic and immigrant group that comes to America. The Irish establish the

Fenian Brotherhood, political clubs, and volunteer fire departments.[7] Italians maintain a close connection to *paisani*, folk from the same region as well as the same country.[8] Japanese Americans first established Gospel Societies,[9] then, at the turn of the century, workers' organizations such as the *Nihonjin Kutsuko Domekai*,[10] and, finally, Japanese Associations.[11] Polish Americans, among others, had their mutual aid societies.[12] Even those ethnic populations that considered themselves temporary "sojourners" in America formed close associations: the Chinese-American *huigans*, the largest of which became the Six Companies.[13] This is not to mention the various urban villages, with their coffinships, mutual benefit associations, politicas, and so on. These organizations were founded for various purposes – from establishing business and political connections to self-consciously attempting to retain some vestige of the *aud sod* in the new – and with various ideas about how one determined a countryman. Their common effect, however, was to establish neighborhoods in which ethnicity was preserved, so that the very urban landscape that was supposedly best suited to erasing ethnicity was in fact changed by it – the new-immigrant presence in New York, Boston, and Chicago being perhaps the best examples, but the African-American presence in those cities and in Memphis, New Orleans, and St. Louis, and the Asian presence in San Francisco being equally appropriate examples. Beyond all self-mythologizing claims of being frontier towns, or cities on the hill, the most significant difference between major American cities and many of their European counterparts was the former's degree of ethnic heterogeneity and the attempt by their various groups to retain some identity. The *landsmannschaft* sensibility of American film comedy was accessible to all these groups, even more because some of its specific ethnicity had disappeared, giving the dynamic a universal appeal.

Performances in the ethnic theater, which provided "a focus for social life" for the various social groups,[14] were sponsored by the various mutual benefit societies, social clubs, and ethnic organizations: the Magyar Egylet for Hungarian Americans,[15] the church and the coffee house for Italian Americans,[16] the temperance societies and the Finnish Socialist Federation for Finnish Americans,[17] and so on. Similarly, the Jewish *landsmannschaft* promoted itself on the stage.[18] [. . .] Ethnicity, community, spectacle, and performance were conflated early on for a newly arrived immigrant audience. Though Jewish-American culture was as stratified as any, the fiction of community created on stage provided an escape through ethnicity from New-World social designations with which the audience did not feel comfortable.

The Marx Brothers play on this discomfort. Though they are German and French Jewish rather than Russian Jewish, the Brothers attempt to find an unofficial *landsmannschaft* with their audience, outside the political parties and outside the class, labor, and social divisions that militate against the integrity of the original ethnic group. Since the Brothers are second generation and can no longer depend on their ethnic identity as a center of value, and since there is no other sacrosanct dimension to replace religion or ethnicity, they define this *landsmannschaft* negatively: anyone unencumbered by mainstream social definitions may join. Of course, this stipulation only defines the Marx Brothers themselves, as they are the only ones with no social agenda in which they genuinely believe.

The Brothers respond to the alazon's official, public self by always assuming the existence of a more genuine other under the disguise of the dowager, gangster, or art connoisseur, Abie beneath the Roscoe. They attempt to locate that other person by creating a scenario in which an official response becomes impossible, replaced by the inappropriate response to an inappropriate provocation. The object of an insult, in acknowledging the slight, reveals an understanding of a world (often sexual) outside the sphere of the officially sanctioned and overtly inhabited. The landsman is glimpsed either when the official other capitulates by behaving anarchically or when his refusal becomes the occasion for anarchic retaliation. The Brothers' treatment of Abie and other authorities contains two related dynamics: the displaced desire to find someone who is more like oneself, a landsman, and a merciless satirizing of the other as social other. This satire is an infantile sadism that has at its root a desire to punish its object for not avowing identity with oneself as well as a desire to correct a condescending social ease by recreating it as disease. When Sig Rumann and Louis Calhern maintain a traditionally condescending stance toward the Brothers, they play the perfect alazons to the Brothers' eirons. The Brothers cut off their coattails and lit cigars; they slap them (not once or twice, but three times) in a continued insult to the body. They paste their pants bottoms to newspapers. They chase their secretaries and, like Harpo with Lassparri, or Harpo and Chico with Trentino, desert to the opposition even while working for them. The Brothers invite the beleaguered party in authority to be either angry in his or her own world or anarchic in theirs – in other words, to be landsmen. The continued oppression of the villains is contingent on their inability or refusal to recognize that they are being oppressed, on their insistence that they inhabit a predictable world, a conventional film *sans* Marx Brothers. As long as they remain conscious of their status as ambassadors, impresarios, gangsters, or gamblers, however, they are abused in a way that constantly invites them to unburden themselves of social designations. In contrast to Abie Kabibble, for example, Louis Calhern's Trentino in *Duck Soup* is suave and debonair to the last degree. But, like Abie, and despite his urbanity, he is something of a failure, a schlimazel. He has failed to start a revolution in Freedonia, and failed to woo Mrs. Teasdale from Firefly. He has even failed to get any scandalously damaging information about Firefly (who is openly corrupt, repressive, and lecherous). Trentino and his various avatars are figures of pity rather than fear because, unlike Coyote or Iago, they are incompetent villains. The one momentary triumph against the Brothers in *Duck Soup* occurs when Edgar Kennedy laughs with Harpo and against himself, thus disarming Harpo for the moment it takes to pour water down Harpo's trousers. Kennedy is capable of momentarily simulating the self-irony necessary to enter the world of the Brothers, possibly because he was himself a Keystone Kop. The search for the self in the other – whether that other is an authority or the landscape – on which so much of comedy is predicated, is in Marx Brothers films motivated by and may be characterized as an immigrant point of faith: that even in an alien environment people and artifacts, despite their exotic facades, will be at bottom comfortably familiar. Marx Brothers comedy is based on a *potential* community of audience, object, and speaker. The attempt to find the self in the social other is like the traditional attempt to fit oneself into the New-World landscape: both are part of the same impulse to identify the ego with all that is not ego, with all that is overtly threatening in its strangeness to the ego.

The search for the landsman in the landscape certainly forces the Marx Brothers films to relocate ethnic Mott Street on the Upper West Side. But while critics routinely remark that the milieux the lower-class Brothers inhabit are most often the haunts of the wealthy, they do not at the same time notice that these milieux are always representations of center and margin, and always represent the Brothers as immigrants. In *Monkey Business* (1931) the Brothers are stowaways in the hold of a luxury liner bound from Europe to the United States; five years later Harpo and Chico are still shipboard stowaways – this time among operatic Italians – in *A Night at the Opera*. In both films, the Brothers become fugitives as a result of their illegal immigrant status; they are policed around the ship's deck in one film and a hotel room and opera house in the other. Two of their films find the Brothers in exotic locales particularly unsuited to nice boys from the Lower East Side: the Old West (Go West [1940]) and Casablanca (A Night in Casablanca). A sort of double jeopardy is at work here, in which the immigrants are Americans in a new environment either not at all American or super-American, either European or Western. In the first scenario, the journey to Europe is a *nostos* of the comic immigrant to the land of his origin (at least to the land of Chico's origin for A Night at the Opera, a fantasy Italy for a fantasy Italian). In the second scenario, the comic immigrant must journey in a direction that became a national imperative of the nineteenth century. Others of their films find the Brothers in intellectual and cultural milieux also (presumed) unsuited to their personae: the worlds of the opera (A Night at the Opera), the university (Horse Feathers [1932]), and high society (Animal Crackers [1930]). These films metaphorize the immigrant experience as a sense of placelessness. They are exposure nightmares; they recreate the experience of being physically, socially, and intellectually vulnerable to hostile environments that reveal the disjunction between one's inadequate personal resources, and the visible, yet inaccessible, abundance of goods.

Whatever the reason, several of the film's verbal and visual jokes refer to Groucho's fragmentation and loss of self; many jokes and gags are discussions of Groucho's absence. In the search for a disgruntled alter self (or "alte cocker"), one's *own* self – especially Groucho's self – may disappear entirely.

Duck Soup seems in some ways the Marx Brothers film most concerned both with the discovery of the self in others, and with the loss of the self to the world. In the first of his scenes, Groucho is waiting for himself in the production number staged to prepare for his entry. In another scene, each time Chico answers Groucho's phone, he insists that Groucho is not at home, until Groucho queries: "I wonder whatever became of me?" Almost immediately after, he slaps Zeppo's face for telling him a dirty joke that *he* had originally told Zeppo, saying "I should have slapped Mrs Teasdale's face when she told it to me" – still another occasion on which he has forgotten himself.

"I wonder whatever became of me?" thus represents an admission of a divided self, half of which has unaccountably disappeared. This rather sophisticated admission of self-fragmentation might be a derivatively modernist representation of the world as fragmented. But the tone in which Groucho delivers the line has none of the angst we have come to associate with such modernism. The tone is insouciant, unconcerned, merely curious. The absent Groucho is the official Groucho: President Firefly, the official whose presence is constantly demanded on the phone, at state functions and inaugural balls, the Firefly who has not received an invitation to Mrs. Teasdale's reception. His verbally abusive self – the landsman – is present, but not his socialized self, which has been effaced.

Where is this Firefly to whom various persons, including Groucho, make application? He is located in part, as we have seen, as an alter ego in Trentino, who though only an ambassador, seems to have full presidential power in Sylvania. He is visually and aurally as ideal as Groucho is abrasive: he is well-groomed, traditionally handsome, tall, and possessed of a cultivated accent. He *appears* to be the perfect diplomat, in opposition to Groucho, who, as always, wears his seedy tails and carries "twofer" cigars. On the other hand, Trentino is dishonest, an adventurer who has tried to foment revolution in Freedonia and who attempts to gain the affections of Mrs. Teasdale for the political power she wields. Groucho succeeds at everything Trentino attempts, thus establishing kinship between Trentino's intentions and his own results. Groucho does in fact begin war and revolution in Freedonia, with his initial song and the declaration of war with Sylvania, and, of course, he wins the hand of Mrs. Teasdale. Both leaders use the two other brothers in civil service posts (spies and minister of defense) and both use the brothers as soldiers in a war that Groucho "wins." That Trentino should be represented as Groucho's dapper doppelgänger is an ethnic inversion of the normative representation of the Jew as insidious shadow.

Ultimately, however, Groucho is inscribed on the whole world of the film in and through the other members of the *landsmannschaft*: his brothers. At Chicolini's trial, Groucho plays judge, prosecutor, and defense lawyer. He even refers at one point to Chicolini's brothers, who are waiting "for him with open arms in the penitentiary," so that he creates an image of himself as defendant and convict as well. At one point during the film, Harpo and Chico are dressed as Groucho in order to hoodwink Mrs. Teasdale into giving them the combination of the safe that contains the Freedonian war plans. The Brothers are not outfitted as traditional Grouchos: only the glasses, moustache, and cigar remain; the usual Groucho costume of tie, tails, and untidy white shirt is absent. The clothes are replaced by a neutral white nightshirt with nightcap that hides the hair, so that even Harpo with his blonde curls can convincingly pass as Groucho. This plot complication provides a rationale for the identical dress that initiates the famous mirror sequence following this scene. The masquerade reveals the Brothers as interested in defining identity as congruence or alienation through the other at several levels. At a primary level, Harpo and Chico assume versions of Groucho's persona in order to undermine that persona. Groucho asks Chico a riddle: "Now what is it that has four pairs of pants, lives in Philadelphia, and it never rains but it pours?" Chico responds: "'At'sa good one. I give you three guesses." Groucho then tries to guess the answer. (There is of course no answer.) Chico thus turns the riddle Groucho asks him into a riddle he is asking Groucho. Then he asks another, overtly insulting riddle. ("What is it got a big black moustache, smokes a big black cigar and is a big pain in the neck?") Insults are supposed to be Groucho's especial ken. This reversal happens because Groucho has momentarily reverted to his socially defined role as president of a country. Chico not only assumes Groucho's role as teller of riddles and dispenser of insults, but makes Groucho accept the role of receiver of a version of himself. Groucho is not only audience and straight man for Chico, he is also the punchline.

As a part of the assault on respectability, this masquerade is another search for kindred sensibilities. Comic deflation works through the comic's caricature of authority, caricature that reveals both the comic's (benevolent) likeness to, and the (insidious) artificiality of, that authority. But while authentic authority does not usually acknowledge the deflation, Groucho does. When Chico or Harpo turns the tables on Groucho's game, Groucho not only does not mind, but he plays along, allowing himself to be victimized in the way he is accustomed to victimizing others:

Firefly: Just for that you don't get the job I was going to give you.
Chicolini: What job?
Firefly: Secretary of War.
Chicolini: All right, I take it.
Firefly: Sold![19]

Self-humiliation is the only possible response to an other whose most useful tool in his search for a kindred other is sadism. The fantasy is that, in an authoritarian world, the only way to be certain of an unmediated dialogue – unfettered by power relations – with the other is to accede to all demands, relinquishing all power.

The *attempt* to discover this self in an other is comic. (The discovery of its presence is epic, of its absence, tragic.) The Marx Brothers' attempt, however, involves insult and hurt, as if to avenge the senseless pain that history tends to disavow.

The fiction of audience

[. . .]

This antagonism between audience and performer is a dramatized version of a central part of the Marx Brothers' dynamic. As their relation to authority within the films is antagonistically fictional, and their relation to their parents is (as every good post-Lacanian structuralist will observe) fictionally antagonistic, so their relation to their audience also depends on a fantasy hostility. Like the Margaret Dumont persona, the audience exercises an economic and hegemonic control over the Brothers. (Whom the fans would destroy they first ignore.) So, as with Dumont, the Brothers must antagonize the audience in order to keep its attention. Like the film dignitaries, the audience is an active foe in a passive stance. With the audience as with the villains, the Brothers are searching for empathetic landsmen in antagonists whose hostility is founded exactly on their desire *not* to be discovered as kindred. Thus, as with the authority figures in their films, the Brothers are attempting to establish a *landsmannschaft* with their audience, a society of hometown Jews with shared sensibilities.

The search for an audience landsman [. . . has] an explicitly sociolinguistic dimension. [. . .] The notion that, because immigrants and ethnics learn to speak in the dominant language, they are as a result completely appropriated is of course a simplistic elevation of the importance of *langue* (the language system) at the expense of *parole* (the particular use of language), in order either to justify the cultural hegemony of a language by its inevitability or to decry (more or less helplessly) the victimization of the subordinated ethnic group. My assumptions about language will be those of a certain line of contemporary socio- or ethnolinguistics that assumes that the analysis of the endurance of language systems is precisely half of the whole enterprise that includes the study – and valorization – of "variations of usage in differing circumstances, the changing meanings of words over time, the specialist practices adopted by specific social groups," and so on.[20]

Voice

In *Modern Times*, [. . .] American film comedy conceives of the comic proletarian as essentially picaresque: a wanderer, a fugitive, immigrating within his own country, constantly and unsuccessfully locating his home in situations necessarily impermanent (a rotting house built over a river, the home furnishings section of a department store, jail). The thematic alliance of the dispossessed with the nomadic wards of Hermes is continued in Hollywood comedy sound films. The most notable comic teams travel: Laurel and Hardy (especially in *Sons of the Desert* [1934], *The Flying Deuces* [1939], and *Utopia* [1951] – this last the French cineastes' sense of the place this wandering should and does end); Abbott and Costello (*Abbott and Costello go to Mars* [1953], *Abbot and Costello in* (pick one) *Hollywood* [1945], *the Foreign*

Legion [1950], *Alaska* [1952]); their co-equals Bob Hope and Bing Crosby (the *Road* pictures, the very titles of which reveal a kind of lebensraum); and their inheritors Dean Martin and Jerry Lewis (*Pardners* [1956], and the remake of *Nothing Sacred* [1937]: *Living It Up* [1954]).

But while the silent comedian tended to face that alien environment alone, or was at least billed alone (in practice Chaplin used villains like Mack Swain over and over again in what amounted to a repertory cast), the sound comedian tended to work with others as landsman. This was true not only of the screwball romantic couple but also of the same-sex partner or sibling. By the early 1930s, Laurel and Hardy were no longer *sui generis*; there were Marx Brothers, Ritz Brothers, Olsens and Johnsons, and so on. Even Buster Keaton tried to pair up with a comic Italian, Jimmy Durante.[21] Sound comics tended to pair up or form teams, in part so that the plots of these sometimes plotless pieces would include some rationale for dialogue but more so because the infinitely ethnic resources of the vaudeville and Broadway stage could then be utilized for film.

Sound enabled the landsman's searches and subversions, enabled a Bakhtinian dialogism in which a multiplicity of voices compete for attention and primacy. One does not have to imagine a completely ethnic Hollywood waiting for a voice to allow it to speak; it had already spoken eloquently in images. But the parallel between the emergent technology and the newly arrived social unit became ever more visible. The positions of film and new-immigrant ethnicity at the end of the 1920s were roughly congruent. The children of new immigrants, now growing up, more often than not spoke only English at about the same time that sound precluded the possibility of American film "speaking" in any other language, as it had in the silent era. A large percentage of these children, unlike many of their parents, lost all contact with their home culture at about the same time as American film had to struggle to keep its international markets.

Despite the corporate urgency to make the early sound film conform to the standards of realism already established by the silent film, a sense of the arbitrariness of the language, of the changeability of the *parole*, was omnipresent in Hollywood: [. . .] Moreover, there came to be a great variety of accents on screen, palpably different from the "legit" and Shakespearean stages. Even though a variety of parent tongues were becoming inaudible in the new, reverse Babel of USA culture, the country's single, hegemonic language changed, not in the direction of appropriation but in the direction of eccentricity and difference. Except in bastions of hegemony – the law courts, the university – eighteenth-century British English was only an echo, to be replaced by a language more tortured and tortuous. It was not merely the inclusion of words like "kosher," and not even the changes in grammar between the eighteenth and twentieth centuries that more and more distinguished American from British English in a manner that continued to elicit a now-familiar satire from the English. Rather, accents – the method as well as the matter of our articulations – changed.

The assertion that the Brothers' voices are "non-U" (non-upper-class) would be under-statement; the Brothers' urban, Jewish, lower-class voices (or in Harpo's case, non-voice) insist on the presence of ethnicity as linguistic intervention. As in most dialect comedy, voice renders the Brothers' *landsmannschaft* as a particular "speech community."[22] Like the most significant American comic heroes – from Sam Slick to Sut Lovingood to Woody Allen to Garrison Keillor – the Marx Brothers' accents define them regionally and economically: they are ethnic and poor, no matter their fictional position within the story. Even the timbre of their voices demands attention. The Brothers are thus set off from the wealthy societies they inhabit by their accents.

[. . .]

The Brothers impersonate two, perhaps three different ethnic accents, a study probably equaled in humorous American literature only by the similar exercise of *Huckleberry Finn*. Chico's accent is not Italian but pseudo-Italian. Chico stands always in an ironized relation to his own character, as if to say that an ethnic posture is always merely a posture. (In *Animal Crackers* one character asks: "How did you get to be an Italian?") Groucho's wisecracking voice, on the other hand, being the accent of lower-class New York, is a genuine inflection, the impossible sound of the Lower East Side in a starring role. This ethnic inflection suggests membership in a speech community familiar with cynicism, hardship, and poverty. The irony and disaffection in Groucho's voice, so comic to audiences, is aggressive and hostile. This quality – present to some degree in Chico's voice as well – characterizes Groucho as a vaudeville comic accustomed to audience hostility. He delivers his one-liners in an offhand manner, as if careless whether his audience laughs or not. He is indifferent, even hostile, to the opinions of his audience, within the narrative as well as without:

Chandler: Captain Spaulding, I think that [yours] is a wonderful idea.
Spaulding: You do, eh?
Chandler: Yes.
Spaulding: Well, then there can't be too much to it. Forget about it.[23]

This vocal indifference is experienced by audiences as comic in part because it is threatening, a shared hostility.

The voice Groucho uses to disempower others reflects the same speech community that, in gangster films, seeks empowerment in that world through more violent means. The voice that for Groucho is deadpan is for the gangster dead serious. This is the wise guy, fast-talking accent of Tony Camonte (*Scarface* [1932]), Rico (*Little Caesar* [1930]), and Tommy Powers (*Public Enemy* [1931]) – two Italians and an Irishman. The foreign accent, or the American accent informed by immigrant parentage, becomes in the criminal a sign of resentful powerlessness. Though invested with the provisional, circumstantial authority of the jester or the criminal these characters cannot speak, except parodically, in the voice of the more truly empowered middle or upper classes. The gangster is always only a parodic version of upward mobility, from the original *Scarface* (1931) to Brian de Palma's remake (1983). The gangsters' "wisecracks" are the same one-liners produced by the new sound comedians, delivered with a defensiveness that reveals an unarticulated insecurity in both performers. Gangsters are also referred to as wiseguys: the one-liner substitutes for educated discourse, for refined speech, for reason. It is threatening, delivered with a staccato speed suggesting the sound of "tommy guns" – another noise so evocative of the early sound-film era.

In Marx Brothers comedy transgression against language, not against specific legal codes, is the most visibly resentful action allowed the antiheroes (including Harpo, for whom *not* speaking becomes an aggressive act). However, ethnic talk is potentially more subversive than ethnic violence because one cannot assume, as with merely violent action, that the speaker acknowledges the values against which his speech is directed. The Marx Brothers – like several early sound comics – do not try, as Camonte, Little Caesar, and Powers try, to gain entry into the cultural mainstream. For both the gangster and the comic, for example, clothes are problematic. But the gangster will not admit to a discomfort in donning the newer and fancier dress he has bought the right to wear. In a consciousness of their clothing that Groucho refuses, gangsters "shoot their cuffs" and wear loud colors, making their clothes icons of the absurd rather than absurdly iconic.[24] While the gangster films are thus comparatively conservative, reinforcing the sense that the conventional world for which the gangsters reach is valuable in proportion to the desperation, violence, and extremity of their attempts to reach it, the early comedy of the Marx Brothers is inherently radical in the sense that they do not act as if they wish to be included in that world at all. Their inertia is thus a form of radical action, as if they affirm a belief that any genuinely motivated action is motivated in the direction of conservatism and hierarchy. Comic speech is contained anarchy, more effective than the gangster's because motivated by the desire to replace power structures not with other structures but with critiques of power. Speech is a substitute for action; it is what one does instead of act. When the possibility of action is effaced by another mode, the desire for action's intended effect disappears as well, and an aesthetic gratification, an enjoyment of speech as speech or play, substitutes for it instead. Because its original ulterior motive has been effaced, this now disinterested play is capable of a kind of subversion inaccessible to mere violence. One cannot talk about the Brothers as spirits of anarchy, as incarnations of the surreal, without realizing that this anarchy and surrealism, as more or less explicit critiques of culture, could have occurred only in the voice of someone outside the high-culture discourse being critiqued, an ethnic voice.

Puns and digressions

In his book *On Puns*, Jonathan Culler asserts, "Puns present the disquieting spectacle of a functioning of language where boundaries . . . count for less than one might imagine and where supposedly discrete meanings threaten to sink into fluid subterranean signifieds."[25] The pun thus works to erode traditional meaning, allowing the imposition of meanings outside accepted etymologies. Of course, since conventional etymologies will ultimately find the derivation of modern English in Old English, French, German, and other Western European roots, puns become a vehicle for the conveyance not merely of some words into English but of a reordering of language.

Though puns and wordplay can be elitist,[26] this reordering of language often works in the service of class and ethnic interests, forcing its audience to re-envision the world through ethnic alienation. The "little man" phenomenon in American modernism, generally associated with such neo-genteel writers as Clarence Day and James Thurber, is most syntactically innovative in the writings of Dorothy Parker, S.J. Perelman, Moss Hart, George S. Kaufman, and other ethnic descendants – some of the most important writers for the Broadway stage, American film, and American magazines.

[. . .]

Of course several of these writers – conspicuously Kaufman, Hart, and Morrie Ryskind – wrote for the Marx Brothers, often thematizing ethnicity and immigration in the Brothers' punning. This dynamic moves one further away from the plot with each ethnically motivated pun. From the stage version of *The Cocoanuts*:

Groucho: We're going to have an auction.
Chico: I came over here on the Atlantic auction.
Groucho: We have a quota. Do you know what a quota is?
Chico: Sure, I got a quota. (He takes the coin out of his pocket.)[27]

It is as if the further one moves from conventional language and plot, the closer the audience is moved toward the ethnic. The further removed from chronological narration, the more apparent is the history narration represses. In *Monkey Business*, Chico and Groucho digress from their roles as stowaways pursued by the ship's captain, in order to participate in a history lesson:

Groucho: Now, one night Columbus' sailors started a mutiny . . .
Chico: Naw, no mutinies at night. They're in the afternoon. You know, mutinies
              Wednesdays and Saturdays.
Groucho, throwing down his cap: There's my argument. Restrict immigration.

The comic bit thus digresses at least two removes from the plot: from a shipboard chase scene to a geography lesson to commentary on international relations. Several stories about immigration and movement are told at the expense of the gangster plot.

This digression from the plot is another antagonistic thrust at the audience meant to recreate it as countersocial. The Brothers, in the kind of move that critics of the canon traditionally abhor even in their own darlings, deviate from the plot of a film through the device of a pun for the sake of a joke or a comic skit. More generally, textual criticism, which has long turned away from plot and story in order better to exploit less visible narrative techniques, is guilty of an odd imaginative failure in objecting to the flimsiness of Marx Brothers plots, which are so constructed in order not to interfere with the elaboration of theme through comic technique. Digression is in fact thematically significant. One is *supposed* to be more or less contemptuous of the plots; audiences are expected to follow the divergence at the expense of the pleasures ordinarily provided by plot and character evolution.

This divergence reflects a Bakhtinian sense of the carnivalesque, an undercutting of the narratives that structure and define identity.[28] At the beginning of a comic sketch the Brothers seem to be aware of the conventions within which they should act, and to subscribe to them just enough to operate within the causal and motivational structure demanded by adherence to conventions. But all seem to forget the conventions and motivations in the elaboration of the sketch, opting instead for a series of nearly motiveless digressions. Chico is on trial for his life, and in an inexplicably short time he is taking bets on whether he will be found guilty. Harpo begins selling peanuts in a sketch that ends with the destruction of the peanut stand by a lemonade vendor. Groucho makes Herculean efforts to get to his inauguration on time, only to begin his term by asking Mrs. Teasdale to pick a card. This absentmindedness does not indicate any lack of intelligence or initiative. On the contrary, the Brothers are impossibly more aggressive and energetic than the characters they antagonize; they are too smart for the social situations they find themselves repeatedly transcending. They become diverted from original goals and social identities through excess rather than lack of consciousness.

Finally, this diversion derives from an irrationality in all "civilized" discourse that insists on one normative code of behavior, habit of thinking, or history, one "master code." To escape the plot of a film about presidents, countries, diplomacy, and war (or about universities, high society, high finance, etc.) is to escape the narrative of history, or, perhaps more properly, to escape from the nightmare of history.

Ad lib

Ad libbing on stage and in film is a special case of digression that throws into great relief the performer's desire to find a community with an audience. [. . .] The Marx Brothers shamelessly exploited the potentiality of the direct address as a way of circumventing conventional modes of audience relation to the drama.

[. . .]

Direct address is almost lost to cinema (except in such exceptional ways as the Tramp's ambiguous glances at the camera). But even on film Groucho ignores filmic convention at moments, deviating from the plot in order to speak directly to his audience. In so doing, Groucho insults Chico several times to the audience: "There's my argument: restrict immigration"; "I have to be here but you can go out for popcorn till this thing blows over." At the end of *Monkey Business* Groucho becomes a radio announcer, giving us a blow-by-blow description of an otherwise pedestrian fight between Zeppo and Alky Brigs, filled with the kinds of quotidian references that would be familiar to a middle- or lower-middle-class audience. Groucho creates a momentary community with the audience by scapegoating someone in the film.

Appreciation for the Brothers' ad libbing derived from, if not the ethnic theater per se, then the kind of audience that had also attended ethnic theater, or whose parents had. As stage performers, the Marx Brothers were most successful in New York, the urban center with the most significant ethnic and immigrant population. Besides providing actors, the ethnic theaters provided several models for mainstream stage dynamics. Though more didactic there, the ad lib was more a part of Yiddish theater than of the genteel stage: "It was not unusual at this time for Yiddish actors to address the audience during some break in the performance – or sometimes, for that matter, in the middle of a scene. The relationship between actor and audience had some of the air of browbeating intimacy that frequently characterized the relationship between rabbi and congregation in a *shtetl* synagogue. Authoritative thundering from a stage, as from a pulpit, often had a dramatic effect upon one's listeners."[29] The liberty to change a part could in fact be seen as fundamentally ethnic, as a way of differentiating the Yiddish theater from other modes of presentation. [. . .]

The stage performances of vaudeville comedy missed by literary America are a perfect trope for the ethnic life that remains untranslatable and unrecordable. These performances are difficult to discuss – they were by their nature ephemeral; references and asides disappeared as soon as they were spoken. They were not immortalized in folio because, though some acts would not vary at all for twenty years, a Marx Brothers performance would change a bit every evening. When, like *Animal Crackers* or *The Cocoanuts*, the stage plays were filmed, only traces of the original performance remained. The original dynamic relationship to the audience was almost completely lost. What in the theater could have been a more authentic contact must in film be a parody of authenticity. Eye contact between actor and camera, or between audience and screen, replaces eye contact between humans. Still, the effect is startling, as if it were an address to an authentic audience, as if we were real. The wider gap – the increased technological barrier – over which the performer has to cross makes the failure to cross it more prominent, as if what was always the point – the attempt rather than its failure or success – highlights more starkly the need and possibility for such a bridging. The enterprise is successful insofar as our attention is called to, and our laughter results from, the attempt.

[. . .]

Theatrical fourth wall/ghetto wall

Ad libbing is already a denial of the existence of a proscenium arch, the tool of an urban culture accustomed to crowded urban spaces in which the privacy assumed by the walls of the Edwardian middle class is simultaneously desired and ridiculed. The Brothers further denied that arch on stage by directly addressing the audience in a manner that assumed an equal response from the audience itself. Not surprisingly, the Brothers' vaudeville and Broadway performances were even less controlled than their films. The Brothers diverged not only from the plots but also from the scripts whenever they had the desire, in a *meshuggah*, parapractic performance of the unconscious. In a frenzy of Artaudian surrealism, they tore clothes off women, insulted people in the audience, and misbehaved in a fashion that at the same time conjured up and denied the presence of an audience in a denial of the invisible partition between audience and actor. The Brothers' wildness presented an image of the ethnic as bad Jew refusing silence and valorizing loudness and impolite, *hamishe* behavior as ways of overcoming arbitrary social distinctions. *The fourth wall was thematized as ghetto wall.*
[. . .]

Despite the assertions of critics like Richard Dyer, who finds the origin of the star system in a moment of Anglo theater at which actors become more important than their roles,[30] the real desire to conflate the world on stage and the world off stage was a phenomenon of the urban ethnic theater. One can see this ethnically sanctioned conflation of audience and actor in, for example, the Friar's Club, a *landsmannschaft* of show-business people that has, since its founding in 1904, taken on a particularly ethnic cast.[31] The Friar's "roast," the series of insulting speeches that commemorates the friendship of the object and the speakers,[32] taking place on a dais in front of other show-business "personalities" who compose the audience, places the private lives of the objects of insult on display, conflating in several ways stage and auditorium.
[. . .]

The favorable audience response to Marx Brothers chaos depended on the belief that these people were who they represented themselves as being, that they were not acting but being. Their offstage behavior (or the stories spread about their behavior) reinforced this conviction, which would occasionally elicit a landsman's impulse in the audience to cross the ghetto/fourth wall.
[. . .]

Doubling

[. . .] The audience desired to see the Marx Brothers double for each other and, finally, to double for the Brothers in a kind of self-abasement that is also an emotional release. Doubling has been a standard comic device at least since *The Odyssey*. But the wrinkle in the Marx Brothers' oeuvre is that, as Hollywood is in fact composed of landsmen, the Brothers are also brothers off stage. They use their physical resemblance to each other (obscured by the costumes they wear) to complicate the skits: all four (badly) imitate Maurice Chevalier; Groucho and Chico rip up their tenor's contract in unison; the three Brothers dress as bedridden Grouchos in *Duck Soup* (and Groucho and Harpo imitate each other in the mirror scene in the same film); all four escape from a ship in identical Russian aviator uniforms; three Brothers dress identically as doctors, all of whom are named Steinberg (the model skeleton is also so named); each Brother performs a version of "I Love You" at different moments in *Horsefeathers*.[33]

The sibling similarity is stressed in the mythology of the Brothers' stage career. When Groucho was ill, Zeppo acted Groucho's part; the audience could not tell the difference.

[. . .]

This insistence on *landsmannschaft* has greater cultural reverberations; in much popular culture one may see the effect of the Brothers' self-multiplication, of their attempt to find versions of themselves in an otherwise remote world. The world responds by looking like Groucho; he stops having to recreate the world in his image because the world learns to recreate itself in his.

[. . .]

The more ideal cinema icons are not nearly as imitated as the Marx Brothers. Cary Grant and Jimmy Stewart, though somewhat imitated, were not adopted by popular culture in the way especially Groucho and Harpo were. The plastic glasses, eyebrows, and nose that may or may not have been modeled on Groucho's inevitably suggest him now. Chaplin is imitated in the same way but, like most popular icons, in the singular, not in the plural. The representations of Groucho are as often as not representations of plurality as if, finally, he represents the entire community of landsmen for which he had always searched.

But that community is never nostalgically hospitable. In opposition to portrayals of other comics, representations of Groucho routinely emphasize the neutrality of his features and the impassivity of the face, despite the outrageousness of his antics or appearance. Groucho does not call attention to the fact that he is joking, in the hysterical manner of comics from vaudevillians through Jerry Lewis. [. . .] The mask Groucho wears is modernist: emotionally neutral, alienated from its own body and the opinion of the world, like the Magritte paintings in which a number of identical subjects inhabiting a single canvas, uniformly dressed, uniformly gaze in different directions but not at each other.

Notes

1 Joe Adamson, *Groucho, Harpo, Chico, and Sometimes Zeppo: A History of the Marx Brothers and a Satire on the Rest of the World* (New York: Simon and Schuster, 1973), 283.

2 Henry Jenkins, *What Made Pistachio Nuts? Early Sound Comedy and the Vaudeville Aesthetic* (New York: Columbia University Press, 1992), 172–84.

3 The most notable of such critics is Gerald Mast, *The Comic Mind: Comedy and the Movies* (Chicago: University of Chicago Press, 1979), 285–88.

4 George S. Kaufman and Morrie Ryskind, *Animal Crackers* (1929; rpt. London: Samuel French, 1984), 14. This is the script of the stage play.

5 Michael R. Weisser, *A Brotherhood of Memory: Jewish Landsmannschaft in the New World* (Ithaca, NY: Cornell University Press, 1989), 4.

6 Weisser finds the *landsmannschaft* even more separatist: "[P]eople who joined a *landsmannschaft* and kept it at the psychic core of their existence were at the same time rejecting the larger society and resisting its opportunities for assimilation" (5).

7 Lawrence Fuchs, *The American Kaleidoscope: Race, Ethnicity, and the Civic Culture* (London: Wesleyan University Press, 1990), 44, 49.

8 Ibid., 5.

9 Yuji Ichioka, *The Issei: The World of the First Generation Japanese Immigrants, 1885–1924* (New York: Free Press, 1988), 23.

10 Ibid., 94.

11 Ibid., 156–57.

12 William I. Thomas and Florian Znaniecki, in *The Polish Peasant in Europe and America*, ed. and abr. Eli Zaretsky (Urbana: University of Illinois Press, 1984), talk specifically about the function of the Mutual Aid Society to preserve Polishness (253–55).

13 Shih-shan Henry Tsai, *The Chinese Experience in America* (Bloomington: Indiana University Press, 1986), 46–47.

14 Maxine Schwartz Seller, "Introduction," in *Ethnic Theatre in the United States*, ed. Maxine Schwartz Seller (Westport, CT: Greenwood Press, 1983), 9.

15 Ibid., 193.

16 Ibid., 240.

17 Ibid., 122–23.

18 "In order to fund themselves, they often gave benefits, and by the early years of this century, the majority of weeknights in Yiddish theater were sponsored in this fashion" (Nalima Sandrow, *Vagabond Stars: A World History of Yiddish Theatre* [New York: Harper & Row, 1977], 82).

19 Kaufman and Ryskind, 130.

20 Penelope J. Corfield, "Introduction: Historians and Language," in *Language, History and Class*, ed. Penelope J. Corfield (Cambridge, MA: Basil Blackwell, 1991), 13. The last ten years have brought the study of various national and international "Englishes," from African-American English to Irish English to pidgin English to various colonial Englishes. See especially John Platt, Heidi Weber, and Ho Mian Lian, *The New Englishes* (London: Routledge, 1984); and Manfred Görlach, *Englishes: Studies in Varieties of English, 1984–1988* (Amsterdam, John Benjamin's, 1991). In *Toward a Social History of American English* (Berlin: Mouton, 1985), J. L. Dillard observes that English was not originally dominant in the American colonies: "Dutch was the official language up to 1664" (91). In both this text and the more recent *A History of American English* (London: Longman, 1992), Dillard attributes the differences between American and British English largely to the formative influence on American English of various ethnic groups.

21 Gene Fowler (*Schnozzola* [New York: Viking Press, 1951], 4–6) compares Durante to the nineteenth-century Italian clown Grimaldi.

22 Elaborated in J. Gumperz, "The Speech Community," in *Language and Social Context*, ed. Pier Paolo Giglioli (Harmondsworth, UK: Penguin, 1972), 219–31. Ethnic humor tends to be first and foremost dialect humor: "There is considerable variation in the qualities eventually associated with the nineteenth century comic Irishman, but one feature remained constant: he spoke with a brogue" (Maureen Waters, *The Comic Irishman* [Albany: State University of New York Press, 1984], 1).

23 Kaufman and Ryskind, 32.

24 The 1930s gangsters differ from the Marx Brothers largely in the amount of faith they invest in the society they are attempting to subvert. Gangsters become a version of the authorities they resent; they come to own the cars and clothes they believe to be the signs of empowerment. Alternatively, the Marx Brothers do not attempt to rise in a hierarchy to which they give only a grudging belief. Such ambition is, for instance, obviated by having Groucho already in a position of power. More significantly, several films – *Monkey*

Business, A *Day at the Races* (1937), At *the Circus* (1939) – employ gangsters and/or swindlers as *ficelles* and foils, as if the films require gangsters in order to exorcise the latent gangsterism in the Brothers by showing them actively repudiating that world, as when the Brothers throw their guns into the mop bucket in *Animal Crackers*.

25 Jonathan Culler, ed., *On Puns: The Foundation of Letters* (New York: Basil Blackwell, 1988), 2. While this volume does in some places treat gender, it treats race and language not at all, despite the fact that the connections should be self-evident.

26 Referring to Hollywood's tendency toward nepotism, Ogden Nash asserted about one mogul that "Uncle Carl Laemmle / Had a very large faemmle."

27 Quoted in Kyle Crichton, *The Marx Brothers* (Garden City, NJ: Doubleday, 1950), 272.

28 Mikhail Bakhtin, *Rabelais and His World*, trans. Helene Iswolsky (Bloomington: Indiana University Press, 1984).

29 Ronald Sanders, *The Downtown Jews: Portraits of an Immigrant Generation* (New York: Harper & Row, 1969), 306.

30 Richard Dyer, *Stars* (London: BFI, 1979), 102.

31 Joey Adams, *Here's to the Friars: The Heart of Show Business* (New York: Crown, 1976), 6. The founding date is about the time of the founding of American *landsmannschaft*. Though the Friars Club was rather Anglo at first, several of its formative members were ethnic: Irish (George M. Cohan), Jewish (Eddie Cantor), and so on. To Dyer's possible assertion that the Club was founded by press agents as a sort of publicity stunt and so was a purely economic phenomenon, one could as easily respond that, as with film itself, ethnics subsequently manipulated the Club to mean whatever they wanted (Adams, 6).

32 The roasts are referred to as "vivisections," "murders," and so on (Adams, 51–52).

33 Even much later, after the dissolution of the Marx Brothers, Groucho stars in a film – *Copacabana* – that contains a *Comedy of Errors* plot: Carmen Miranda must play two different kinds of exotic singers (Brazilian bombshell and "Madame Fifi") in order to help her boyfriend/agent Groucho live up to a contract he has made.

PART FOUR

COMEDIAN COMEDY AND GENDER

Introduction

Women have not found the same opportunities for comic licence in Hollywood as their male counterparts, despite the contributions of a wide range of female performers, including Flora Finch, Mabel Normand, Constance Talmadge, Louise Fazenda, Dorothy Devore, Marie Dressler, Gale Henry, Alice Howell, Fay Tincher, Polly Moran, Charlotte Greenwood, Willie Lightner, Billie Burke, Beatrice Lillie, Carole Lombard, Thelma Todd, ZaSu Pitts, Patsy Kelly, Fanny Brice, Gracie Allen, Patsy Moran, Marjorie Main, Lupe Velez, Martha Raye, Mary Wickes, Vera Vague, Judy Canova, Eve Arden, Joan Davis, Cass Daley, Lucille Ball, Renie Riano, Alice Pearce, Edie Adams, Phyllis Diller, Goldie Hawn, Lily Tomlin, Carol Burnett, Gilda Radner, Shelley Long, Whoopi Goldberg, Janeane Garofalo and – most famously – Mae West. In her book *The Unruly Woman: Gender and the Genres of Laughter* (1995), Kathleen Rowe ascribes the marginalization of the female comedian in mainstream cinema to an entrenched cultural taboo regarding women and comedy. Women's comedy and women's laughter are potentially subversive, she argues, because they have the power 'to challenge the social and symbolic systems that would keep women in their place' (Rowe 1995: 3). Even though the dominance of male comedians inevitably skews the representational focus, so that male fantasy and problems with male identity tend to hog the spotlight, the selections within this part of the Reader illustrate that the comedian film can nevertheless permit a disorderly rewriting of the traditional scripts of gender and sexuality.

The opening selection, from Kathleen Rowe's book, provides a brisk analysis of *She Done Him Wrong*, one of the scandalous commercial hits featuring Hollywood cinema's most flamboyant and enduring unruly woman. Before the Hays Code forced her subjugation in the mid-1930s, Mae West flaunted herself as an outspoken and sexually forward female grotesque who spurned the decorous repressions of seemly womanhood. Rowe's lively account explores West's significance as a carnivalesque unruly woman by considering both her distinctively ironic performance style, which overturns cultural conventions of femininity, and its narrative contextualization. She focuses in particular upon West's manipulation of her image and her challenge to the authority of the male gaze. Although West provides an astonishing example of a woman who demonstrates her prowess both as bearer of the sexually active look and as joke-maker, Rowe cautions that West herself remains very much an exceptional case whose singular success highlights the fact that Hollywood screen comedy ultimately permits few narrative options for such a strong example of female unruliness.

As Patricia Mellencamp illustrates in her contribution to this Reader, female performers may have faced restricted options in Hollywood comedy but from the early 1950s they found new opportunities in television – even if these were strongly wedded to the domestic imperatives that dominated network broadcasting. Before her debut in CBS's phenomenally successful situation comedy *I Love Lucy*, Lucille Ball had spent almost two decades in Hollywood. Working for several studios, she had played a range of glamorous, comic and dramatic roles without establishing a secure star image (Doty 1990: 4–5). The initial concept for *I Love Lucy* was a sitcom that would also incorporate the vaudevillian musical-comedy shtick that Ball and husband Desi Arnaz had been performing in a live act they toured through the USA. Ball would be cast as a famous actress, with Arnaz as her bandleader husband. CBS baulked at this concept, however, because it felt there was a better chance of attracting a sponsor if the star couple were transformed into characters 'with whom the average person can associate – everyday people' (Doty 1990: 8). While Arnaz was permitted to 'play himself', the Cuban bandleader, Ball bore the brunt of servicing the network's insistence upon everyday domesticity. Forced to relinquish her desired role as a witty and accomplished movie star, Ball had to play 'ordinary' housewife Lucy Ricardo whose desire for showbiz success is continually thwarted.

Patricia Mellencamp's discussion of Lucille Ball was published initially in conjunction with an account of Gracie Allen, another embodiment of female unruliness within a domestic context (Mellencamp 1986, 1992). As with *I Love Lucy*, the focus upon professional entertainers in the *George Burns and Gracie Allen Show* (1950–58) inherently qualified the heterodomestic norms that ruled other contemporary sitcoms. As professional showbiz folk who were familiar to audiences across three decades of appearances in vaudeville, Hollywood films and radio, Burns and Allen were integrated only loosely within the world of everyday domesticity. A law unto herself, Gracie Allen was a disorderly woman who specialized in a deconstructive derailing of the laws of language and logic (Mellencamp 1992: 316). She may have reduced everyone she encountered to speechless bewilderment, but Gracie was nonetheless ultimately subordinated to George Burns in his role as the straight mediator between herself and the world, the show and the audience. A different dynamic operates in the case of Lucille Ball's impersonation of would-be entertainer Lucy Ricardo.

Examining the relations sustained between performance, physical comedy and narrative, Mellencamp explores how *I Love Lucy* negotiates the opposition between rejection and acceptance of female domestic confinement. Lucy Ricardo continually and energetically schemes to escape the stranglehold of domestic confinement by transforming marriage and housewifery into vaudeville. Mellencamp stresses that even though Lucy Ricardo's plots to escape her domestic options fail *narratively*, they succeed in terms of Lucille Ball's *performance*. The intriguing dynamic that Mellencamp identifies in Ball's incarnation of Lucy Ricardo was recently echoed in elegant assessment of *I Love Lucy* by television scholar Christopher Anderson:

> It is possible to see *I Love Lucy* as a conservative comedy in which each episode teaches Lucy not to question the social order. In a series that corresponded roughly to their real lives, it is notable that Desi played a character very much like himself, while Lucy had to sublimate her professional identity as a performer and pretend to be a mere housewife. The casting decision seems to mirror the dynamic of the series; both Lucy Ricardo and Lucille Ball are domesticated, shoehorned into an inappropriate and confining role. But this apparent act of suppression actually gives the series its manic and liberating energy. In being asked to play a proper housewife, Lucille Ball was a tornado in a bottle, an irrepressible force of

nature, a rattling, whirling blast of energy just waiting to explode. The true force of each episode lies not in the indifferent resolution, the half-hearted return to the status quo, but in Lucy's burst of rebellious energy that sends each episode spinning into chaos. Lucy Ricardo's attempts at rebellion are usually sabotaged by her own incompetence, but Lucille Ball's virtuosity as a performer perversely undermines the narrative's explicit message, creating a tension which cannot be resolved. Viewed from this perspective, the tranquil status quo that begins and ends each episode is less an act of submission than a sly joke; the chaos in between reveals the folly of ever trying to contain Lucy.

(Anderson 2001)

The Hollywood comedian film may prioritize male concerns but, as the final two contributions to this section affirm, this does not necessarily result in an orthodox handling of male identity and desire. Joanna Rapf examines the strange case of Jerry Lewis, the final comedian signed to a Hollywood major of the classical studio era. Drawing attention to the way Lewis' comedy disarms the protocols of patriarchal masculinity, Rapf's perceptive analysis discerns in his films a tendency towards both 'involuntary surrealism' and 'involuntary feminism' that makes them a productive site for feminist analysis. In a consideration of comedies that position men as surrogate mothers, such as Chaplin's *The Kid* (1921) and Laurel and Hardy's *Their First Mistake* (1933), Lucy Fischer argues that in substituting the clown for the mother they 'sustain female absence while positioning maternity at centre stage' (Fischer 1991: 67). Fischer claims that 'male absorption of women' and the devaluation of the maternal is a ubiquitous stratagem in comedy, which serves to consign women further to the regime of lack (ibid: 60). She underestimates, however, the degree to which the grotesque clown-figure can disarrange established gender roles and hierarchies by sanctioning a more disorderly perspective upon American manhood and the conformist scripts of achievement and cultural integration. As I have argued elsewhere, a film such as Lewis' *The Ladies Man*, examined closely in Rapf's chapter, provides a curious unravelling of the Oedipal narrative structures that sustain the majority of Hollywood's male-centred fictions (Krutnik 2000: 144–9).

Rapf's discussion foregrounds how the comedian's play with culturally determined norms and expectations can qualify established gender binarisms. Like other male comedians, she suggests, Lewis parodies patriarchal ideals and assumptions rather than exalting them. Steve Cohan's chapter also considers how the comedian film plays with gender expectations. His study of the series of *Road to . . .* films made by Bob Hope and Bing Crosby explores the queer dynamics of this extraordinarily successful screen partnership. Like my own work on Dean Martin and Jerry Lewis (Krutnik 1995a, 2000, 2002), Cohan's chapter outlines how the male buddy relationship encompasses a complex range of emotional and quasi-erotic intensities between men. Arguing that the phenomenal popularity of Hope and Crosby in the 1940s was rooted in the male homosocial order of wartime, Cohan's engaging study raises new possibilities for considering the dynamics of same-sex comedy. Cohan also sheds new light upon the critically neglected figure of Bob Hope, a major screen comedian whose continual slippages from normative possibilities of heterosexual masculinity are examined in relation to the shifting discourses of male homosexuality in the 1930s and 1940s.

She Done Him Wrong

Spectacle and narrative

KATHLEEN ROWE

[. . .]

She Done Him Wrong is set in a Bowery saloon during the Gay Nineties and tells the story of Lou, a singer of great beauty and sexual allure who enjoys the attention and gifts of many male admirers. Cummins, an undercover cop played by Cary Grant, disguises himself as a mission worker to investigate a crime ring involving Lou's current beau. By the end of the film, he cracks the case. He also convinces Lou to settle down and marry him. The plot isn't the major interest in the film, however, but merely a backdrop for West's performance – as "Lou" and as actress/author/unruly woman "Mae West." That performance displays a number of motifs traditionally associated with the unruly woman: a carnivalesque openness toward sexuality; an ironic attitude toward romance; the presentation of her self, especially her gendered self, as visual construct or image, created through a performance of femininity that exaggerates its attributes and thus denaturalizes it; and a comic gender inversion that reduces men to interchangeable sexual objects while acknowledging, as Lou does, that men make the rules of the game ("I'm just smart enough to play it their way," she says). West's famous invitation – "Why don't you come up and see me?" – mocks not only Puritan attitudes toward sex but Victorian ideals of female delicacy and sentimentality.

These themes are evident from the earliest moments of the film. While Lou's admirers become fools for love, she remains supremely detached from sentiment about men, using them only for her own pleasure and for gifts that secure her independence. During the film, five past or present lovers move in and out of Lou's life, and when she strolls by a row of jail cells, one abject prisoner after another greets her fondly, even though love for her has brought many of them there. But Lou doesn't waste time grieving for them. "I ain't the sentimental kind," she says. As she tells a young woman who tried to kill herself after losing her virtue, men are all alike, whether they're married or single, and they are good for only two things: money and sex. "Diamonds is my career," she tells Cummins, who knows that as long as she has her diamonds, she remains out of his control.

Lou eludes male control by controlling men herself, which she does by creating and manipulating herself as spectacle. For Lou, as for West, being a spectacle doesn't make her vulnerable to men but ensures her power over them. Even before we see Lou, she is introduced as a spectacle. The film begins with a montage of street scenes then moves into a saloon filled with men who are drinking, brawling, and making business deals. In the foreground men at the bar discuss a prize fight, while another man gazes at an object concealed from our view. His comments soon reveal it to be a painting of Lou. Another man, Gus, boasts of his plans to wrest control of the saloon from Dan, its current owner, and to take Lou as his prize. Other men discuss a dispute between calendar companies fighting over the right to use Lou's image on their New Year calendars. In the meantime, the camera gives its first glimpse of the painting, which depicts a nude Lou in a reclining position.

The scene recalls John Berger's analysis of sexual representation and social power. According to Berger, business in early capitalism was often conducted in rooms lined with paintings of passive female nudes, whose display of sexual difference and availability reassured the businessmen of their own power. In this case, however, West turns the tables on the men, asserting both her power over – and desire for – them. She draws on what Gaylyn Studlar describes as the masochistic pleasure men may experience in giving themselves over to the image of a female who evokes the all-powerful mother.[1] Lou displays her savvy manipulation of her image and her ability to actively control the male gaze in an early scene with Dan and the crooked couple, Serge and Rita. After passing around a series of photographs of herself – with all her "rocks," the signifiers of her power – she fixes her own provocative gaze on Serge, invites him to come up and see her, then saunters up the stairs. The camera and the gaze of the men follow her until she poses on the balcony, back-lit to display her corseted figure. She positions herself in front of her bedroom door, with one hand resting suggestively on a pillar. For several lingering moments, she leers provocatively at the men below her and offers her image to their gaze.

West, of course, didn't create her persona out of a cultural vacuum. The unruly woman flourished in other popular traditions of the late nineteenth and early twentieth centuries. As Henry Jenkins has shown, a popular figure in early sound film was the "wild woman." While not the comic sex goddess West portrayed, the wild woman disrupted gender norms about feminine restraint and humiliated male characters to comic effect. This figure, he argues, provided an alternative to the dominant comic paradigm of the time, which centered on male suffering from domestic power (as in the films of W. C. Fields). In So Long Letty (1929), Charlotte Greenwood overturns ladylike decorum with her "ear-piercing voice and thrashing movements," disrespect for authority, and vulgar use of language (Henry Jenkins, "Don't Become Too Intimate", 3). However, unlike West, who exaggerates her apparent allure, many of these women derived their comedy from their *failure* to meet traditional standards of feminine beauty. Winnie Lightner, for example, offers her own unfeminine appearance as a "grotesque parody" of femininity, "an unfit object for male desire" (Henry Jenkins, 22).

A more suggestive context for West's explicit celebration of female power and sexuality can be found in the tradition of burlesque. As Robert C. Allen argues, burlesque created an "upside-down world of enormous, powerful women and powerless, victimized men."[2] The burlesque queen, epitomized by the exoticized stripper, enacted a range of sexual transgressions, from impersonating men to aggressively returning the male gaze. In her own career, West brought elements of burlesque into the more middle-class performance form of vaudeville. She alludes to the connection in She Done Him Wrong, when a chorus line of bare-legged women introduces Lou's singing act. The film, in fact, is set during the heyday of burlesque, when, as its opening titles remind us, "legs were confidential."

West was unique, however, both in her control of her image and in its impact. As she explains in her autobiography, Goodness Had Nothing to Do With It (1959), "I became a writer by the accident of needing material and having no place to get it. At least not the kind of writing I wanted for my stage appearance. . . . Yes, I had to create myself, and to create the fully mature image, I had to write it out to begin with" (72). That image took on a life of its own, she noted:

> Few people knew that I didn't *always* walk around with a hand on one hip, or pushing at my hairdress and talking low and husky. I had created a kind of Twentieth Century Sex Goddess that mocked and delighted all victims and soldiers of the great war between men and women. I was their banner, their figurehead, an articulate image, and I certainly enjoyed the work. (163)

Furthermore, the image she did create was multivalent and powerful, consistent with the topos of female unruliness. While some reviewers praised her skills as a comedian and her appeal as an entertainer, *Variety* reviewed her act in terms of the grotesque: "She is one of the many freak persons on the vaudeville stage where freakishness often carries more weight than talent."[3] The ambiguity of her sexual image is well known. From the outset of her career, as she notes in her autobiography, she had special appeal to gay men as a female female impersonator, presenting sex largely as a matter of style – a theme that would be taken up, though more conventionally, in the stylish, playful couples of the classical romantic comedy. The element of camp about West points to a strain of female unruliness that exists, like her own work, outside conventional romantic comedy, in the figures of Joan Crawford and Carmen Miranda, for example (see Robertson), as well as in Jack Lemmon's female impersonation in *Some Like It Hot* (1959). Parker Tyler opens *Screening the Sexes* (1972) with a lengthy tribute to her as "The Mother Superior of the Faggots" (1). As film reviewer Stark Young observes, it is the "abstraction" of her image that most fully accounts for the "howling, diverting mythology" that clings to her. He compares her to Harlequin, Pierrot, Chaplin, and Sarah Bernhardt, "as abstract as . . . a song, good or bad; or as the circus." That abstraction, he writes, comes to a single conclusion affirming the power of the woman on top: "that every woman has the lure and that every man can be had" (91–92).

    This abstraction – or more precisely, fetishization – largely accounts for West's success as an image of female unruliness based on sexuality.[4] Because the "real" sexuality of any woman presented as image or spectacle is always hidden, that image heightens desire for what is missing while at the same time defusing the potential threat of unruly and unmediated female sexuality. West's image, like Dietrich's, is fetishized – redolent with signs (the phallic attire, the husky voice) that reassure male viewers that femininity is not so different from masculinity. In *She Done Him Wrong*, West heightens the irony surrounding her image by reinforcing distance through both setting and style. The film is a period piece. Despite its musical numbers and its dependence on West's delivery of her lines, it has the feel less of the sound film than of silent cinema, with its opening montage of street scenes and intertitles. West's parodic tone further puts her in the realm of excess, "freakishness," or the "horrible prettiness" (in Allen's words) of the burlesque queen, removing any real erotic charge – and therefore danger – from her persona.

    She Done Him Wrong concludes with Cummins making Lou his personal "prisoner," taking from her fingers her many diamond rings and replacing them with a small solitaire. The ending is entirely conventional; leading ladies are paired up with the right man at the end of almost all comedies and indeed most other films, and the arbitrariness of such endings is usually overlooked or accepted as an inevitable part of narrative.[5] That is hard to do in the case of this film, however. The power of West's personality, the independent and cynical character she plays, and her age at the time of the film (she was 40, compared with Grant's 29) make Lou's willing surrender laughable, even to a man as suave as Cummins. Cummins must be given all the authority of the Law – from his masquerade as a mission worker to his job as a police officer – to give his character sufficient weight to bring Lou/West into the social fabric of marriage, family, and bourgeois respectability.

The film's ending illustrates the difficulty of emplotting the unruly woman in a traditional narrative. The Chaplin Tramp as Everyman can be himself – perform himself – in virtually any narrative, since narrative is built around the activity or agency of a male hero. Chaplin simply uses those narratives of male action – whether prospecting for gold in *The Gold Rush* (1925), or working on an assembly line in *Modern Times* (1936), or taking his place in the front lines of history in *The Great Dictator* (1940) – as fuel for his comic performances. Chaplin's performances indeed dominate the narratives of his films, as West's do hers, but, for Chaplin, narrative generates an abundant storehouse of material for performance. (This is true whether he is working entirely in mime and physical comedy, as in the silent films, or using verbal humor as well, as in the less successful sound films, although silent comedy's dependence on "activity" may well contribute to its effectiveness in undercutting the heroic "man of action.") In contrast, West is limited to the single narrative of a woman's life: that of her relation to men. West's persona bursts out of the narrative of the whore with a heart of gold, which is the only narrative that would make her acceptable to a mainstream audience. And yet, that narrative confines her to a single-note performance. There are few narrative options for strong examples of female unruliness.

At the same time, the appetite *for* narrative is tremendous, as the history of Hollywood film has proved. The pull of narrative over simple performance is evident in another film released a year after *She Done Him Wrong* – Frank Capra's *It Happened One Night* – which was equally popular and ultimately more influential than *She Done Him Wrong*. *It Happened One Night* set the pattern for a kind of comedy that had unique appeal to a country finding its way out of the social crises of the 1930s. Much of the appeal of this genre depended on its use of female unruliness. That unruliness, however, was associated no longer with sexual experience, as in West's case, but with something quite different: virginity. The unruly virgin retained much of the essence of the West persona – its foregrounding of gender, resonances of sexual ambiguity, dominance of men – but tempered into a form more amenable to traditional narrative.

Notes

1 Studlar criticizes Laura Mulvey for overlooking in her early work the pre-Oedipal, masochistic desire to give oneself over to the power of the female/mother figure and for emphasizing, exclusively, the sadistic drive of scopophilia to strengthen the political power of her argument – its extension to relations of power under patriarchy. Studlar's analysis is primarily based on Dietrich but also draws on West.

2 See "The Leg Business" (1990, 44), and *Horrible Prettiness* (1991). Allen links burlesque with such traditions of carnival as the Feast of Fools. He argues that burlesque's play with gender helped refigure femininity outside a sentimentalized notion of the bourgeois family and that, in fact, its transgressive gender inversions extended to class. Unlike vaudeville, which was aligned with a middle-class family audience, burlesque offered both a comic

inversion of the bourgeois world and a vulgar "other" against which the bourgeoisie defined itself.

3 Quoted in Seidman (1981, 71). However, West's persona obviously meant other things as well to audiences at the time. For example, her reassuring speech to the fallen woman takes on special significance at a time when unemployment was increasing the ranks of prostitution. See Curry 1991.

4 See Studlar 1990; Kaplan (1983, 49–59); and also Johnston ("Women's Cinema as Counter-Cinema" (1976)), who is sympathetic toward stylized rather than "realistic" representations of femininity in cinema but also suspicious of the image of the fetishized woman, such as West.

5 It is worth remembering here that most narrative endings are problematic from a feminist point of view, and that a feminist criticism that is unwilling to bracket the conventional ending, at least temporarily, in order to consider what precedes it will be a discouraging project.

References

Allen, Robert C. (1990): "The Leg Business: Transgression and Containment in American Burlesque", *Camera Obscura* No. 23: 43–70.

Allen, Robert C. (1991): *Horrible Prettiness: Burlesque and American Culture*, Chapel Hill: University of North Carolina Press.

Berger, John (1972): *Ways of Seeing*, New York: BBC and Penguin Books.

Curry, Ramona (1991): "'Mae West as Censored Commodity': The Case of *Klondike Annie'*", *Cinema Journal* Vol. 31, No. 1: 57–84.

Jenkins, Henry (1991): "'Don't Become Too Intimate With That Terrible Woman!' Unruly Wives, Female Comic Performance and *So Long Letty*", *Camera Obscura* nos 25–6 (January–May): 202–23.

Johnston, Claire (1976): "Women's Cinema as Counter-Cinema", in Bill Nichols (ed.): *Movies and Methods*, Berkeley: University of California Press: 208–17.

Kaplan, E. Ann (1983): *Women and Film: Both Sides of the Camera*, London: Methuen.

Mulvey, Laura (1989): "Visual Pleasure and Narrative Cinema", in *Visual and Other Pleasures*, Bloomington: Indiana University Press (originally published 1975).

Robertson, Pamela (1993): "'The Kinda Camp That Imitates Me': Mae West's Identification With the Feminist Camp", *Cinema Journal* Vol. 32, No. 2: 57–72.

Seidman, Steve (1981): *Comedian Comedy: A Tradition in Hollywood Film*, Ann Arbor, MI: UMI Research Press.

Studlar, Gaylyn (1990): "Masochism, Masquerade, and the erotic Metamorphosis of Marlene Dietrich", in Jane Gaines and Charlotte Herzog (eds): *Fabrications: Costume and the Female Body*, New York: Routledge: 229–49.

Tyler, Parker (1972): *Screening the Sexes: Homosexuality in the Movies*, New York: Holt, Rinehart & Winston.

West, Mae (1959): *Goodness Had Nothing to Do With It*, New York: Macfadden-Bartell.

Young, Stark (1977): "What Maisie Knows: Mae West", in Karen Kay and Gerald Peary (eds): *Women and the Cinema*, New York: E.P. Dutton, 90–92.

THE LIBRARY
GUILDFORD COLLEGE
of Further and Higher Education

Lucille Ball and the Regime of Domiculture

9

PATRICIA MELLENCAMP

> Since we said "I do," there are so many things we don't.
>
> — Lucy Ricardo

> This is a battle between two different ways of life – men and women.
> The battle of the sexes!?
> Sex has nothing to do with it.
>
> — Gracie Allen and Blanche Morton

During the late 1940s and 1950s, television, linked to or owned by the major radio networks in the US, recycled radio's stars, formats, and times through little proscenium screens, filling up the day. Vaudeville and movies fed both these voracious domestic media, each reliant on sound, and each influential in the rapidly developing suburbs. With a commercial collage of quiz, news, music, variety, wrestling/boxing, fashion/cooking, and comedy shows, both media were relatively irreverent toward well-fashioned narrative and worshipful of audiences and sponsors. TV was then (and continues to be) an ecology, a repetition and recycling through the years, and a family affair, in the 1950s conducted collectively in the living room, the dial dominated by Dad. A TV set was a status symbol, a rooftop economic declaration, and an invitation to other couples to watch. The agenda was familialism. Or as George Burns put it: "There are more husbands and wives on television than at home watching."

Coincident with the massive licensing of broadcast air and time, women were being urged to leave the city, work force, and salaries; move to the suburbs, leisure, and tranquility; raise children; and placate commuting, overworked husbands for free. In reality, of course, not all women did so. Most women over 35 remained in the paid work force; when allowed, instead of building battleships, they took other jobs. That TV, and particularly situation comedies, would, like radio, both serve and support the new, imaginary blissful domesticity of a ranch-style house, a backyard barbecue, a tree, and a bath and a half, seems logical – it is, of course, historical. "Containment" was not only a defensive military strategy developed as US foreign policy in the 1950s, it was practiced on the domestic front as well, and it was aimed at excluding women from the work force and keeping them in the home. For Andrew Ross in *No Respect*, "This mechanism of containment is a process of identification, not an act of annexation. It results in the formation of new audiences, new cultural identities . . . not in

. . . homogenizing of . . . cultural production and consumption."[1] For women, however, containment was a double whammy – identification *and* (by or with) annexation. The "New Traditionalist," fashionably dressed to stay at home as were Gracie and Lucy, is a revision of an earlier campaign, a "situation" which occurs when jobs are fewer and too many men are unemployed. For women in the 1950s, consumption for the family home became a full-time, unpaid job. "I *Love Lucy*" brilliantly documents this process of "upward mobility," with Lucy always aware that her talents might be wasted on full-time housewifery.[2]

The self-sufficient/contained family home – the locus of situation comedy – is a haven for consumer durables and services, along with marriage. The "household" is the setting for the neo-Fordist regime: domiculture.[3] For example, the introduction of TV (a piece of furniture and entertainment) into the home in the late 1940s and 1950s was accompanied by redecorating or the construction of a rec or family room. As Lynn Spigel demonstrates, it was a marketing campaign addressed to women, urged to alter predetermined spaces. The campaign was contradictory: TV was disruptive and hence demanded spatial change, but it would bring the family together.[4] In the beginning, there was one set per family, in a central viewing space. Now, TVs sit in many rooms of the house, watched by individual family members while babies are monitored by closed-circuit surveillance cameras. TV is not only a stationary piece of furniture but a mobile appliance. It can be bought as a series of components and then hooked up to other high-voltage electronic durables – VCRs, computers, and stereo systems. With men now included in on the purchase, the latest redecorating phase is designing costly "entertainment centers." The electronic expansion capacity might be endless.

To argue that television was and is a powerful machinery of familial containment of women is hardly original. Yet, the disparagement of situation comedy suggests that more is going on in these twenty-four minutes than meets the eye. Because this form has been dominated by middle-aged women, often mothers, its lowly stature might be a symptom of disrespect for, particularly, housewives (the least regarded and the most crucial job). Yet, this cultural disrespect is promising, especially for women of a certain age. The history of sitcom women is my history – one of contradiction.

Lucy

In its original version, I *Love Lucy* debuted Monday, October 15, 1951, at 8:00 p.m. (It ran until May 6, 1957.) The means of filming involved the simultaneous use of three 35mm cameras with ten-minute magazines (the discontinuous stop-and-start method) for a live audience in a converted sound stage. The *mise-en-scène* was of minimal sets – kitchen right, bedroom left, central living room – and uniform lighting, "invented" by the German Expressionist cameraman Karl Freund. The method, attributed to Desi Arnaz, was and continues to be hailed as a technological rather than economic innovation; and, indeed, this style and apparatus set the pattern of three cameras, a live audience and laugh track, and a filmed/edited product. Under the rubric "Desilu" (his name first, the name of their ranch in the valley, eventually a corporate studio logo), they owned a tangible product (after sacrificing salaries for ownership) which could be corrected by postproduction editing, unlike live broadcasts or the low-resolution kinescopes (filmed from the TV screen).[5] The postproduction schedule was from six to eight weeks. Each episode was edited on a Moviola, producing a master print which included opticals such as wipes, fades, and dissolves. Prints were sent to CBS outlets prior to air date. There were thirty-nine episodes per season. And unlike the two-camera setup without an audience (which accounts for *Burns and Allen's* [his name first] multiple sets and scene changes), this system seemed to encode presence and the status of live performance.

Perhaps most important, the standardization of product and broadcast times was achieved. The system was economically brilliant, if (visually) artistically retrograde – a profitable hybrid of nineteenth-century staging techniques and B-movie continuity style and abbreviated conventions, necessitating, for example, the center-frame, frontal, uniformly lighted *mise en-scène*. Desilu went on to make hundreds of hours of programming, employing the same system in their own studio empire, purchased, through the presumed economic savvy of Arnaz, the independent producer/entrepreneur, with the profits from the first series. In 1954, Arnaz produced, for example, *December Bride*, *Make Room for Daddy*, *The Ray Bolger Show*, and later *The Untouchables*, totaling some 229 half-hour shows.[6] The three-camera format, the central living room and women's place within the home, the studio audience, frontal staging, and the laugh track – tied to reactions – have become an institutionalized, familiar style which has endured, with minor stylistic revisions, for forty years. The major locale was the family dwelling (with forays to workplaces), significant in that situation means, among other things, "a place of employment" – so true for female stars and viewers.

Held to the domesticity of situation comedy's conventions, Lucy Ricardo was barely in control, constantly attempting to escape domesticity – her "situation" – always trying to get into show business by getting into Ricky's "act," narratively fouling it up, but brilliantly and comically performing in it. Lucy endured marriage and housewifery by transforming them into vaudeville: costumed performances and rehearsals which made staying home (a lack of choice and economic power) frustrating, yet tolerable. Her dissatisfaction, expressed as her desire for a job, show business, and stardom, was concealed by the happy-ended resolutions of hug/kiss (sometimes tagged with the line "Now we're even")/applause/titles/theme song, over the famous heart logo. Her discontent and ambition, literally and weekly stated, were the show's working premises, its contradictions massively covered up by our sheer pleasure in her performances, her "real" stardom and brilliance. The series typified the both/and logic and the paradox of women and comedy (and work) – the female performer/spectator caught somewhere between narrative and spectacle, always having two effortless jobs, historically held as a simulation between the real and the model. The serious contradictions of women's lives were blatantly there, often spoken, but covered up by laughter and by Lucy's childish antics.

[. . .] On a more general level, the series dramatized the social phenomenon of "upward mobility." One version is embedded in Raymond Williams's analysis of the function of "consumer durables": "Socially this complex is characterized" by a paradox of (1) upward "mobility" and (2) the "apparently self-sufficient family home."[7] For Williams, there is as yet "no satisfactory name" for this "paradoxical" tendency of "modern urban industrial living," a technology which is both "mobile and home-centered," the phenomenon he describes as "*mobile privatisation*" (26). Williams places "broadcasting institutions" as the resolutions of these contradictory pressures: consumer durables improved small homes for families, which then needed new forms of contact, services which TV, like radio, provided. Consumer durables also covered up the contradictions in marriage and domestic labor. (Electric appliances were supposed to make housework easier and faster, along with providing cheaper entertainment at home. Arguing "the freedom to stay at home" or the virtue of saving money, audiences could accept the infinitely lower resolution and bad sound of television when compared to movies. Purchase and debt still hold marriages together.)

Lucy and Ethel crave dishwashers, freezers, and other domestic appliances, as well as clothing. Shopping for these two close friends is a pleasure, a rebellion, and an occupation – they always run the risk of spending too much and being chastised. Their lack of economic independence is a given, a source of comedy and plot, yet a frustrating one familiar to many women in the 1990s as well as the 1950s. "Pioneer Women" involves a bet on whether Lucy and Ethel can go without modern conveniences; the episode is also a parody on baking, the reality of women's work, which Lucy transforms into a comic routine. ("Job Switching" poignantly exemplifies women's economic subservience and the difficulties of housework, at which Fred and Ricky fail miserably. Housework is gender-determined.) In "Oil Wells," broadcast on February 15, 1954, the Ricardos and the Mertzes buy Texas oil stock; then come the fur coats and "custom-built periwinkle blue Cadillacs." As always, Lucy's scheme is initially right, hailed, and finally wrong; she loses the money in the end after a great performance with a microphone in her pant leg. Their dreams of wealth vanish. Situation comedy is destined to be middle class. In "Ricky Loses His Temper," the bet is on that Lucy cannot refrain from buying. She can't, but neither can Ricky keep his temper. Again, they are "even." It should be noted that while she was the emblematic 1950s consumer, Lucy (like Buster Keaton's one-reelers) also gleefully and offhandedly trashed possessions, suggesting their irrelevance and the risk of her endeavors.

The Ricardos' upward mobility is apparent throughout the series, including the early move to an apartment with a window. In fact, the series neatly coincides with newly introduced products and advertising campaigns in picture magazines such as *Look*. In the twenty-seven episodes devoted to the California sojourn (where the series originated, although it claimed New York as its setting) – Ricky's stint at becoming a famous movie star – aired during the 1955–56 season, Ricky buys a car (for all the bad women-driver jokes that the series had so far avoided). In ad campaigns increasingly pitched to women, the family car was the big consumer item, along with the family home. Family travel and vacations (by car, and a bit later by plane) were increasingly advertised. [. . .] Two episodes of *Lucy* are devoted to the purchase of an automobile (which Lucy will then predictably crash).

Now the couples, constantly together, are mobile and drive cross-country. In the Hollywood episodes, they stay in a luxurious hotel suite and concoct schemes to meet movie stars, which are wildly successful. In May 1956, "Lucy Goes to Monte Carlo" (and makes, then loses, piles of money), and after seventeen episodes devoted to Europe, she returns to New York, carrying her cheese "baby" on the plane. In November 1956, they're "Off to Florida" and "Deep Sea Fishing" (with another bet between women and men, wives versus husbands, the battle of the sexes which has nothing to do with sex, over who will catch the biggest tuna). In December that year, "The Ricardos Visit Cuba."

Finally, the ultimate 1950s seal of upward mobility – the move to suburban Connecticut, with the Mertzes as entrepreneurial chicken farmers (they also try some other small-time business schemes, which fail). This enterprise, "Lucy Does the Tango," resulted in the longest laugh on the series – Lucy doing the tango with Ricky (who apparently *wants* her in his act!), with dozens of eggs stuffed in her clothing. After a long dance routine, they finally collide, and the audience breaks up. The scene builds on that laugh when Ethel is slammed by a swinging door, squishing her concealed eggs. One episode is devoted to Lucy's redecorating; she spends too much money on furniture because she is afraid to let the decorator know she, and Ricky, can't afford to spend so much. [. . .]

At the same time, Ricky has moved from performer, to manager, to movie star, to owner of the Club Babaloo. Lucy has also been working: "Little Ricky Gets a Dog," "Little Ricky Plays the Drums," and everyone goes to "Little Ricky's School Pageant." It goes without saying that the latter are among the least interesting episodes. [. . .]

Outside the fiction (which was always elided with the real, particularly the Arnazes' marriage), Desilu purchased RKO, Lucy's former studio. In addition to their seven-acre, nine-stage lot, purchased in 1953, they now owned RKO's fifteen-stage, fourteen-acre Hollywood lot as well as RKO's Culver City Studio of eleven stages. Desilu, consisting of thirty-five movie stages, a forty-acre backlot, and offices, along with the Motion Picture Center, was bigger than MGM or Fox. Charles Higham called it "the biggest production facility on earth."[8] Along this corporate way, in the best entrepreneurial fashion, they crossed media boundaries, staging the series live in Las Vegas and releasing combined episodes on film for movie showings. They "tied in" with the American Export Lines, in return for a plug on the European voyage, and General Motors, for a car plug on the California trip. The lucrative sponsorship/ linkage with Phillip Morris is apparent in almost every episode; Lucy and Ricky frequently smoke or handle cigarettes. In the famous "Lucy Makes a TV Commercial," Lucy imitates the Phillip Morris boy in the TV set which she has trashed.[9]

In the best Walt Disney fashion, hundreds of Lucy products were manufactured: Lucy and Little Ricky dolls, Lucy bedroom suites, Lucille Ball dresses, Desi Arnaz smoking jackets (then very much out of style), he-and-she pyjamas, Desi Denims, Lucy Lingerie. There was a syndicated comic strip for King Features from December 8, 1952, to May 30, 1955, records, Dell comic books, and I Love Lucy one-act plays for amateur theatrical groups. However, in an intrusion of the real, after a season of one-hour shows with famous guest stars, the couple separated and then divorced. Rather than bringing the couple together, which Lucy commentators never cease to repeat was the virtual reason for the program (Lucy's stymied, flat film career might be as significant), upward mobility led them apart, along with gossip's (and a TV movie's) later reports of Desi's drinking and infidelity and Lucy's "workaholism" and demanding perfection. The "real," incorporated into the series, was carefully managed until much later, after Lucy's death. After the divorce, Lucille Ball bought Desi Arnaz out and continued on in a successful single-parent series. In the 1980s, she began a new sitcom, as a grandmother, which was soon canceled. In Stone Pillow, a TV movie, she played the lead bag lady. Just prior to and after her death, she was hailed as an entertaining genius.

Along with the consumption of consumer durables and upward mobility, the series portrayed irrevocable, stereotypical differences between men and women. Fred is cheap, Ethel eats too much, Ricky loses his temper, and Lucy plots and shops. Like George Burns, Fred is a 1950s expert on female psychology, with constant commentary on women and marriage. In "Oil Wells," he labels Lucy and Ethel "the snooper patrol," followed by "Nosiness is just part of a woman's charm, like hanging stockings in the bathroom and nagging." In "Job Switching," Fred divides the world sexually into "earners and spenders." Ethel gets almost equal time for her "men" and "husband" jokes. At least TV, unlike the movies, presumed that women occupied other subject positions, with different identifications possible. This double-directed strategy was also apparent in the gender base of 1950s television, with sports and news shows for men, cooking and fashion shows for women, and "kidvid" for children, differences which "family shows" elided. However, while acknowledging women's existence,

US television scheduled few daytime programs for women. As Jack Gould, the TV critic for the *New York Times*, wrote: "The idea of a nation of housewives sitting mute before the video screen when they should be tidying up the premises or preparing the formula is not something to be grasped hurriedly."[10] Neither is Gould's remark easily grasped.

The series is a compendium of references to 1950s popular culture. The 1950s fashion of full skirts and crinolines, tight waists, capri pant outfits, casual and formal aprons, and hats was seriously acknowledged in episodes devoted to designer clothing, parodied, as are many upper-class forms, including ballet and *House Beautiful*, in "Lucy Gets a Paris Gown." Her style was glamorized in 1953 with the hiring of award-winning Elois Jensen as costumer. Max Factor's brother-in-law was Lucy's constant makeup man, taking her age down from more than forty to the program's stated twenty-nine – a process aided by Freund's diffused lighting and the presence of Ethel, beside whom Lucy looked younger and more glamorous. Her trademark, along with her huge, false-eyelashed eyes, was, of course, her strawberry or hennaed hair, clearly not natural and a source of endless jokes.[11]

Additional references include the Kinsey report, Joe DiMaggio, and Marilyn Monroe. "Second Honeymoon," broadcast in January 1956, re-enacts the scenario of *Gentlemen Prefer Blonds*, with Lucy as Lorelei and Kenny as the young boy, Spofford; they restage the scene where Monroe gets stuck in a porthole. (As anecdote has it, Lucy's impersonation of Monroe on another episode amazed passersby.) The show's brilliant writers, Marilyn Pugh, Jess Oppenheimer (the producer), and Bob Carroll, admitted to combing films for stories and bits. Lucy imitated Katharine Hepburn and Tallulah Bankhead. "Lucy's Italian Movie," which contains the grape-stomping sequence, dissects 1950s art films, specifically Italian neo-realism. An Italian director, Vittorio Fellipe, approaches Lucy (the couples are vacationing in Italy) with the question, "Have you ever considered acting?" Huge laugh. Lucy, imagining herself as Anna Magnani, dresses as an earthy, disheveled peasant in order to gather "local color" and prepare for her part in the film *Bitter Grapes*; her hilarious sequence with the female peasant in the wine vat *is* the film, including subtitles, which in the end she doesn't make. As usual, she broke her promise to Ricky, disobeyed, is purple from the grape catfight in the vat, and must be narratively punished or contained.

Although not as reflexive as *Burns and Allen* (the forebear of Gary Shandling), the series also alluded to television. One example – the consummate testimony to Lucy's ability to endlessly vary a bit – is "Lucy Does a TV Commercial." The episode is predicated on the pretense of the live while acknowledging that *Lucy* is not live – it only pretends to be. The "real" Lucy stages a commercial in her living room, dressed as the Phillip Morris guy in the now-trashed TV set. Ricky tries to change the channel. Later, in the television studio of Ricky's show, Lucy rehearses for Vitametavegamin, a health product with a high dosage of alcohol, becoming drunker with each runthrough. (She is as brilliant as Chaplin.) Fade. Ricky is broadcasting *his* live show; the delightfully drunk Lucy walks on stage, upstaging Ricky and disrupting his act.

During the Hollywood episodes, she imitates star behavior – wearing dark glasses and scarves, carrying a long cigarette holder, and walking with an affected, hip-swinging gait. She sits on drugstore stools waiting to be discovered and tells stories about overnight fame. Like the audience, Lucy is starstruck, the consummate fan who will do anything to get star mementoes, including a huge block of cement from Grauman's Chinese Theatre with John Wayne's footprints in it. Being a star, viewed as an effortless and pleasurable job, is the show's ultimate fantasy and narrative gimmick. In "The Ballet," Lucy says: "Here I am with all this talent bottled up inside me and you're always sitting on the cork . . . I'm going to get into that show or my name is not Lucy Ricardo." She goes on work and hunger strikes to get either clothes or a shot at a job performing. In order to work, she will lie, cheat, and even blackmail Ricky. In "Don Juan Is Shelved," Lucy tries to steal Ricky's big screen test by upstaging him. She is strapped to a couch, which doesn't stop her; finally, she pulls off Ricky's pants. In "Lucy's Fake Illness," she and Ethel are sitting in the kitchen, the scene of so many openings. Lucy is reading a psychology book: "I'm learning to act abnormal." Already by air date, January 1952, this bit receives laughter. After she decides to have amnesia, she says: "Ricky has kept me from becoming a famous actress."

Like Gracie, Lucy was a comic clown, a fashion model, and a "typical female": she was stylishly dressed, with extravagant tastes for hats; she loved gossip and was prey to jealousy; she was zany, without inhibition – the child whom the husband or father, Ricky, tried to control. His noble tolerance was particularly evident in the Hollywood episodes. All the stars – Rock Hudson, Richard Widmark, John Wayne, and Dore Schary, the producer – know about Lucy's wild antics and empathize with Ricky and presumably tolerant husbands everywhere.

As was the case with the *George Burns and Gracie Allen Show*, the entire series was biographically linked to the marriage of the two stars. Lucille Ball, movie star, and her husband Desi Arnaz, Cuban bandleader, became disguised as Lucy and Ricky Ricardo; their friends appeared on programs as bit players or as "themselves." At the end of "Harpo Marx," in which Lucy and Harpo re-create the famous mirror scene of *Duck Soup* (with Lucy wearing a Harpo wig and baggy coat, as earlier in the episode she dressed as Clark Gable, Gary Cooper, and Jimmy Durante), the voiceover announcer said: "Harpo Marx played himself." Image/person/ star are totally merged as "himself"; the real is a replayed image, a scene, a simulation – what Baudrillard calls the "hyperreal." The most extraordinary or bizarre example of the elision of "fact" and fiction, or the "real" with the simulation, was Lucy's hyperreal pregnancy. In 1952, with scripts supervised by a minister, a priest, and a rabbi, seven episodes were devoted to Lucy's TV and real pregnancy (without ever mentioning the word, except in Spanish). The first episode was aired in December, timed in accordance with Lucy's scheduled caesarean delivery date of Monday, January 19, 1953. Lucy's real baby, Desi, Jr., was electronically delivered, after a seven-week TV gestation, on January 19 at 8 p.m. as Little Ricky, while 44 million Americans watched. (Only 29 million tuned in to Eisenhower's swearing-in ceremony. We liked Ike. We loved Lucy.) Like all the episodes in this series, this one was given a children's book title, "Lucy Goes to the Hospital."[12]

But if the "real" domestic and familial details of the stars' lives (including the state of their marriage and Desi's reputation as a producer) were so oddly mixed up with the fiction, perhaps the supreme fiction of the series was that Lucy was not star material and hence needed to be confined to domesticity. Thus, the weekly plot concerned her thwarted attempts to break out of the home and into show business. Unlike Gracie's implausible connections and overt machinations, all of Lucy's schemes failed, even if failure necessitated an instant and gratuitous reversal in the end. Lucy was the rebellious child whom the husband/father Ricky endured, understood, loved, and even punished, as, for example, when he spanked her for her continual disobedience.

However, if Lucy's plots for ambition and fame *narratively* failed, with the result that she was held, often gratefully, to domesticity (and Ricky was therefore right), *performatively* they succeeded. In the elemental, repetitive narrative, Lucy never got what she wanted: a job and recognition. Weekly, for six years, she accepted domesticity, only to try to escape the next week. During each program, she not only succeeded but demolished Ricky's act, upstaging every other performer, including Orson Welles, and got exactly what she and the television audience wanted: Lucy the star, performing off-key, crazy, perfectly executed vaudeville turns – physical comedy as few women (particularly beautiful ones, formerly Goldwyn girls, with gorgeous legs and face) have ever done.

The typical movement of this series involves Lucy performing for us, at home, the role that the narrative forbids her. She can never be a "real" public performer, except for us: she must narratively remain a housewife. In the episode entitled "The Ballet," for example, Ricky needs a ballerina and a burlesque clown for his nightclub act; Lucy pleads with him to use her. Of course he refuses. Lucy trains as a ballet dancer in one of her characteristic performances: resplendent in a frothy tutu, she eagerly and maniacally imitates the dancer performing ballet movements, which she then transforms through automatic, exaggerated repetition into a Charleston. Whenever Lucy is confident that she has learned something new, no matter how difficult, she gets carried away. (To a degree, these moments recall Chaplin's bodily transformation into an automaton of repetitive motions.) These are the great comic scenes, occurring after the narrative setup: pure performances during which the other characters show absolutely no reaction.

This is the first "story" line, before the mid-program "heart break" – "curtains" as halves of a heart lovingly open/close, or frame and divide each episode. Then, the second: Lucy will now train to be a burlesque comic. Her baggy-pants clown/teacher, an old vaudevillian partner of Fred, arrives at their apartment with a bit for two men. Lucy says, "Just pretend I'm a man. He tells his melodramatic tale of woe about Martha and betrayal; Lucy becomes involved, says the Pavlovian name, Martha, and is hit with a pig bladder, sprayed with seltzer water, and finally, gets a pie in the face. The scene ends with Lucy saying, "Next time, you're going to be the one with the kind face" – in other words, the victim of the sketch. By assuming the mantle of male clothing and slapstick in the "Slowly I Turned" routine, she will become the perpetrator. Lucy never could be the straight woman. (Like the bet between men and women, turning the tables, or getting even, is another story gambit. Here, Lucy demonstrates her mastery of physical comedy, burlesque, and vaudeville, historically a male domain. In a style which she made her own, there are overtones of Keaton and Chaplin.)

Then, as in all the episodes, in this one more literally than most, the two stories are condensed in a final, on-stage performance. At his nightclub, Ricky is romantically singing "Martha" in Spanish. Ethel calls Lucy to inform her that Ricky needs someone in his act. She dresses up as the burlesque clown (not the needed dancer) and steps on stage with her wrong props. When Ricky sings his refrain, the word "Martha" is now her Pavlovian cue: she beats the male ballet dancers with the pig bladder, squirts the female ballerina with seltzer water, and, in a conclusion which uses up all the previous setups, slams a pie in the singing face of tuxedoed, romantic crooner Ricky. The Saudi Arabian government noticed the gentle subversion of this series, banning it because Lucy dominated her husband.

This episode, like so many others, is a rehearsal for a performance, involving in the end a comical, public upstaging of (or getting even with) Ricky. We are simultaneously backstage and out front, in the audience, waiting for the surprise and pleasure of Lucy's performance and Ricky's stoic, albeit frustrated, endurance; thus, expectation is connected not to narrative but to anticipation of the comic – a performative, or proairetic, expectation.

An exemplary instance of Lucy's upstaging, or humiliation, of Ricky may be seen in the episode entitled "The Benefit," in which Ricky's attempts to be the comedian rather than the straight man are utterly foiled. In this episode, Lucy, along with the audience, discovers that

Ricky has re-edited their benefit duo, taking all the punchlines for himself. Fade. On stage, in identical costumes of men's suits, straw hats, and canes, Ricky and Lucy perform a soft-shoe sketch. Ricky stops, taps his cane, and waits for Lucy to be the "straight man." Of course, she won't comply. While Ricky sings "Under the Bamboo Tree" about marriage and happiness, Lucy, with camera closeups as her loyal accomplice in the reaction shots, outrageously steals all of his lines, smirking and using every upstaging method in the show-biz book. Applause, exit; the heart, this time as a literal curtain, closes. Lucy gets the last word and the last laugh during this ironic "turn" on the lyrics of the romantic song.

It is interesting to compare Ricky, the would-be comedian forced by his partner/wife to be the straight man, to George [Burns], the "straight man" who always gets the final, controlling laugh. That Ricky can be so constantly upstaged and so readily disobeyed is not insignificant, for with his Cuban accent (constantly mimicked by Lucy), he does not fully possess language, and is not properly symbolic as is George, the joker or wielder of authoritatively funny speech. The program's reliance on physical rather than verbal comedy, with Lucy and Ethel as the lead performers, constitutes another exclusion of Ricky. Unlike George, who stays at home, Ricky is not given equal, let alone superior, time. He constantly leaves the story, and his departure for work becomes the cue for comic mayhem and audience pleasure. The comedy cannot begin until he leaves. Although he is "tall, dark, and handsome," not the usual slapstick type, his representation as the Latin lover/bandleader/crooner and slapstick foil for Lucy's pies in the face suggests that Lucy's resistance to patriarchy might be more palatable because it is mediated by a subtle racism which views Ricky as inferior.

At the same time, Ricky is clearly the father figure, albeit a funny one. A sample of his responses: in the TV commercial episode, "I don't care if you talk to me, just give me my breakfast." In "Lucy Plays Cupid," aired in January 1952, Ricky is at the breakfast table, talking about marriage, men, and Lucy's scheme to arrange a date for another woman. He threatens Lucy, "If you're gonna act like a child . . .," followed by a spanking, then a fade. Fortunately for the series, Lucy always disobeys. In "The Adagio" (December 1957), Ricky repeats the inevitable "I'll teach her a lesson she'll never forget." In "The Saxophone," he best summarizes his position:

Ricky: When I go on the road, I want you to stay home and be a good little girl.
Lucy: Well, I'll stay home.
Ricky: What do you mean by that?
Lucy: Oh, nothing . . . [sauntering away, swinging her key chain, wearing her man's zoot suit – for her audition].

Typically, Ricky says: "No funny business." Lucy promises. Door closes. Lucy: "Let's go, Ethel." That Ricky could be so readily disobeyed is not insignificant. That marriage was a series of one-upwomanships within a structure of domination/subordination, that independence involved disobedience and deceit, should not go unremarked, covered up by laughter as these inequities were. At the same time, this very structure of marriage was the comic premise.

In "Vacation from Marriage," the underside of situation comedy's reiteration of the same is briefly revealed. Lucy, with Ethel in the kitchen, is talking about the boredom and routine of marriage. "It isn't funny, Ethel, it's tragic." The rest of this show and the series make marriage funny and adventurous. Week after week, the show keeps Lucy happily in her confined, domestic sitcom place after a twenty-three-minute *tour-de-force* struggle to escape. That neither audiences nor critics noticed Lucy's feminist strain is curious, suggesting that comedy is a powerful and unexamined weapon of subjugation, escape, and survival. The most famous episode, "Job Switching," in which Lucy and Ethel sit at an assembly line making chocolates at Kramer's Candy Kitchen, a brilliant staging of comedy, is also a commentary on women and work. The double plot – women at work in uniforms and men at home cooking in aprons – is a bet and a role reversal. Lucy and Ethel, like Siamese twins moving and responding as one, interview for a job at the Acme Employment Agency with A. Snodgrass: "What do you do?" Lucy: "What kind of jobs do you have open?" Snodgrass: "What do you do?" Lucy: "What kind of jobs do you have open?" This bit repeats. Snodgrass suggests another rhetorical method; Lucy agrees and asks: "What do you do?" He in turn asks: "What kind of jobs do you have open?" Finally, as always, Lucy wins, and he asks whether they are (of course) stenographers; then he reads a list, including candymakers.

Housewives, on this program and in the series, can't *do* anything except housework, which isn't taken seriously; and while Lucy and Ethel are great comedians on the assembly line, they can't handle the system when it speeds up. Wearing a hat, Lucy, with Ethel beside her, as always receiving fewer shots, imitates the female candymaker, thinks she's got it, makes a mess of things, and with a child's pleasure of playing in messes of chocolate, gets into a candy fight with her co-worker before the fade. Comically she makes it; narratively she fails, losing her job and returning home to clean up the kitchen, which Ricky has demolished with his rice and chicken. "Now we're even." At the end of "The Ballet," her return home is met with a bucket of water dumped on her head, rigged over the doorway by Ricky. She smiles, "Now we're even." But women were not then, and are not now, even. And Gracie Allen was right: sex has nothing to do with the battle between the sexes.

In most of the programs' endings, the narrative policy was one of twofold containment: every week for seven years, Lucy was always wrong and duly apologetic; and while repeating discontent, her masquerades and escapades made Monday nights and marriage pleasurable. Allen, on the same network, untied legal language and the power polarities implicit in its command; Ball took over the male domain of physical comedy, revising history, with few imitators. Both unmade "meaning" and overturned patriarchal assumptions, stealing the show in the process; yet neither escaped confinement and the tolerance of kindly fathers. "That's entertainment!" – for women a massive yet benevolent containment.

[. . .] Trying to revive Lucy for feminism (although younger scholars have recently questioned my interpretation),[13] I have suggested that throughout the overall series and in the narrative structure of each episode, she is the victim, confined to domesticity and outward compliance with patriarchy and consumer capitalism's 1950s contradictory mandates. Yet this series is complex; Ricky is often the immediate victim of Lucy, a role more easily accepted because of his Cuban rather than Anglo-Saxon heritage. Given this perhaps critical quali-fication, Lucy is, finally, rebelliously incarcerated within situation comedy's domestic regime and *mise-en-scène*, acutely frustrated, trying to escape via the "comic of movement," while cheerfully cracking jokes along the way to her own unmasking or capture. She also became the star she wanted to (and couldn't) be.

Importantly, humorous pleasure comes from "an economy in expenditure upon feeling" rather than the usual lifting of inhibitions that is the source of pleasure in jokes – not a slight distinction, suggesting a displacement of affect or emotion, which I argued earlier might be one critical effect of television, a medium so reliant on comedy. In contrast to the supposedly "liberating" function of jokes, humorous pleasure "saves" feeling because the reality of the situation is too painful. As Lucy poignantly declared to Ethel: "It's not funny, Ethel. It's tragic." Or as Freud states: "The situation is dominated by the emotion that is to be avoided, which is of an unpleasurable character." In "I Love Lucy," the avoided emotion, the "unconquered emotions submitted to the control of humor" (235), is anger at the weekly frustration of Lucy's desire to escape the confinement of domesticity. Her desire is caricatured by her unrealistic dreams of instant stardom in the face of her narrative lack of talent – her wretched, off-key singing, mugging facial exaggerations, and out-of-step dancing. Her *lack* of talent is paradoxically both the source of pleasure and the narrative necessity for housewifery. Using strategies of humorous displacement (the "highest of defensive processes," says Freud – a phrase that takes on interesting connotations in light of 1950s containment policies) and the comic, both of which are "impossible under the glare of conscious attention" (233), situation comedy avoids the unpleasant effects of its own situations (a logic of creation/cancellation). The situation of Lucy was replicated by the female spectator, whether working as a wife or in another "job," moving between comic and humorous pleasure, from spectator to victim, in tandem with Lucy.

Notes

1 Ross, p. 60.
2 I refer to Raymond Williams's notion of "privatized mobility" in relation to the family home and television, in *Television: Technology and Cultural Form* (New York: Schocken Books, 1975).
3 This is a referral back to Alliez and Feher, Part I.
4 As Lynn Spigel has described in *Logics of Television*.
5 Bart Andrews, *Lucy & Ricky & Fred & Ethel* (New York: E. P. Dutton and Co., 1976). This invaluable sourcebook includes a concluding synopsis of shows by air date and title without which I could not have historically organized my textual analyses; it was also used for anecdotes.
6 Charles Higham, *Lucy: The Real Life of Lucille Ball* (New York: St Martin's Press, 1986).
7 Williams, *Television: Technology and Cultural Form*.
8 See Higham, *Lucy*.
9 See Andrews, *Lucy & Ricky*.
10 Jack Gould, TV critic for the *New York Times*.
11 For more on Lucy's history and image as a star in films, see Alex Doty, "The Cabinet of Lucy Ricardo: Lucille Ball's Star Image," *Cinema Journal* 29, no. 4 (Summer 1990). Presumably, Doty is in disagreement with me regarding Lucy's childish antics; yet I fail to see where he differs in theory, if at all.
12 Bart Andrews's book contains a synopsis of shows by air date and title, an invaluable listing.
13 See, for example, Doty, "The Cabinet of Lucy Ricardo".

Comic Theory from a Feminist Perspective

A look at Jerry Lewis

10

JOANNA E. RAPF

> I ask you, learn to go and see the "worst" films; they are sometimes sublime.
>
> – Ado Kyrou[1]

[. . .]

Critics stumble when faced with the subject of women and comedy. A typical sidestepping of the problem is Steve Seidman's in his interesting work on "comedian comedy" where he states that the role of the comedienne in comedian comedy is a topic definitely worth pursuing. "Basically, I agree with Molly Haskell's observation that comedians were essentially misogynistic in their films, and as a result they had a limited appeal to female audiences. This may be why so few women thrived in comedian comedy, but I am unable to either amplify or refute this observation" (1981: 13). There are two issues here: (1) the assertion that women do not like comedians as much as men, and (2) that there are very few successful female comics. The second issue is beyond dispute. If we look at the history of what Seidman calls "comedian comedy" – and this will exclude "situation" or "screwball" comedy, where men and women confront each other as comic equals – Mae West stands almost alone as a successful solo comedienne. The reasons for this are enormously complex, and beyond the scope of this chapter, but as Linda Martin and Kerry Segrave have noted in their landmark book, *Women in Comedy,* "society in general has thrown up a huge resistance to the idea that females can be comedians" (1986: 13). According to Freud, humor is the "highest of defensive processes," whereby the ego asserts its own invulnerability.

> It refuses to be hurt . . . or to be compelled to suffer. It insists that it is impervious to wounds dealt by the outside world, in fact that these are merely occasions for affording it pleasure. Humour is not resigned, it is rebellious. It signifies the triumph of not only the ego but the pleasure principle . . . it [repudiates] the possibility of suffering . . . all without quitting the ground of mental sanity . . . it is a rare and precious gift. (1964: 162–163)

In this light, we can see the source of the idea that women, traditionally "longsuffering," self-sacrificing, and ego-effacing, do not have a sense of humor. And if humor is "rebellious," it is also aggressive, especially that form of humor known as farce, an affirmation of what Henri Bergson called *"une énergie vivante"* which is *"le principe même de la vie intellectuelle et morale"* (1901: 51). But women are not supposed to be aggressive. As Martin and Segrave express it, women "are supposed to be nice to men, children, and animals. Being pervasively nice is not conducive to comedy" (1986: 20).

But the first issue raised by Seidman, that women are not as responsive to solo comedy as men, is disputable. Haskell qualifies this idea by limiting the dislike to *physical* comedy which she calls "masculine" in that it "instinctively sets out to destroy, through ridicule or physical assault, the props of an orderly society over which woman presides."

> Comedy is a gust of fresh air, anarchic and disruptive; it spills the tea, shatters glass and conversation; it is a mad dog that shreds the napkins and the tablecloth, and along with them the last vestiges of romantic illusion. (1977: 36)

If women are indeed primal earth mothers, sources of life and order, comfort and reassurance, apple pie, chicken soup, and everything that builds a foundation to give others the strength to grow, then comedy, as Haskell defines it, is anathema to the feminine.

A third issue is involved here, however, that Seidman does not raise in discussing women and comedy: the issue of theory as opposed to practice or response. Here, the problem is that feminist theory has been largely informed by psychoanalysis, discourse theory, and narrative theory, particularly the work of Lacan and Foucault. Some recent feminist writing suggests that these theoretical models might be limiting. Talking about the issue of male versus female spectatorship, Diane Waldman states, "For me this dilemma points to an inadequacy in a theoretical model drawn solely from psychoanalysis" (1988: 83). And Patricia Mellencamp notes in a perceptive essay on Gracie Allen and Lucille Ball that theories of narrative are of little help "in trying to determine how comedy works to contain women and how successfully it does so" (1986: 91). For this we must turn to theories of the comic and humor. Mellencamp uses Freud, who finds the comic in "embarrassments in which we rediscover the child's helplessness" (1986: 92). From this Freudian perspective, the comic is found in victimization, and the typical comedian is the little man at odds with a big bully of a world where he does not seem to fit. Jerry Lewis defines his own persona this way: "I am nine years old when performing comedy. At that age, hurt is possible but degradation seldom possible" (1971: 161). Curiously, as victim, the comedian can often be seen as a feminine figure persecuted by the patriarchy for his refusal or inability to conform. Structurally, the comic narrative usually involves a growth into a masculine identity: the overcoming of childishness or femininity so that son becomes father. This is beautifully illustrated in *The Delicate Delinquent* where in the end Jerry Lewis, an orphan, becomes a mirror of the father-figure who has had faith in him, a policeman, the upholder of *the law*. This patriarchal evolution can also be mocked, as Keaton does at the end of *College*, where marriage and fatherhood lead eventually to the grave, The difference between the two, Lewis and Keaton, is the difference between what I have elsewhere defined as the difference between moral and amoral comedy, one asserting that meaning precedes existence and the other, that existence precedes meaning.[2]

As a genre, Hollywood comedy tends to follow "the rules of the game," where community and social values win out over the individual and anarchic creativity. According to Rick Altman, all genres can be conceived in terms of a dialectic where "cultural drives are constantly opposed to counter-cultural drives," but in the end, the cultural drives must triumph, the comic figure must either be integrated into or expulsed from society (1977: 38). Ultimately, the patriarchy will be upheld, but between that "fade in" and "fade out," comedy is free to work its subversive purpose which makes it particularly interesting for feminist analysis.

Laura Mulvey's ground-breaking essay, "Visual Pleasure and Narrative Cinema," does not mention a comic film (comic films are often non-narrative), and indeed, it would be very difficult to apply her thesis to comedy because her ideas involve *identification* with screen characters whereas comedy asks for distance:

> The scopophilic instinct (pleasure in looking at another person as an erotic object), and in contradistinction, ego libido (forming identification processes) act as formations, mechanisms, which mould this cinema's formal attributes. (1989: 25)

One of the great strengths, and also the dangers, of film, as André Bazin has stressed, is that it allows us *to identify* in our imaginations "with the world before us, which becomes *the* world" (1967: 21–22, italics mine). One of the recurring subjects of feminist film theory is the nature of this identification. Mary Desjardins has suggested that the "female spectator is in some way constituted as a hysteric, for she overidentifies or overinvests with the story and the character."[3] The image that comes to mind here is Mia Farrow lost in the screen world of *The Purple Rose of Cairo*, a striking exploration of female over-identification. But we need to remember that Woody Allen explored the same theme in *Play It Again, Sam*, only this time the spectator was male. As Waldman suggests, it may be that the patriarchy has constructed "male spectators out of all of us" (1988: 88).

Gaylyn Studlar, moving from Mulvey's post-Oedipal perspective to a concept of pre-Oedipal masochism, argues that the female in this aesthetic is more than the passive object of the male's desire for possession. "She is also a *figure of identification*, the mother of plenitude whose gaze meets the infant's as it asserts her presence and her power" (1984: 275, italics mine). But again, this perspective necessitates the concept of identification. Ruby Rich: "What is there in a film with which a woman viewer identifies?" (Citron *et al.* 1978: 87). Although the rhetorical answer implies very little, the question is not really even applicable to the genre of comedy.

Man's illusions are the basis of comedy, and laughter arises from the gap between illusion and reality, a gap that it is difficult to perceive without psychological distance. This need for distance explains why many of the landmark concepts of feminist film theory do not work well when applied to comedy. E. Ann Kaplan's thesis about "the male gaze," for example, holds true in some respects. The gaze in comic films usually belongs to the male; he controls the point-of-view of the camera and has the power to act on the gaze whereas the woman does not (1983: 31). But – and this is significant – comic films *do not* give back to the male spectator "his more perfect mirror self" (1983: 28). The Lacanian mirror phase works only in inversion here, for comic effect. In *The Patsy* Jerry Lewis stands in front of a three-sided mirror, admiring a new suit coat. The salesman tells him it was made for George Raft, and the camera moves back to reveal Raft, in the same coat, reflected in one of the sides. Like the old Marx Brothers' mirror routine from *Duck Soup*, Raft mimics Lewis perfectly so that Lewis, giving us, as he so often does, a psychological rather than a *real* world, exclaims, "That's terrific! I look just like George Raft." The mirror has indeed given him *his* "ego-ideal," but the comedy comes from our superior awareness of his folly. Rather than an "ego-ideal," the comic hero gives the spectator a sense of superiority, a position which makes laughter easier. Jerry Lewis's *persona* of The Idiot or The Kid, childhood frozen at the age of 9, allows him freedom from the repressions of adult rationality, but makes it hard for adults to form any kind of *identification* with him. The Lewis character is not dislikable and hostile like W.C. Fields (whom we envy for doing all those things we do not dare do). He is not a sympathetic underdog like Charlie's tramp, nor a self-absorbed, over-anxious intellectual like Woody Allen, although none of these characters is an ego-ideal. Bernard Davidson has described Lewis in terms of a game of attraction and repulsion, concluding that "Jerry reminds us of those madmen with strangler's hands" (Durgnat 1972: 47). J.P. Coursedon is harsher: "Jerry Lewis is a pathological case . . . let us say no more than that Lewis seems to us to represent the lowest degree of physical, moral and intellectual abasement to which a comic actor can descend" (ibid.).

Far from presenting idealized masculine images, Lewis and other male comics often present parodies of such images; in this light they may be seen as critiquing the patriarchy, not exalting it. Note Lewis's extreme portrayal of *machismo* with the character of Buddy Love in *The Nutty Professor*, or the glorious put-down of the tough guy boyfriend in *The Ladies Man*, a scene that begins with an assertion of male power on the part of the tough ("my middle initial is 'C' for 'killer'") which reduces the Lewis character to a victimized state of inarticulate stammering drivel, and ends with a Freudian reversal. The Lewis character sits on the tough's hat, a familiar phallic image. His symbol of potency destroyed, the tough demands that Lewis put it on him and try to fix it. The scene is charged with sexual overtones, as the formerly powerless Lewis gradually becomes the dominant male trying to please a whimpering female. The tough is reduced to a ragged reminder of his former self; the masculine ideal uncomfortably deflated.

This deflation involves the use of stereotypes. Comedy thrives on stereotypes because if the characters seemed real, it would be difficult to laugh at them. Again, distance is the key here, abstracting pain and frustration, as in the scene with the tough, forbidding the *identification* that is so crucial to the classical feminist approach to film theory. The women in Lewis's films, for example, may seem like powder puffs or monsters. The tight-waisted blondes in *The Ladies Man*, the mighty operatic mother, Mrs. Wellonmellon, who can onehandedly push aside a mound of furniture with which a "scared" Lewis character has blocked a door, are the equivalent of Harpo's beauties or Margaret Dumont in the Marx Brothers' films. They are parodies of patriarchal ideals of womanhood, sexual fantasy and motherhood, and in this they may be seen as a critique of such socially constructed models rather than an affirmation of them.

The Lewis character is more complex than the simple parodies with which he surrounds himself. He does, as Bukatman suggests, make "problematic the social construction of masculinity" (1988: 203). Through continual devices of self-referentiality, it is impossible to view the character with any sense of realism. Although he plays "a kid," he makes no effort to hide his grown man exterior; in fact, he makes no effort to hide the fact that he is really Jerry Lewis. In *The Ladies Man*, he continues to wear his wedding ring, constantly reminding us of the performer playing the part. In *The Bellboy*, where he plays a character named Stanley, he also appears as himself with an entourage at a Miami Beach hotel. His persona is both child and man, both male and female, and even both mother and son. The curious androgyny is set out directly in the titles of many of Lewis's films: *The Delicate Delinquent* (1957), *The Geisha Boy* (1958), *Cinderfella* (1960). *The Ladies Man*, of course, is ironic because it is established at the outset that the Lewis character wants nothing to do with girls. But nowhere is there a better illustration of sexual ambiguity than in the character's name in that film: *Her* bert H. *He* bert (italics mine). This dual sexuality is seen a number of times as the movie unfolds. One of the most striking examples is at the beginning. Herbert, having been "two-timed" by his girl, ironically named "Faith," runs to cry to his parents. He is facing the camera in a close shot so that we see only the back of his parents' heads, his mother's covered in a wide-brimmed hat.

First he cries on his father's shoulder, and we see the man's face as he responds, "How could this happen to my son?" Then Herbert turns to his mother, and when we finally see her heavily made-up, grotesque and twitching face, crying "my baby, my baby," we recognize that Jerry Lewis is playing his own mother!

In a wonderfully intertextual confrontation with George Raft (again), Herbert Hebert refuses to believe Raft is *the* movie actor. He asks him to prove it by doing the coin flip from *Scarface*. Raft obliges, but drops the coin. Desperate to prove that he really *is* who he is – the problem of identity reinforced – he says he used to dance in his pictures. When he asks Herbert to dance, Herbert naturally refuses. How would it look, a guy dancing with a guy? But Raft insists: "Give me your hand and *you be the girl*." The camera pulls back, a spotlight goes on, and from a stunning high angle we watch these two small dancers whirl in each other's arms, dwarfed by the surreal construction of Mrs. Wellonmellon's house.

A figure playing Stan Laurel – in "real" life one of Lewis's heroes – makes ongoing cameo appearances throughout *The Bellboy*, a film in which the Lewis persona is identified with Laurel through his name, Stanley. One of the times we encounter the Laurel figure is in the course of a telephone conversation. With bellboy Stanley we overhear a girl saying to her mother, "There's no one I can go out with; they only want to drive my Rolls Royce." This makes us as interested as Stanley, even more so when the conversation ends and Stan Laurel comes out of the booth! Lewis loves to play with incongruity between sound and image and here it serves to blur sexual identity.

The techniques used to evoke this sexual ambiguity are techniques that disorient us, destroying the illusion of reality that film so persistently evokes. Lewis likes to refer to the "nonsense I make" although he says that "the making of comedy is a very serious business within the dramatic structure of entertainment" (1971: 183). But where the worlds of Chaplin and Keaton tend to be based on slapstick (and Keaton tended to have the "impossible" occur only within dream sequences), Lewis creates a world capable of going topsy-turvy at any time, It indeed reminds us of that other Lewis, Lewis Carroll, who gave us a Wonderland, or counter-world, populated by counter-identities. Lewis's technique might also remind us of what Claire Johnston, in a call for a cinema by which women can express their power, labeled a "counter-cinema":

> Romanticism will not provide us with the necessary tools to construct a women's cinema: our objectification cannot be overcome simply by examining it artistically. It can only be challenged by developing the means to interrogate the male bourgeois cinema. *Furthermore, a desire for change can only come about by drawing on fantasy.* . . . *Any revolutionary strategy must challenge the depiction of reality* . . . the language of the cinema/the depiction of reality must be interrogated. (1976: 215, italics mine)

Is this not the strategy of Lewis's comedy? His devices are essentially those that Seidman has defined as belonging to "comedian comedy": performing to the spectator, references to the comedian's star persona (such as Lewis's own appearance as "star" in *The Bellboy*), "guest stars" (such as George Raft in *The Patsy* and *The Ladies Man*), the use of movie lore (Raft's coin flipping from *Scarface*), exposing the falsity of certain filmic codes and the revealing of narrative as a contrivance. *The Bellboy*, in fact, begins with a producer, Jack Emulsion, talking directly to the audience in order to tell it that the film will have no plot, no story. And *The Patsy* ends with the Lewis character apparently falling from a balcony to his death. When his girl, Ellen, starts to cry, Lewis re-enters the frame, calls her by the name of the actress who plays her, "Ina Balin," and says, "Aren't you over-acting a bit? . . . It's a movie. See, I'm fine." He then looks directly at the camera in order to talk to us: "The people in the movie theater know I ain't gonna die. Here, it's a movie stage." He then removes a section of the balcony ledge, revealing its construction as a set and its inner workings of lights and wires. "I'm gonna make more movies, so I couldn't die. It's like make-believe," he says, then with Ina Balin, and followed by a set technician, he walks back through the soundstage on lunch break. Both the falsity of certain film codes and the contrivance of narrative are laid bare.

Acknowledging his use of fantasy, Lewis challenges our easy acceptance of what is real in film after film. In this, he not only fulfills Claire Johnston's criteria for a counter-cinema and critiques patriarchal assumptions through what can only be called his "involuntary feminism," he also becomes an "involuntary surrealist." Little has been written on the obvious connection between feminist and surrealist aesthetics, perhaps again because of the problematic nature of women and comedy. Laura Mulvey's essay, "Film, Feminism and the Avant-Garde," originally written in 1978, clearly articulates that "feminists have recently come to see the modernist avant-garde as relevant to their own struggle to develop a radical approach to art" (1989: 112). "The twentieth century," she observes, "has seen the growth of oppositional aesthetics, under various avant-garde banners and movements" (1989: 121), and here I assume she would include surrealism, for her oppositional aesthetic criteria are surrealist to the core. She discusses the problem of the dominant cinema, which has privileged content and encouraged an identification between spectator and screen, obliterating the possibility of experiencing contradiction. The first steps towards a feminist film practice, she argues, must involve "dislocation between cinematic form and represented material," and a "splitting open [of] the closed space between screen and spectator," inviting "structures to become visible and the bare bones of the cinematic process [to] force themselves forward" (1989: 119) – just as they do in a Jerry Lewis film! The strategy of this oppositional response is "to foreground the cinematic process, privilege the signifier, disrupt aesthetic unity, and force the spectator's attention on the means of production of meaning" (1989: 120–121). Citing Freud as crucial for positing the importance of the workings of the unconscious and making the point that things can seldom be what they seem, she notes Kristeva's work on modernist poetics which suggests that femininity is the repressed in the patriarchal order.[4] To the extent that one of the stated aims of surrealism was to reveal the unconscious life of things, from Kristeva's perspective what the surrealist strives to do is to uncover and unsilence the feminine.

Linda Williams stresses that *identification* is an issue in surrealist film also, but it differs from other kinds of film because it

> focuses on the processes of identification without reproducing its effect in the spectator. Rather than simply using the identification process to create an illusion of a fictive time, space, and character in the way most fictional films do, Surrealist film exposes the fundamental illusion of the film image itself to focus on its role in creating the fictive unity of the human subject. (1981: xiv)

In terms of the screen/spectator relationship, so important to current feminist film theory, surrealist aesthetics, according to Williams, is "a very sophisticated attempt to work against the identification process inherent in this relationship" (ibid.). With respect to theories of spectatorship, then, surrealism and feminism are on the same track. Both, as Mulvey stresses in her essay on the avant-garde, "point toward a desire and a need for rupture with closed, homogeneous forms of representation," for both question bourgeois ideology (1989: 123).

In discussing the work of Yvonne Rainer, Mulvey points to how her films *distance* us "by an ironic handling of familiar self-doubts and self-questioning" (1989: 125). This again is essential to the way Jerry Lewis creates, from a young man's fear of women in *The Ladies Man*, to the "fat lady" gag in *The Bellboy*. In this film, a woman who has dieted down to svelt elegance gains back her original bulk when she eats one box of chocolates. Although there is no physical realism to this scene, it *is* psychologically real, as anyone who has ever dieted knows. True to surrealist tenets, what Lewis gives us is inner reality, the world of dreams, the world of imagination, the world that throws a wet rag in the face of culturally determined norms and expectations.

A stunning example is in a sequence from *The Ladies Man* cited by Seidman as "one of the strangest fantasy projections in comedian comedy" (1981: 129). In this, Herbert finally gets up the courage to enter the forbidden room of Miss Cartilage. Behind the white door is a white room and as Herbert gropes his way through it, a white-painted face encased in a tight black hood slowly drops upside down into the center of the frame. Miss Cartilage has been hanging upside down from out of nowhere, and she emerges into the film to lead Herbert through a wall which magically lifts to reveal another, larger room. Herbert re-enters the frame, only now he is wearing a tuxedo, and he and Miss Cartilage end up dancing to Harry James' band. At one point he runs from her to open a door to escape, only to encounter another version of her seductively standing in the doorway, blocking his escape.[5] When he finally returns to the original room, he is no longer wearing a tuxedo. The girl goes to her bed and Herbert exits with the remark, "Boy, what imagination can do to you." But there has been no cinematic clue that what we've witnessed is imagined. Indeed, the whole film is so surreal that it perfectly embodies what Hammond sees as the crux of that aesthetic: "the contamination of reality by the imaginary" (1978: 19).

It is well known that the surrealists admired Buster Keaton, the Marx Brothers, and W.C. Fields, whom Ado Kyrou called a "surrealist in everything," with the Marx Brothers as "his worthy continuators" (1963: 98). But Jerry Lewis was also on their "to see" lists.[6] His comic techniques are, consciously or unconsciously, theirs, utilizing what André Breton saw as the power of cinema to *disorient [son pouvoir de dépaysement]*. These techniques include Freud's basic devices of the unconscious: condensation, displacement, symbolisation, co-existent opposites, a disregard for time, space, and causality" (Hammond 1978: 8). Kyrou might have been thinking of Lewis when he wrote in *Le Surréalisme au cinéma*: "A freedom of thought is often present in these 'popular' productions, films that don't address themselves to pretentious pseudo-intellectuals. . . . You don't have to look for long to find films in your local cinema that are more often than not involuntarily sublime, films scorned by the critics, charged with cretinism or infantilism by the old defenders of rationalism. . . . And as often as not, these are involuntary dadaistic or surrealistic films" (Hammond 1978: 40).

This is why, with Lewis, we must talk of "involuntary feminism" and "involuntary surrealism." As a conscious artist, he differs from his more radical and consciously surreal and/ or feminist counterparts in the fact that if there is protest embodied in his work, it is not against the dominant ideology. Although films like *The Bellboy* and *The Ladies Man* do exemplify an attitude towards the world, it is not much more than the simple message that people should learn to treat each other better. Matthews has said that "film comedy promises to be a noteworthy form of involuntary surrealism so long . . . as it steers clear of the sentimental"

(1971: 30). Lewis's films do not. The sentimental, as Matthews puts it, "argues for acceptance of social values, often rehearsing them in the last reel, for the audience's edification" (ibid.), This, of course, is exactly what Lewis does, which is part of the "problem" people like Gerald Mast see in his films.[7]

Another problem in terms of looking at Lewis as "revolutionary" is that although he experiments with the conventions of cinema, playing with time and space, illusion and reality, he does it all in the name of entertainment and comedy. Comedy, Susanne Langer reminds us, comes from Comus and *komos*, linked with springtime revelry and fertility, a celebration of enduring as opposed to tragedy, which celebrates death.[8] Lewis's films are about enduring. In *The Total Film-maker* he writes that comedy is "man's emotional safety valve. If it wasn't for humor, man could not survive emotionally. People who have the ability to laugh at themselves are the people who eventually make it" (1971: 160). "Making it," working within the system, surviving in a world that is not always fun: this is a perspective that maintains the status quo and reinforces our culturally encoded values. It is not feminist, avant-garde, or surrealist. As Matthews puts it: "Any comedy is totally alien to surrealism in which comic effect functions as a safety valve" (1971: 30).

So with Lewis we are left with only contradictions – and laughter. Theme and technique conflict, auteur and persona conflict, sentimentality and surrealism conflict. But then again, we must remember that Mulvey, envisioning an aesthetics of feminist filmmaking, stressed the importance of "experiencing contradiction" (1989: 120), and Hammond reminds us that true surreality is a "point of the mind where contradictions cease to trouble us" (1978: 8). It may be that the distaste many people experience while watching a Jerry Lewis film is indeed an involuntary destruction of "visual pleasure," much as Mulvey would like. With the connection between the avant-garde and feminist aesthetics in mind, Jerry Lewis's paradoxical mixture of surrealism and sentimentality, his flagrant rejection of conventional standards of realistic and narrative expectation, and his ambiguous approach to gender and sexuality all put him in what can only be called an unexpected and surprisingly revolutionary camp. Like the English poet, William Blake, he challenges our horizons, speaks to the prerational, presexual child buried within us, and ask us to see not with, but *through* our eyes to a better world.

Notes

1 From *Le Surréalisme au cinéma* (1953), quoted in Hammond 1978: 41.
2 See my essay, "Moral and Amoral Visions: Chaplin, Keaton, and Comic Theory." *The Western Humanities Review*, 37 (Winter 1983).
3 70. In this connection, Scott Bukatman has suggested that the Jerry Lewis character may take the position "of the nineteenth-century female hysteric." He writes, "Jerry, taking on the persona of the female hysteric, acts out his own ambivalence towards an inscribed and proscribed social position (masculinity)" (1988: 196).
4 Julia Kristeva, "Signifying Practice and Means of Production." *Edinburgh '76 Magazine: Psychoanalysis, Cinema and Avant-Garde* (1976).
5 This sequence is in many ways reminiscent of Gene Kelley's dance with Cyd Charisse in Singin' in the Rain (1952).
6 A list, entitled "Some Surrealist Advice," is given in Hammond 1978: 25–26. While Lewis,

Sennett, Langdon, and Méliès are listed as "See," Walt Disney, Frank Capra, D.W. Griffith and Lumière are listed under "Don't See." The repudiation of realism and sentimentality is obvious.

7 See "The Problem of Jerry Lewis," in *The Comic Mind*, Chicago: University of Chicago Press, 1973: 303–306.

8 See Susanne Langer, "The Comic Rhythm," from *Feeling and Form*, rpt. in Corrigan 1981: 67–83. She writes, "Comus was a fertility rite, and the god it celebrated a fertility god, a symbol of perpetual rebirth, eternal life" (p. 71). Strictly speaking, then, it is not necessary for comedy to be funny. "Comedy," Langer writes, "may be serious" (p. 72).

References

Altman, Rick. "Toward a Theory of the Genre Film." *Film Studies Annual*. NS 2 (1977).

Bazin, André. *What is Cinema?* Vol. 1. Berkeley: University of California Press 1967.

Bergson, Henri. *Le rire*. Paris: Ancienne Librairie Germer Baillère & Cie, 1901.

Bukatman, Scott. "Paralysis in Motion: Jerry Lewis's Life as a Man." *Camera Obscura*. 17 (May 1988).

Citron, Michelle, *et al.* "Women and Film: A Discussion of Feminist Aesthetics." *New German Critique*. 13 (1978).

Corrigan, Robert W. ed. *Comedy: Meaning and Form*. 2nd edn. New York: Harper & Row, 1981.

Desjardins, Mary. "(Re)Presenting the Female Body." *Quarterly Review of Film & Video*. 2 (1989).

Durgnat, Raymond. *The Crazy Mirror: Hollywood and the American Image*. New York: Delta, 1972.

Freud, Sigmund. "Humour," in *The Standard Edition of the Complete Psychological Works of Sigmund Freud*. Vol. XXI. London: The Hogarth Press, 1964.

Hammond, Paul, ed. *The Shadow and its Shadow: Surrealist Writings on Cinema*. London: British Film Institute, 1978.

Haskell, Molly. "Women and the Silent Comedians," in *Movie Comedy*. Eds Stuart Byron and Elisabeth Weis. New York: Penguin Books, 1977.

Johnston, Claire. "Women's Cinema as Counter-Cinema." Rpt. in *Movies and Methods*. Ed. Bill Nichols. Berkeley: University of California Press, 1976.

Kaplan, E. Ann. *Women and Film: Both Sides of the Camera*. New York: Methuen, 1983.

Kyrou, Ado. *Le Surréalisme au Cinéma*. Paris: Édition Mise à Jour, 1963.

Lewis, Jerry. *The Total Film-maker*. New York: Random House, 1971.

Martin, Linda and Kerry Segrave. *Women in Comedy*. Secaucus, New Jersey: Citadel Press, 1986.

Matthews, J.H. *Surrealism and Film*. Ann Arbor: University of Michigan Press, 1971.

Mellencamp, Patricia. "Situation Comedy, Feminism, and Freud: Discourses of Gracie and Lucy," in *Studies in Entertainment: Critical Approaches to Mass Culture*. Ed. Tania Modleski. Bloomington and Indianapolis: Indiana University Press, 1986.

Mulvey, Laura. *Visual and Other Pleasures*. Bloomington and Indianapolis: Indiana University Press, 1989.

Seidman, Steve. *Comedian Comedy: A Tradition in Hollywood Film*. Ann Arbor, Michigan: UMI Research Press, 1981.

Studlar, Gaylyn. "Masochism and the Perverse Pleasures of the Cinema." *Quarterly Review of Film Studies*. 9.4 (1984).

Waldman, Diane. "Film Theory and the Gendered Spectator: The Female or the Feminist Reader?" *Camera Obscura*. 18 (September 1988).

Williams, Linda. *Figures of Desire: A Theory and Analysis of Surrealist Film*. Urbana: University of Illinois Press, 1981.

Queering the Deal

11

On the road with Hope and Crosby

STEVEN COHAN

> *Lamour*: Why didn't you tell me you had a friend in Karameesh – and such a friend?
> *Crosby*: So you didn't tell her about me, huh?
> *Hope*: Well, I didn't want to dicker too much. It might have queered the deal.
> — *Road to Morocco* (1942)

> Dear Bing and Bob:
> All I want is a date with you two fellows when I get back – NO females, just we three.
> I'm sure the laughs I'd get that one day would make up for all I have missed and will
> over here. I sure would like to have you send me the "word" even if it is just a "maybe."
> — Lt. A. L. G., 3rd Marine Division, "Letters from GIs"[1]

The most popular male stars of the 1940s – whether together or apart – were Bob Hope and Bing Crosby, whose series of "Road to" films for Paramount helped to make the studio the most profitable one throughout the decade. The success of *Road to Singapore* in 1940 was followed by *Road to Zanzibar* in 1941, *Road to Morocco* in 1942, *Road to Utopia* in 1945, and *Road to Rio* in 1947. All were among the highest grossers of their respective years. Five years later Paramount released a successful revival of the series in Technicolor, *Road to Bali* (1952), and a decade after that, somewhat less successfully, Hope and Crosby reunited for the last time in *Road to Hong Kong* (1962), the only "Road to" movie made independently of Paramount, filmed outside of the United States, and without Dorothy Lamour as the female lead opposite the two male co-stars.

The popularity of the "Road to" series is particularly notable because it builds its comic value primarily out of a buddy relation. While there were major male comedy teams before and after Hope and Crosby, the buddy relation had unusually strong cultural significance during the 1940s because of the intensity with which men formed close friendships in the all-male military environment of World War II. The Army, in fact, formally organized men into pairs as its primary means of instilling loyalty on a personal level. Giving official sanction to the male couple, the military's buddy system structured masculinity in terms of same-sex bonding, problematizing what we now take for granted as the heterosexual/homosexual binarism that differentiates between "normal" and "deviant" masculinities according to sexual orientation. In his history of gays and lesbians in the armed forces, Allan Bérubé reports:

"Veterans of all kinds describe the love they felt for each other with a passion, romance, and sentimentality that often rivaled gay men's expressions of their love for other men and made gay affections seem less out of place." To be sure, "during the war the combat soldiers' acceptance of one another's pairing and physical intimacy was more a recognition of their need for closeness in life-threatening situations than any conscious tolerance of homosexuality."[2] But it was also the case, Bérubé observes, that "[b]uddy relations easily slipped into romantic and even sexual intimacies between men that they themselves often did not perceive to be 'queer.'"[3] Army life, moreover, while never entirely free of homophobic aggression and harassment, allowed for all sorts of transgressions (and digressions) from the norm, such as drag performances. "Military officials," Bérubé comments, "used soldiers' shows and drag routines for their own purposes – to boost soldier morale by allowing soldiers without women to entertain each other and affirm their heterosexuality. Once they had established their masculinity by becoming soldiers, men in these shows could enjoy the benefits of the same wartime relaxation of rigid gender roles that had allowed women to enter both industry and the military."[4]

The team of Hope and Crosby needs to be read in terms of the gender slippages occurring during the 1940s, when, as institutionalized by the Army buddy relation, the homosociality underlying American masculinity could all too easily "queer the deal," as the bit of dialogue from *Road to Morocco*, which serves as the first epigraph of this chapter, suggests. Lamour and Crosby both ask Hope why he has kept his buddy a secret, and the comic's response condenses the logic by which his pairing with Crosby invariably interrupts straight coupling in the "Road to" series by triangulating it, to the point where one has to wonder: does Hope not tell Lamour about Crosby in order to prevent the crooner from stealing her away, or does he refrain from mentioning Crosby in order to keep his buddy all to himself? In evoking the queer subtext of the Hope–Crosby teaming, I do not mean to propose that the "Road to" films openly represent a gay sexual relation between the two male stars; but I am arguing that the comedic framework of the series plays upon intimations of homoeroticism, and that the queer shading of their buddy relation must be taken into account when understanding the immense popularity of Hope and Crosby's teaming in the 1940s. After all, they were enough of a bona fide couple to prompt, in this chapter's second epigraph, that marine's request for "a date" on his return home from the war. "NO females," he specified, "just we three."

Fighting over girls?

The first film in the series, *Road to Singapore*, establishes the buddy relation of the two male stars as a respite from heterosexuality. Crosby and Hope, who is sarcastically called his pal's "boyfriend" at one point in the film, forswear women entirely as their motive for taking off to Asia, vowing, in Hope's words: "No more women. . . . Why if even one of us looks at anything in skirts, the other one can clip his ears off and stuff it down his throat." Crosby observes that "if the world was run right, only women would get married," and he tells his millionaire father that he refuses to follow the family tradition of running their shipping company, preferring instead to tramp the seas with his pal Hope, because "I want to be one of the boys. A regular guy." Of course, once these boys meet Lamour, they change their tune entirely; while the narrative allows Crosby to reject the stuffy values of his upper-class family through his unconventional attraction to Lamour, playing a Eurasian woman whom he and

Hope rescue, it also shows that he can only be a "regular guy" through heterosexual coupling. Nevertheless, the initial bonding of the two men over their rejection of women establishes the pattern that the rest of the series more knowingly and comically plays up. The "Road to" films typically open with Hope and Crosby performing as a vaudevillian song-and-dance team or engaged in some confidence game with the local yokels, or doing both. After a musical number (usually on the subject of their friendship) establishes buddy camaraderie – and we see the two men taking more pleasure in performing together than their onscreen audience does – their chicanery is exposed, often at the same time as their womanizing off-stage comes to light. Chased out of town and swearing off women, they end up in a remote but exotic colonial outpost, "wide open spaces," as Crosby describes it in *Road to Rio* "where the men are men." "And the women?" Hope asks him. "No women," Crosby reminds him. "That's how we got into this in the first place."

Once on the road, Crosby tricks Hope into going along with a surefire scheme that invariably subjects the comic to the crooner's selfish manipulations. This comedic setup differentiates the two men in terms of Crosby's active, sadistic, and arrogant personality and Hope's passive, masochistic and gentler one, or as *Road to Bali* puts it, Crosby carries a blue toothbrush as his "luggage" (because "blue is for boy"), while Hope's is red. When Lamour then enters the plot, tricking the boys into serving a scheme of her own while falling in love with Crosby once he sings his big ballad, she appears in order to gloss over the sexual asymmetry suggested by the men's differences from each other. Lamour's presence sets up a good-natured rivalry between the two buddies that, curiously enough, does not divide them or make them enemies but, on the contrary, intensifies their close relation. "Do you always fight over girls?" Lamour asks Crosby in *Road to Bali*, to which he replies: "What else can we fight over? We've never had any money."

Clearly, the "Road to" films offer a classic instance of Hollywood's narrativization of homosocial masculinity. As Eve Kosofsky Sedgwick explains in *Between Men*, the bonding of two men through their rivalry for a woman not only creates a relation between them, "as intense and potent as the bond that links either of the rivals to the beloved," but it also structures "male heterosexual desire, in the form of a desire to consolidate partnership with authoritative males in and through the bodies of females."[5] In the "Road to" films, Lamour provides Hope and Crosby with a common but also socially permissible object of desire. The expectation that she will inevitably turn up on the scene gives these two "friends of Dorothy" more license than usual for transgression, for pushing the buddy relation past its official limits. Once Lamour triangulates their relation, she legitimates their obvious pleasure – and physical intimacy – as a pair of buddies who have sworn off women in order to be together. At one point in *Road to Zanzibar*, Lamour snuggles up to Crosby, who's seated almost as close to Hope. "See what I mean," Hope whispers to his buddy. "She's just using you to get to me."

Through two extended gags about the buddies kissing, *Road to Morocco* shows how the logic of the Hope–Crosby–Lamour triangle actually works the other way around: the buddies use her to get even closer to each other. The first kissing gag occurs very early in the film, after the two men, castaways from an exploded ship, land on an empty beach. Seated alongside Hope in front of a row of bushes, Crosby apologizes for his abusive treatment of his pal while the two were on a raft, confessing, "You know how I feel about you. I guess in my own way I sorta love you." A camel peers over from behind the bushes and nuzzles Hope on the cheek. "All right," Hope replies, assuming that Crosby has just kissed him, "but you don't have to slobber all over me. . . . I guess I kinda love you, too." The camel then nuzzles Crosby on the ear.

Crosby: There now, wait a minute, Junior, stop kissing me.
Hope: What are you talking about? I didn't –
Crosby: You did, too.
Hope: Look, are you crazy? I don't mind being kissed, but this is ridiculous.

The camel "kisses" Hope again, and the two men repeat their accusations, both stating that they felt something: "I thought it was you," each says. They assume what they felt must be the handiwork of the ghost of Hope's Aunt Lucy come back to haunt them and, as the camel raises its head and emits a roaring noise, the two frightened men jump into each other's arms. The gag arises from their misrecognition of the kiss's origin, to be sure, but also, more subtly, from the unmistakable impression that each man does have a strong inclination to kiss the other. After all, Hope says that he doesn't mind being kissed; his protestation, like Crosby's, has more to do with the slobbering than with the kissing itself.

Much later in the film, a similar gag repeats the transgression these two buddies seem to have in mind when seated on the beach. Stranded in a desert and walking a mile without a camel in search of Lamour, who has been kidnapped, Hope and Crosby come upon a desert mirage: Lamour approaches them, singing a reprise of Crosby's ballad, "Moonlight Becomes You." When the two men join her in the song, their voices become disconnected from their bodies, so that Lamour opens her mouth and out comes Crosby's voice, Hope opens his and we hear Lamour, and so on. At the close of the song, the three stars harmonize, restoring voice to body; then Hope and Crosby step back in profile to look at Lamour desirously, but she disappears just as each man leans forward to kiss her. With her fantasized body gone, there is nothing to prevent the two men from kissing each other on the lips, and they do, spitting and wiping their mouths afterward. As the buddies continue their trek through the desert, Hope complains that he is too weak to go any further. Crosby remarks: "I guess that kiss took too much out of you, huh?" Before he spits and wipes his mouth again, Hope mutters, "yeah," and Crosby then carries his buddy on his back. The affectionate gesture on Crosby's part, which reminds us of the physical intimacy of their relation, rhymes this second kissing gag with the earlier one, which began with Crosby carrying Hope out of the water. But whereas in the first gag the camel both motivates and explains each buddy's mistaken if nonetheless desired impression that his pal is kissing him, the second more clearly displays how the cover of Lamour's presence can enable a kiss between Hope and Crosby to take place and, more importantly, to be acknowledged *as* a kiss.

Taken together, the two kissing gags in *Road to Morocco* illustrate quite plainly how the series achieves its particular take on the homosocial bonding of men through an inversion of the pattern Sedgwick analyzes. Instead of serving to cover up the homosexual desire that motivates the heterosexual competition of two men, in the "Road to" films Crosby and Hope's rivalry for Lamour makes their intimacy more visible as a celebration of their bonding and, moreover, shows how it structures the possibility of a queer desire. In the manner of comedian-comedy films generally, as Frank Krutnik has shown about this genre, the "Road to" films invariably close with gags that break the narrative's diegetic illusion, interrupting the heterosexual trajectory of the Crosby–Lamour romance.[6] For instance, in the closing moments of *Road to Utopia*, circumstances separate Hope and Lamour from Crosby, and he does not find them again for thirty-five years. When he finally returns, Crosby discovers that Hope and Lamour married and have a son, Junior – who is the spitting image of Crosby! "We adopted," Hope explains directly to the audience with deadpan expression, and the film then cuts to the Paramount logo. The gag's implication that Crosby has somehow cuckolded Hope has the effect of closing upon the buddy rivals instead of the straight couple, confirming that the homosocial buddies rather than the heterosexual lovers comprise the "true" romantic couple in a "Road to" film.

If there were any doubt that the buddy couple drives the romantic energy of the series, one only has to watch *Road to Bali*. Late in this film, Hope, Crosby, and Lamour are all taken captive by a Balinese tribe that *will* allow the two men to imagine what, beginning with *Road to Singapore* (when the three stars set up house together midway through the film), the series as a whole has always appeared to be proposing as the impossible desire of these two buddies: namely, polygamy, a bride's marriage to two men as the best means of maintaining the homosocial triangle. However, when the villains take over the tribe and decide to keep Lamour for themselves, they want to get rid of Hope and Crosby by arranging for what the series also has always suggested is the unthinkable desire of the two buddies when they fight over Lamour to be near each other – as one of the villains puts it, an unconventional marriage of "two grooms with no bride." At the wedding ceremony each man is masked in a head-dress and feathers, and the costuming causes each to assume the other is his intended partner, Lamour. Afterward, the two are asleep with their backs to each other in a large matrimonial bed. They awake; slyly, each moves backward to touch the other's buttocks; with a pleased smile, each leans his arm behind him to clasp hands with his "bride." Crosby moans, "Oh, honey," and a startled Hope cries out, "There's a man in our bed!" As they turn around, both exclaim at the same time, "You!" Given the sexual transgression implied by such a marriage of "two grooms with no bride," it's not surprising that Hope and Crosby escape from this situation without having to consummate it, but, in its gag ending, the film itself does not entirely evade the queer implications of their unconventional wedding. After Lamour finally chooses Crosby over Hope, *Road to Bali* then reconfigures the heterosexual pair in another bisexual triangle with a cameo appearance by Jane Russell (in her costume from Hope's *Son of Paleface*, released the same year [1952]), who goes off with Crosby and Lamour to establish a new *ménage à trois*, much to Hope's chagrin.

[. . .]

"Nightingale Blush": Hope's queer persona

According to historian George Chauncey in *Gay New York*, American culture during the first half of the twentieth century did not follow "the now-conventional division of men into 'homosexuals' and 'heterosexuals,' based on the sex of their sexual partners" but instead categorized men according to their gender behavior. "The abnormality (or 'queerness') of the 'fairy,' that is, was defined as much by his 'woman-like' character or 'effeminacy' as his solicitation of male sexual partners."[7] Chauncey further explains in the conclusion to his study that the systematic "exclusion of homosexuality from the public sphere" in the 1930s worked to repress what had been, particularly in working-class culture, the fairy's tolerated role in urban life as the queer defining the normality of other, more masculinized men, even those who had homosexual liaisons.[8] The visibility of the fairy reached its high point in the so-called pansy craze of vaudeville, nightclub, and live theater during the early 1930s; later in that decade, public censorship of this obviously queer sissy figure on stage and then in film (with the renewal of Production Code Administration restrictions on subject matter) resulted in a shift in register from a denotative encoding of queerness (the well-known fairy character) to a more complex, because more covert, one of connotation (sexual innuendo and camp) that, in the postwar era, was crucial in reshaping gay culture in all modes of its representation.

Outwardly, however, the fairy continued to define queerness through effeminacy even after the pansy craze of the early 1930s had run its course. For one thing, the fairy celebrated by the pansy craze influenced comedic conventions of the entertainment industry for several decades afterward, as in the sissy personae of stage, screen, radio, and, later, television stars like Eddy Cantor and Jack Benny, as well as Hope.[9] For another, the fairy supplied the characteristics identifying the gender inversion that military induction centers had institutionalized as the Army's means of pinpointing the homosexual personality for exclusion. The official mentality followed a psychiatric profile of gender deviancy that concentrated on "three major traits – effeminacy, a sense of superiority, and fear": "Effeminacy was by far the most common characteristic psychiatrists attributed to the typical homosexual. At a time when national survival depended on aggressive masculinity, military psychiatrists paid special attention to effeminacy as a sign of homosexuality expressing on the hospital wards the same interest in gender characteristics that their colleagues had shown at induction stations. Researchers described their gay male patients as womanly in their bodies, mannerisms, emotional makeup, and interests."[10]

In his solo films, as in the "Road to" series, Hope's persona is unmistakably readable as queer because of the way his screen personality folds together the fairy of the 1930s pansy craze and the invert of 1940s military diagnostic practice, which identified queerness through the very same signs of gender disorder that his persona exaggerated: effeminacy, superiority, and fear. In *Caught in the Draft* (1941), for instance, made after the first two "Road to" films, Hope plays a movie star of action films who, as he confesses, actually "can't stand the sight of bullets," fainting on the set whenever he hears the sound of phony gunfire. "I'm sort of a Madeleine Carroll with muscles," he explains in his own defense. Though a sissy, he is also a lady's man, which causes him to balk at his agent's suggestion that he get married to avoid the draft. "That's like cutting your throat to avoid laryngitis," he complains. However, after disregarding all of the women he has dated, Hope settles on proposing to Dorothy Lamour, a general's daughter who initially cannot stand him because of his cowardice. His plan backfires, though, as a chain of events leads him right into the Army, where, after he repeatedly displays his incompetence as a soldier, he ultimately gets a chance to redeem his manhood by proving his courage.

Bruce Babington and Peter William Evans point out that Hope's films are, like *Caught in the Draft*, routinely structured in terms of jokes, gags, and comic situations characterizing a screen persona that inverts traditional assumptions about masculinity. Recurring references to Hope's gender ambiguity and sexual ineptitude, his narcissistic self-absorption and undeserved bravado, and his infantilizing cowardliness, passivity, and overall "perversity" all construct what amounts to a fairy persona.[11] Hope's films place him in what is visible as a feminizing position (as when, in *Morocco*, he takes so enthusiastically to being costumed as Shalamar's intended or appears in drag as his own Aunt Lucy), just as they verbally link him to effeminacy by making jokes about his manhood. "Remember, you're a man, not a mouse," a grizzled prospector tells Hope in *Son of Paleface*. Hope coyly replies, "You peeked." Later, the prospector repeats this advice when reminding Hope to behave in a more manly style if he wants to win Jane Russell away from Roy Rogers. "Don't forget, this is the West, where men are men." "That's what she likes about me," Hope explains, "I'm a novelty." With the "novelty" of his gender inversion emphasized all the more by the parodic backdrop of established male genres that serve as the premise for most of his comedies – like the war film in *Caught in the Draft*, the swashbuckler in *The Princess and the Pirate* (1944), the Western in *The Paleface* (1948) and *Son of Paleface*, the spy thriller in *They Got Me Covered* (1943) and *My Favorite Brunette* (1947), and the imperial adventure tale in the "Road to" series – Hope's fairy comic persona cannot help queering what, as narrativized by his films, otherwise appear to be decidedly straight male characters lusting after glamorous leading ladies like Virginia Mayo (in *Princess*), Russell (in the two *Palefaces*), and Lamour (in the other comedies named, as well as the "Road to" films).

Thus, while Hope's films usually contextualize his gender inversion in a narrative of progression and disavow its queerness by his (often unsuccessful) hyperactive hetero-sexuality, his screen persona, which all his comedies reiterate, always has the potential to disturb the straight poles of sexual difference because his roles so routinely refer to the fairy stereotype. His best comedies make full use of that potential, with the gags promoting Hope's persona as a gender invert openly insisting upon the queerness of his masculinity. In *The Princess and the Pirate*, Hope disguises himself as an old crone in order to escape the Hook (Victor McLaglen), a notorious pirate. "Why don't you die like a man?" Virginia Mayo asks the cross-dressed Hope, who replies, "Because I'd rather live like a woman." When the wizened and seemingly crazy Walter Brennan then seems attracted to him, Hope tries to resist the homoerotic dimension implied by his transvestic disguise: "Now I'm not so sure." But later, Hope also ends up in the bath with the villain, Walter Slezak, who keeps asking the comic to take off his clothes: "You wash my back and I'll wash yours." The script gives Hope a reason for declining (because he has a treasure map tattooed on his chest) but the scene itself is played as sexual farce, the attempted seduction of one man by another. Indeed, at the end of this film, Hope does not even pair up with his leading lady, since it turns out that Mayo has been using him to return to her true love, a sailor played by Crosby in a gag guest appearance.

The Paleface, produced at the height of the "Road to" series' success, exploits the queerness of Hope's persona even more broadly and explicitly. "Painless" Peter Potter (Hope), an inept dentist wanting to return East, "where men may not be men but they're not corpses either," checks into a hotel with his new wife, Calamity Jane (Jane Russell), and the desk clerk asks, "Would you like a boy?" In response, Potter does not answer but giggles and smiles, looks at Jane, and then the clerk rings the bell, which clarifies his meaning for Potter, who finally mutters, "oh, yes, yes." Babington and Evans claim that the joke in this exchange results from Potter's thinking that the clerk is asking him if "he wants to produce a son," with the gag meant to make fun of Potter's sexual naiveté.[12] Although the two critics parenthetically note "the homoerotic element lurking" in his confusion, the film itself does not exactly conceal the implication that the giggling and smiling Potter may be mulling over in his mind what he takes to be the clerk's offer of a boy for sex. How could a viewer ignore this possibility since *The Paleface* queers the deal for Potter at almost every opportunity? Welcomed into town as an Indian fighter (though Calamity Jane has in fact done the shooting for him), Potter picks up a cowboy – in order to obtain the latter's clothes so that he can dress appropriately for the West – by asking him: "How would you like a little conversation with a hero? . . . Well, follow me." And the cowboy does, right into the shadows of an alleyway. When Hope emerges following a discreet fade-out, he and the cowboy have exchanged clothes, which means, at the very least, they have also had to take them off.

Even more outrageously, when he marries Calamity Jane Potter, hands the ring to the minister, who gives it back so that the groom can place it on the bride's finger, but Potter pockets the ring instead, as if he does not fully comprehend the heterosexual component of this ceremony – and that's not because of his naiveté, either. "And now the kiss," the minister announces, and Potter kisses *him*. As in *Road to Morocco*, kissing in *The Paleface* results in a gender slippage that aligns Hope's persona with queer desire. Since Jane wants to avoid consummating their relationship, every time they kiss she knocks him out with the butt of her gun, which he misinterprets as evidence of her ability to overwhelm him sexually, as if a kiss were an orgasm. On their wedding night, when Jane sneaks out of the cabin to escape the nuptial bed, Potter does not even notice her absence. A male Indian lurking outside samples Potter's laughing gas and, giggling, takes Mrs. Potter's place. Closing his eyes to respect what he assumes is his new wife's modesty, Potter admires her/his smooth skin, long braided hair, and muscles; they kiss, and the Indian hits him on the back of his head with a tomahawk, the effect of which is indistinguishable from kissing his wife. "Boy, can you kiss!" Potter exclaims as he falls unconscious. Since the next morning he assumes that he has consummated his marriage, it seems perfectly clear that, for Potter, a kiss is still a kiss, regardless of his bed partner's gender.

"Two grooms with no bride"

Hope's solo films refer to his partnership with Crosby because of the frequency with which they include a gag premised on the singer's guest appearance, usually in the role of an unexpected rival for the leading lady. Since the partnership with Crosby homoeroticized the queer dimensions of Hope's persona by linking it to a buddy relation, it is worth noting that the most popular of his solo comedies, such as *The Princess and the Pirate* and *The Paleface*, are also the ones most open in their intimations of his fairy persona's ambiguous sexuality, and that these films followed in the wake of the successes of *Road to Zanzibar* and *Road to Morocco*. By the same token, the "Road to" series itself did not take off until the studio appreciated the full importance of Hope's persona in complementing Crosby's. According to Hope's biographer, Arthur Marx, when the time came to make *Road to Zanzibar*, the sequel to *Singapore*, Paramount "had learned some valuable lessons. . . . First of all, don't let the romance [between Crosby and Lamour] get serious or in the way of the story. And second, Crosby was better when he was the schemer and Hope the victim."[13] Whereas the first film bills Hope after Lamour, he received second billing in *Zanzibar*, in acknowledgment that the buddy team was the primary attraction, and this ranking remained in place for the rest of the series.

Because of Hope's persona, his position in the "Road to" films as the comic playing off of Crosby's straight man also had the crucial residual effect of his playing the fairy to his partner's "trade": a man who, though sexually active with other men as well as with women, was not himself stigmatized "so long as [he] maintained a masculine demeanor and played (or claimed to play) only the 'masculine,' or insertive, role in the encounter – so long, that is, as [he] eschewed the style of the fairy."[14] That an implied fairy–trade relation informs Hope and Crosby's teaming in *Road to Zanzibar* is evident in the jokes that arise from their carnival act, which opens and closes the film. Crosby collects money from the crowd while Hope performs a dangerous stunt parodying masculine prowess (posing as "The Human Dynamo," "The Human Bat," "The Living Bullet"); a montage shows how this carnival act keeps resulting in severe physical injury to the comic even though it is rigged. The act sets up the occasion for jokes that differentiate Hope from Crosby by emphasizing the comic's gender inversion (in much the same way that fairy jokes feminize Hope and masculinize Russell in *The Paleface*). As "The Living Bullet," for instance, Hope is seemingly shot out of a cannon, though a dummy is ejected while he remains safely hidden inside the machine. "Everything all right?" Crosby asks after finding Hope in a faint. Upon awakening, Hope reassures him, adding, "But I think we'll have to have a little more room when the baby comes." Another scheme Crosby plans is to have Hope wrestle an octopus: "We'll dress you like a pearl diver, maybe a sarong or something," he tells his pal excitedly. When the team revives their act at the end of the film, Hope refuses to go along with Crosby's latest gimmick, which would require the comic to impersonate a bearded lady. Hope's reply underlines his standing as the fairy to Crosby's trade in this partnership: "You think I want those sailors chasing me?"

In the "Road to" films, Hope's persona instantly evokes comparisons to the fairy because his characters invert the normal behavior and outward manner of Crosby's masculinity: recall that in *Bali*, Crosby carries a blue toothbrush to signify the properly masculine color, while Hope carries a red one, to signify his odd gender standing. Their different masculinities appear to motivate the placing of the comic, not the straight man, in the subordinate position of the effeminate male, Crosby's "victim." Crosby thus routinely refers to Hope by diminutive nicknames like "Junior" or "son," signifying his own superior masculine standing. In much the same vein, whenever the plot requires the team to masquerade, Crosby wears a man's disguise whereas Hope resorts to drag (as when he puts on a Carmen Miranda costume in *Road to Rio*). Even more significantly, given the official discourse about homosexuality in place at the time, Crosby's occasional wisecracks about the comic's large rear end suggest the homoerotic direction of his gaze while allowing him to maintain a "masculine" position in their partnership. At the start of *Road to Utopia*, Hope thinks he has finally gotten the better of Crosby by refusing to accompany the latter to the Klondike and getting away with their bankroll. "I never thought I'd have the bigger end," the comic boasts, and Crosby replies, "Oh, you've always had the bigger end." Hope then eyes his friend suspiciously, asking, "Where do you keep *your* butter?" According to Bérubé, in 1942 the Army "listed three possible signs for identifying male homosexuals, all of them based on gender deviance: 'feminine bodily characteristics,' 'effeminacy in dress and manner,' and a 'patulous [expanded] rectum.' All three of these markers linked homosexuality with effeminacy or sexually 'passive' anal intercourse and ignored gay men who were masculine or 'active' in anal intercourse."[15] Hope's fairy persona thus implicates Crosby's seemingly straight masculinity in this queer deal, too, as the kissing gags in *Road to Morocco* – not to say the wedding of "two grooms with no bride" in *Road to Bali* – recognize.

Still another evocation of this couple's queerness as a team arises from the frequency with which the "Road to" series draws on "show business" through asides, gags, and so on as a frame of reference that substantiates their onscreen rapport. In each film Hope and Crosby regularly disrupt the diegesis with their direct address, resorting to show business "shtick" to put forward their star personae over their characters. On one hand, these recurring references to show business follow the conventions of comedian-comedy generally in breaking the diegetic illusion but, on the other hand, they also allude to the way that, in the 1940s, the queer camaraderie of "show business" had already begun to supply gay men with another, much more covert, lexicon of self-identification. One of the ex-GIs interviewed for the film version of Bérubé's *Coming Out under Fire* remembers: "There was a group of us who met and hung out together. I knew they were homosexual, although I never spoke to another man about it, because they were funny, and they were gay, and they were happy, and they knew show biz."[16] In the "Road to" films, Hope and Crosby are not only "funny . . . gay . . . and . . . happy" every time they stop the story to make a joke about Hope's nose or acting pretenses, Crosby's stable of racehorses or his singing style, Lamour's star persona as a jungle princess, their home studio, other entertainers, and so on, but it is also clear from these extradiegetic gags that these two buddies certainly know their "showbiz"!

With their potential for a camp reading, Hope and Crosby's show business jokes register the shift at mid-century from the denotative marking of queerness as a gender inversion (the fairy, defined through his effeminacy and not his sexual practices) to the much more covert encoding of a gay subculture through connotation. As already mentioned, this transformation in the semiotics of queerness, in its turn, manifested what Chauncey describes as "a reorganization of sexual categories and the transition from an early twentieth-century culture divided into 'queers' and 'men' on the basis of gender status to a late-twentieth-century culture divided into 'homosexuals' and 'heterosexuals' on the basis of sexual object choice."[17] As an illustration of how this shift in thinking about homosexuality redefined the relation of queer identity and queer desires, it is revealing that Hope himself once boasted to his writers about doing trade with a fairy, describing for them "a one-night stand he'd had back in his vaudeville days with the premier drag queen of the time." Decades later Hope recounted how he allowed the transvestite to perform oral sex on him, telling his story without embarrassment even though his stunned audience could themselves only understand it from the more contemporary perspective as an admission "that he'd had a homosexual affair." "The only thing he didn't tell us," Marx later recalls, "was whether or not he enjoyed it."[18]

According to Chauncey, until the 1950s the contemporary heterosexual–homosexual binarism, which conflates gender and sexuality, was a middle-class ideology that did not dominate the entire culture. In the first half of the century, the fairy was primarily a gender position in working-class culture. Like Hope himself in his anecdote about his youthful adventure with the drag queen while on the road touring in vaudeville, "many working-men thought they demonstrated their sexual virility by playing the 'man's part' in sexual encounters with either women or men." In this earlier era, middle-class "queers," by contrast, consciously distanced themselves from the fairy's gender inversion in part to distinguish their own social position and in part because, in their own class, "normal middle-class men increasingly believed that their virility depended on their exclusive sexual interest in women," defining "their difference from queers on the basis of their renuciation of any sentiments or behavior that might be marked as homosexual."[19] Generally speaking, whereas the 1950s saw the homogenization of the culture through middle-class hegemony, so that "normal" masculinity became exclusively heterosexual, the 1940s marked a crucial turning point in the reorganization of the culture's understanding of homosexuality, the traces of which continued to permeate postwar representations of gender and sexuality.[20]

To be sure, the war years resulted in the repression of queerness and pathologizing of the homosexual that characterized the postwar mentality. However, the war also caused, because of its massive disruption of US society and the integration of all classes (but not races) in the military, the momentary collapse of the boundaries between middle-class and working-class masculinities. While an ideology of "home" motivated patriotism by equating a normative masculinity with the national character, setting the terms by which the working class was induced to identify with middle-class hegemony in the decade following, the institutions of wartime also repositioned masculinity in a same-sex environment that challenged the middle-class presumption of heterosexual normality as defined in opposition to homosexual deviance. During the war, the military privileged and encouraged the buddy relation and, in camp drag shows, gave renewed prominence to the fairy as a projection of male desires. Furthermore, while the military officially targeted homosexuality as a specific category of deviation (the sissy), homoerotic desire was nonetheless allowed to diffuse throughout the same-sex culture of the armed forces because of the circumstances of sexual deprivation. As (working-class) novelist Harold Robbins remembers about his wartime bisexuality: "I was on a submarine, and if you're on a submarine for 22 days, you want sex. We were either jacking each other off or sucking each other off. Everybody knew that everybody else was doing it. . . . So we did it, it was fun, and it was over. I don't know whether any of them were really homosexual."[21] Because of its apparent detachment of gender from sexuality, the fairy stereotype did not outwardly threaten the heterosexual basis of normative masculinity but instead defined queerness in such a way that men could engage in homosexual activity without having to acknowledge as "really homosexual" the queer desire that fueled it.

The pairing of Hope and Crosby in the "Road to" series needs to be contextualized in both the war's disruption of middle-class masculinity and the postwar era's reconstitution of gender in sexuality. The series uses its homosocial plot trajectory (can Crosby steal Lamour away from Hope?) simply as the narrative mainstay of the more important, more ambiguous, and more fluid buddy relation, which Hope's comic persona repeatedly queers. As the numerous examples that I have cited from his solo films as well as the "Road to" series illustrate, in his queer persona Hope not only represents a gender inversion, he also incites the possibility of homoerotic desire: hence the number of gags that materialize his fairy persona in a same-sex kiss. The imbrication of his fairy identity in homoerotic desire establishes what is transgressive about Hope's queer persona and helps to historicize the disruption that he personifies as the odd man out – or, more accurately, the "out" odd man – in the homosocial triangle driving the star power of the "Road to" series. It explains, too, why Crosby's "straightness" cannot be so easily extricated from the queer buddy relation of the series – precisely because it is a relation and one formed on the road, away from the heterosexual normality of the home front.

In private life, according to Marx, Hope and Crosby maintained a strict heterosexual image, having numerous extramarital affairs and even passing women back and forth between them. We might infer, then, that the two stars themselves did not intend such a queer resonance to be read off of their buddy relation, which they promoted offscreen in radio and TV appearances, as well as in their USO shows. However, how else can we interpret the full weight of the jokes and sight gags that abound in the "Road to" films to dramatize the intimacy and rapport of their teaming? The series casts an unmistakable queer shading onto their onscreen partnership, because the 1940s buddy relation, like the era's fairy stereotype, historically placed the coupling of two men in a larger cultural setting. For the same reason, after the "Road to" series effectively ran its course with Bali in 1952, it would be much harder for movie buddies to queer the deal with either the innocence or audacity that Hope and Crosby, those "two grooms with no bride," so outrageously put on display when they kissed onscreen or woke up in bed together.

Notes

All quotations of dialogue in this chapter are my own transcriptions from laser disc versions of the films or, if unavailable in that format, video-cassettes.

1 "Letters from GIs." *Bob Hope: Memories of World War II*. Online. *Bobhope.com*. 18 August 1996. This home page from Bob Hope Enterprises publicizes the special aired by NBC on 5 August 1995 and subsequently released on video-cassette. This letter is also one read in voice-over on the program (but was omitted on the video-cassette).

2 Alan Bérubé, *Coming Out under Fire: The History of Gay Men and Women in World War Two* (New York: Plume, 1990), 186.

3 Ibid., 188.

4 Ibid., 68.

5 Eve Kosofsky Sedgwick, *Between Men: English Literature and Male Homosocial Desire* (New York: Columbia University Press, 1985), 21, 38.

6 Frank Krutnik, "The Clown-Prints of Comedy," *Screen* 25, nos. 4–5 (1984): 50–59.

7 George Chauncey, *Gay New York: Gender, Urban Culture, and the Making of the Gay Male World, 1890–1940* (New York: Basic, 1994), 13.

8 Ibid., 356.

9 On Cantor, see Hank Sartin, "Eddie Cantor, the Pansy Craze of the 1930s, and the Intersection of Jewish and Gay Stereotypes" (paper presented at Society of Cinema Studies Convention, 4 March 1995); and on Benny, see Alexander Doty, *Making Things Perfectly Queer: Interpreting Mass Culture* (Minneapolis: University of Minnesota Press, 1993), 63–79.

10 Bérubé, *Coming Out under Fire*, 156.

11 Bruce Babington, and Peter William Evans, *Affairs to Remember: The Hollywood Comedy of the Sexes* (Manchester: Manchester University Press, 1989), 103–18.

12 Ibid., 102.

13 Arthur Marx, *The Secret Life of Bob Hope* (New York: Barricade, 1993), 148–49.

14 Chauncey, *Gay New York*, 68.

15 Bérubé, *Coming Out under Fire*, 19; brackets in original.

16 Dialogue from Arthur Dong, dir., *Coming Out Under Fire* (1991).

17 Chauncey, *Gay New York*, 22.

18 Marx, *Secret Life of Bob Hope*, 41–42.

19 Chauncey, *Gay New York*, 41–42.

20 I make this argument in greater detail in my book *Masked Men: Masculinity and the Movies in the Fifties* (Bloomington: Indiana University Press, 1997).

21 Quoted in Gerry Kroll, "Master Harold," *Advocate*, 22 August 1995, 42–43.

PART FIVE

POST-CLASSICAL COMEDIAN COMEDY

Introduction

As I have discussed elsewhere, the period from the late 1930s to the early 1960s saw the entrenchment of the comedian film as a staple fixture of the Hollywood system, one which provided a familiar and predictable combination of fiction-making and entertainment spectacle (Krutnik 1995b). The standardized format of comedian comedy could accommodate various performative styles and persona – from Bob Hope, to Danny Kaye, to Red Skelton, to Jerry Lewis. As Steve Seidman details, the comedian was generally cast as misfit, underdog or outsider who is faced with securing an integrated psychological and social identity – which is frequently defined through generic and romantic codes, with the comic hero faced with the prospect of overcoming a villainous plot and winning the girl). This standardized format suited the oligopolistic imperatives of the Hollywood industry, geared as it was to the regulated production of diverse films.

Comedian comedy proved one of the casualties of the decline of classical Hollywood, its studio system and its star system. Cast adrift as a regular generic presence in Hollywood production, comedian comedy splintered in the 1960s into a range of cycles and tendencies. Most notably, the epic slapstick spectacles *It's A Mad Mad Mad Mad World* (1963), *The Great Race* (1965), *Those Magnificent Men In Their Flying Machines* (GB, 1965), *Monte Carlo Or Bust/Those Daring Young Men In Their Jaunty Jalopies* (GB-France-Italy, 1969) signified an ultimate dispersal of the concept of centralizing personality that is so crucial to the comedian film. Aiming to deliver multiple forms of entertainment within the loosely organized structure of a chase, these grandiose collages of slapstick comedy, adventure, romance and travelogue saw comedians such as Milton Berle, Sid Caesar, Jerry Lewis, The Three Stooges, Tony Hancock, Peter Cook and Dudley Moore and Phil Silvers competing for the central focus with light comic performers (Jack Lemmon, Tony Curtis, Terry-Thomas) and legitimate 'actors' (Spencer Tracy, George Macready, Stuart Whitman).

Of the Hollywood old guard, Danny Kaye and Bob Hope continued to make films in the 1960s, but they did so far less frequently and with far less reward. Under the protection of a record-breaking $10 million contract with Paramount, Jerry Lewis ploughed his own idiosyncratic furrow until the mid-1960s, by alternating film appearances as a star comedian with more ambitious auteurist projects that he directed, wrote, produced and starred in (Krutnik 2000: 121–64).

However, Lewis' long run as a top-flight cinematic attraction came to an end when he quit Paramount in 1965 (ibid: 165–74). At the same time as Lewis' film career was winding down, that of another, more assertively Jewish comedian was just beginning to crank up. Within a few years of his screen debut as writer and performer in the 1965 sex comedy *What's New Pussycat?* Woody Allen had begun to write and direct the films he starred in.

Intriguingly, for the first of his long run of auteurist projects, *Take the Money and Run* (1969), Allen actively courted Jerry Lewis for the directorial chores and only took on this project himself when United Artists, the film's backers, vetoed Lewis' involvement. Although he followed in Lewis' footsteps as a comic auteur, over the next three decades Allen's career as a screen comedian would take a very different route. He eschewed Hollywood for New York, a city lovingly commemorated in his films, and after *Love and Death* (1975) moved progressively away from the framework of comedian comedy towards more ambitious areas of creative endeavour. Like Lewis, too, Woody Allen has not only emerged as a highly controversial celebrity but has also made films that engage directly with his convoluted public image. The subject of a devotional biographical cult himself, Allen's film work has also played teasingly with autobiographical structures and resonances (see such diverse films as *Take the Money and Run*, 1969; *Annie Hall*, 1977; *Zelig*, 1983; *Radio Days*, 1987; *Husbands and Wives*, 1992; and *Deconstructing Harry*, 1997).[1]

One crucial difference between Lewis and Allen is that where the former specializes in a flamboyantly inarticulate body comedy, Allen is an expressly verbal and cerebral comedian. And while Lewis persistently asserts his commitment to the values of showbiz culture (through the Vegas memorial of the annual MDA Telethon, for example), Allen has become something of a standard-bearer for the intellectual culture of New York. Thus, where Lewis eulogizes such showbiz heroes as Al Jolson, Charlie Chaplin and Stan Laurel, Allen is more likely to be found tipping his hat to the European art cinema of Ingmar Bergman and Federico Fellini. Allen's stand-up monologues may develop a distinctively surreal narrative logic that resembles Lewis' strangely ordered bodily disorder, but ultimately he has more in common with another of his comic heroes, the verbal comedian Bob Hope. Where Hope is a master of precisioned wisecracks, Lewis' extremist physical comedy most frequently ends up gagging the gag (Krutnik 1994).

The film comedians who have succeeded Jerry Lewis have rarely been content to stick with comedy alone. Like Woody Allen, for example, Steve Martin has moved on from broad comedian comedy (such as his expressly Lewisian 1979 debut *The Jerk*), towards more 'refined' situation comedies such as *Roxanne* (1987) and the *Father of the Bride* films (1992, 1995). Jim Carrey has also aimed beyond his trademark physical shtick towards straight acting assignments in *The Truman Show* (1998) and *Man on the Moon* (1999). Robin Williams and Eddie Murphy have similarly attempted a more diversified portfolio of performances beyond 'mere' comedy. Mel Brooks is one of the few comic performers of recent years to keep faith with the principles of 'low' physical comedy, having been responsible (as writer, director, producer and performer) for a lengthy series of old-style generic parodies – including *Blazing Saddles* (1974), *Young Frankenstein* (1974), *Silent Movie* (1976), *High Anxiety* (1977), *Spaceballs* (1987), *Robin Hood: Men in Tights* (1993), and *Dracula: Dead and Loving It* (1995).

Like Woody Allen, Brooks began his comedy career as a writer for live television shows in the 1950s (both worked for the versatile small-screen comic Sid Caesar). Television has proved increasingly influential in providing training and exposure for subsequent generations of Hollywood performers and writers. Steve Martin, for example, started his professional work in comedy as a writer on the cult 1960s satire show *The Smother Brothers Comedy Hour* (for which he won an Emmy award). Martin's ironic performance style of 'wild and crazy' comedy was honed in a series of rock-style gigs in the mid-1970s, and he secured national popularity with the aid of a series of television comedy specials and guest-hosting stints on *The Tonight Show*. In 1976 Martin also made the first of numerous appearances as a guest on the cult NBC sketch show *Saturday Night Live*. Since its launch in 1975, *Saturday Night Live* has proved the single most influential showcase for filtering comedians into the mainstream. The first generation of *SNL* performers included Chevy Chase, Bill Murray, John Belushi and Dan Ackroyd, who all went on to careers in Hollywood, while among the show's later alumni were Eddie Murphy, Mike Myers, Dana Carvey, David Spade, Chris Farley, Chris Rock, Janeane Garofalo and Adam Sandler. Other performers who have migrated from the small screen to Hollywood include Pauly Shore, Jim Carrey, the Wayans Brothers, Paul Reubens (Pee Wee Herman), Will Smith, Chris Tucker and Martin Lawrence.

Throughout its history, the comedian-centred film has shared a vital relationship with other performance media in which comedians appear and build a familiarity with audiences. These intermedia contexts have not remained constant – theatrical variety forms, for example, were displaced in prominence by both the synchronized sound film and broadcast radio. From the 1950s, competition from the home-based mass-entertainment medium of broadcast television has contributed to the wide-scale redefinition of the role and character of mainstream cinema. Broadcast television from its inception invested substantially in comedy, incorporating and adapting many pre-existing comic forms. As well as re-presenting such earlier cinematic comedy attractions as the feature film, the comedian-centred short and the animated short, the medium also provided an important showcase for comic performers experienced in other media (for example, Lucille Ball, Phil Silvers, Abbott and Costello, Bob Hope, Jack Benny and Milton Berle). Television has provided more widespread exposure for comic performers long marginalized in the cinema: especially women (including Lucille Ball, Goldie Hawn and Rosanne Barr) and black comedians (including Bill Cosby, Flip Wilson, Eddie Murphy and Chris Rock).

Bambi Haggins' chapter in this section of the Reader focuses specifically upon the question of how African-American comedians have fared in their sometimes rocky road into the main-stream during the post-Civil Rights era. Where comedians from white ethnic minorities could potentially mask their ethnicity (for example, Jerry Lewis, born Levitch, never played explicitly Jewish characters on film), it was not possible for black comedians to escape so easily from their visible difference – nor from the second-class status this used to bring with it. As Mel Watkins illustrates in his magisterial history of African-American comedy, prior to the 1960s black performers faced limited options in mainstream cultural contexts (Watkins 1999). Concentrating upon the careers of Eddie Murphy and Chris Rock, Haggins suggests that contemporary African-American comedians still face problems in negotiating the distinct cultural regimes of blackness and the mainstream. Access to the mainstream, she argues, too often requires a series of comedic colour adjustments in which the enunciation of cultural specificity (that is, of uniquely African-American experience) must be sacrificed to the demands of accommodation. Haggins posits that contemporary black performers are faced with steering between the various possibilities incarnated by an earlier generation of black comics: the comic activism of Dick Gregory, the assimilationist universalism of Bill Cosby, or the 'Crazy Nigger' of Richard Pryor.

Murphy shot to fame as a result of his appearances on *Saturday Night Live* from 1980 to 1984. He became the leading black cinema star in the 1980s as a result of such films as *Trading Places* (1983) and the action-adventure comedies *48hrs* (1982) and *Beverly Hills Cop* (1984). Thereafter Murphy had mixed fortunes at the box office owing to several ill-chosen screen vehicles (including a sequel to *48hrs* and two further replays of *Beverly Hills Cop*). In the early 1990s he attempted to reinvigorate his film career with the more restrained comic persona he displayed in *Boomerang* and *The Distinguished Gentleman* (both 1992). His 1996 remake of Jerry Lewis' *The Nutty Professor* attempted to capitalize upon the vogue for gross body comedy and proved a huge box office success. He followed this with the even more profitable family comedy *Dr. Dolittle* two years later. Despite the waywardness of his cinematic career from the mid-1980s, Eddie Murphy's success made it possible for other black comedians to gain acceptance as screen performers – including Damon and Keenan Ivory Wayans, Robert Townsend, Martin Lawrence and Will Smith.

Although, like other contemporary black comedians, Rock has clearly been influenced by Murphy's phenomenal cross-over success, Haggins argues that his stand-up act (and its televisual rendition) has been far more successful in confronting the issues of class and race that Murphy himself downplayed. It still remains to be seen, however, whether Rock can successfully resist the conformist compromises that have dogged Murphy's Hollywood enterprises.

Phil Drake's chapter deals with one of the most successful and distinctive Hollywood comedians to emerge in the 1990s. Like Murphy and Rock, Jim Carrey's success also owes a great deal to television: he first achieved widespread exposure as the only white member in the cast of the Fox network's African-American sketch show *In Living Colour* (1990–92). Dave Kehr has suggested that in 'one way or another, all of Carrey's characters are marked by television. Born in 196[2], he is the first major American comic to grow up with television in his bloodstream' (Kehr 2000: 12). Television has continued to figure as a crucial reference point in his work, most explicitly in the dystopian media fantasies of *The Cable Guy* (1996) and *The Truman Show* (1998). Carrey rocketed to cinematic success with three films released in 1994 – *Ace Ventura, Pet Detective, Dumb and Dumber* and *The Mask*. In his comic performances, Carrey specializes in a style of excessive physical comedy that owes an acknowledged debt to Jerry Lewis – while Adam Sandler has effectively appropriated Lewis' Idiot/Kid persona. Taking his cue from Steve Seidman's earlier work on comedian comedy, Drake uses Carrey's hyperbolic physical style to expose the inadequacy of existing theorizations of screen performance. Besides the insights he offers into this most high profile of 1990s 'dumb comedians', Drake's incisive account offers a fresh and stimulating perspective upon issues of performance that are fundamental to the comedian film, to its showcasing of comic talent, and to its figuration of identity and the body.

Note

1 The intensive industry of biographical speculation that Allen has inspired may be gauged by such books as: John Baxter (1999): *Woody Allen: a Biography*, London: HarperCollins; Robert Benayoun (1986): *Woody Allen: Beyond Words*, London: Pavilion; Stig Bjorkman in conversation with Woody Allen (1994): *Woody Allen on Woody Allen*, London: Faber; Douglas Brode (1988): *Woody Allen: His Films and Career*, San Francisco: Columbus; Julian Fox (1996): *Woody: Movies from Manhattan*, London: Batsford; Foster Hirsch (1991): *Love, Sex, Death & the Meaning of Life: The Films of Woody Allen*, New York: Limelight Editions; Graham McCann (1992): *Woody Allen: New Yorker*, Cambridge: Polity Press; and Stephen J. Spignesi (1992): *The Woody Allen Companion*, London: Plexus.

Laughing Mad

12

The black comedian's place in American comedy of the post-Civil Rights era

BAMBI L. HAGGINS

Chris Rock's breakthrough HBO special *Bring The Pain* (1998) begins by invoking a personal canon of stand-up comedians. 'Ladies and Gentlemen, are you ready to bring the pain? Give up the love for Mr CHRIS ROCK!' The sound of crowd pandemonium accompanies a medium close-up of Rock's black and white leather shoes as he swaggers towards the stage. A series of comedy album covers is then superimposed over his strut, including Bill Cosby's *To Russell, My Brother, Whom I Slept With*, Dick Gregory's *In Living Black And White*, Richard Pryor's *Is It Something I Said?*, Steve Martin's *Comedy Isn't Pretty*, and self-titled albums from Woody Allen and Eddie Murphy. The sequence provides both a historical context within which to view Rock's comedy and a genealogy of comedians who have stepped out from behind the mike to ply their wares as comedic actors. Murphy and Rock represent, respectively, the first and second waves of black comedians in the post-Civil Rights era.[1] Upon examining the play between the black comic's stand-up act and the mainstreamed persona constructed for cinematic consumption, the inherent tenuousness of his or her *place* in contemporary American film comedy becomes clearer. One might be tempted to assert that the edges of the African-American comic's rant are trimmed to fit into the construct of movie star's shtick, with the comedic social commentary – along with the critical bite – left on the cutting-room floor. However, as this chapter will illustrate, the trade-offs are far less transparent. Such analysis also provides insight into how these performers make us laugh when dealing – or not dealing – with race. The nature of that laughter is key to understanding the significance of these comic forces within blackness in American comedy. Is it nervous laughter, or patronizing laughter? Or are the comic players themselves, like some of us in the audience, laughing mad?

Setting the stage: comics of the Civil Rights era

Dick Gregory, Bill Cosby and Richard Pryor all came of comic age during the era of Civil Rights and Black Power. Setting the stage for later black performers seeking to move from stand-up to screen, they emblematized distinct socio-political threads in black comedy during this time. Gregory was the comic activist, Cosby an assimilationist observer, while Pryor played the 'Crazy Nigger' cultural critic. Such comedic and cultural possibilities for 'performing' blackness would exert considerable influence on subsequent black comedians such as Murphy and Rock. Besides the impact of their carefully cultivated personae, these three performers also provided crucial lessons in the logistics of cross-over through the ease or difficulty of their transformation from comic to comedic actor. As one of the first black comedians to bring issues of racial injustice into his act, Dick Gregory was painfully aware of what it took to make this transition:

> I've got to go up there as an individual first, a Negro second. I've got to be a coloured funny man, not a funny coloured man. I've got to act like a star who isn't sorry for himself – that way they can't feel sorry for me. I've got to make jokes about myself before I make jokes about them and their society – that way they can't hate me. Comedy is a friendly relation.
>
> (Berger 2000: 121)

Despite this insight, Gregory later complicated his 'friendly relation' to the white audience by openly blasting the hypocrisies of racial injustice and, as a result, became famous for his unrelenting social and political critique (Anonymous 2000). As Mel Watkins suggests, by 1967 Gregory had become a self-proclaimed 'social commentator who uses humour to interpret the needs and wants of Negroes to the white community, rather than . . . a comedian who happens to deal in topical social material' (Watkins 1999: 503).

Whereas Gregory's critique was deemed 'controversial', Cosby's material embodied the optimism of the integrationist New Frontier: his squeaky-clean likeability and universalist comedic approach won over audiences regardless of race, creed or colour. Despite the semi-autobiographical inflections of his comic pieces on friends and family, specific issues of race and/or black culture are notably absent. Much of Cosby's stand-up material is rooted not in the social turmoil of the era but in a sanitized and universalized version of growing up poor in an urban setting. Richard Pryor's career bears traces of both Gregory's social commentary and Cosby's universalist riffing. It was not until the early 1970s, when Pryor 'killed the Cosby in his act', that he began to challenge 'traditional show business assumptions about the viability of ungentrified black material and an unmoderated black voice . . . [and broke] with blacks' long standing tradition of subterfuge and concealment of inner community customs' (Watkins 1999: 544). Pryor's new persona, the uncontainable and unpredictable 'crazy nigger', had almost nothing in common with the easily assimilable 'Super Negro' types. Embodying both the rage and the vulnerability inherent in the burgeoning tide of heightened black awareness, Pryor's routines refused to de-emphasize the cultural, economic and political disparities between black and white lives.

Then, as now, the black comic's act is informed by the tension between enunciating cultural specificity and being sufficiently 'Anglo-friendly' to cross over into the Hollywood mainstream. Access to mainstream American film and television comedy requires a series of comedic colour adjustments that often dilute or erase black cultural specificity. Gregory's outspoken-ness, both on and offstage, made him unpalatable to Hollywood comedy, even at a time (the early 1970s) when, as controversial comic Dick Davy ('the whitey who scored at the Apollo') puts it, there was a 'big rush to give black comedians a push on television. . . . To keep black people from rioting, let's put them on television but not controversial black faces . . . not Dick Gregory' (Berger 2000: 192). Cosby's stand-up success translated into small screen stardom and iconic status within popular culture: first, as televisual 'Super Negro' Alexander Scott in I-Spy and later as the father who knows best in a colorized American Dream (in his book Fatherhood as well as his playing of Dr Cliff Huxtable on The Cosby Show). Pryor, on the other hand, was truly unfriendly to prime time, with even his forays into late-night television sparking controversy.[2] Unlike Gregory or Cosby, however, Pryor was able to succeed on the big screen with two distinct personae: as a stand-up performer and as a 'sampled' and sanitized version of the 'Crazy Nigger' in Hollywood films.

The tenuous nature of the black comedian's grasp on his cinematic performance of blackness is especially well illustrated by Pryor's performance in Silver Streak (1976) and Cosby's in Uptown Saturday Night (1974). Despite the success of such concert films as Richard Pryor: Live On The Sunset Strip (1982), Pryor only really hit box-office pay dirt with a succession of interracial buddy comedies that paired him with Gene Wilder. Silver Streak, Stir Crazy (1980), See No Evil, Hear No Evil (1989) exemplify a strategy of cultural and racial appropriation in which stereotypical performances of blackness masquerade as cultural critique while actually reiterating conventions of minstrelsy. As Ed Guerrero notes, the 'teaching Blackness' moment in Silver Streak 'turns out to be a comic interpretation of black urban "cool" and toughness' that would have been considered inflammatory if not for the 'mediating presence of Pryor' (Guerrero 1993: 22). One of Cosby's few big screen successes came in the black caper comedy Uptown Saturday Night. While Cosby's portrayal of the angling Everyman, 'Wardell Franklin', departs from the Anglo-friendly comic persona of his TV show, the roles that sought to capitalize on his televisual persona – such as the harried spirit version of Cliff Huxtable in Ghost Dad (1990) and the retired secret agent of Leonard Part VI (1987) – proved to be box office poison.[3] Although commercially successful, however, Silver Streak and Uptown Saturday Night were not cross-over blockbusters, nor did they offer a liberatory cinematic discourse on black identity.[4]

As this brief account of the comics of the Civil Rights era suggests, the persona of the black comic is constantly being retooled, reframed and re-envisioned for mainstream consumption. Cross-over acceptance requires the black comic to separate troubling questions of racism from his articulation of race. Thus Dick Gregory's socio-comedic rebellion ultimately caused him to reject the mainstream, just as the inherent social reassurance of Cosby's comedy served to embrace it. For Pryor, the negotiation process proved decidedly more complex than the black and white binaries of rejection or acceptance. The rest of this chapter will examine how subsequent black comedians such as Murphy and Rock have attempted to deal with the problem of negotiating blackness and the mainstream.

Black comedians: the next generation

During the Civil Rights era black comedians generally had to work their passage through the Chitlin' Circuit before they could access the white comic venues that filtered entertainment talent into the mainstream. By the 1980s there were two frequently intersecting roads into American film comedian comedy – one through Saturday Night Live (SNL, 1975–), the other through comedy programming on the Home Box Office channel. Although the first era of SNL may be hailed as cutting-edge television humour, it was not a place for black comics to shine. Over three decades the 'black guy' (or girl) on SNL has often been an underused player whose screen time is minimal and whose characters are ancillary to another player's central role (from Garrett Morris' 'Chico Escuela' on Chevy Chase's 'Weekend Update' to Tim Meadow's lampooning of Oprah Winfrey). Eddie Murphy was the notable exception to the 'black guy syndrome'. Before the end of his freshman season (1980–81) on SNL, Murphy was a major presence on SNL. In fact, Murphy's recurring characters (the grown-up Buckwheat as a post-*Little Rascal* celebrity; a Borscht-Belt, cigar-chomping version of Gumby; and Mr Robinson, the Mister Rogers of the hood) ended SNL's first comic slump era in the early 1980s. By the time Murphy left the series in 1984, he was already a bona fide cross-over star on stand-up's main stage – an act captured in *Eddie Murphy Delirious* (1983) – and was well on his way to big screen superstardom with 48 *Hours* (1982) and *Trading Places* (1983).

Clad in the type of red and black leather suit that Axel Foley would later lampoon in *Beverly Hills Cop* (1984), Eddie Murphy prowled the stage in *Delirious* with all the swagger of a stand-up virtuoso turned sex symbol. Parading a new sort of audaciousness, Murphy's routines used the blue tone of Pryor (particularly in terms of language and sexually explicit content) while excising his sociopolitical edge. Murphy's stories of family and childhood are jadedly nostalgic, touching upon issues of race and class in uncritical terms. They are neither 'cleaned up' for a mainstream audience like Cosby's idealization of childhood, nor are they intended as points of departure for a larger discussion of Black life. One routine begins with the joyous moments a child spends with his freshly scooped ice-cream cone:

> You don't eat your ice-cream for, like, a half hour, you'd be dancin' around singing, 'I have some ice-cream, I have some ice-cream. And I'm gonna eat it all . . . eat it all' . . . [The joyous song transforms into a musical taunt directed at 'that one kid on the side who didn't get no ice-cream.'] 'Kids didn't give a fuck,' they'd say, 'You didn't get no ice-cream. You didn't get none. You didn't get none. You didn't get none cuz you are on the welfare and can't afford it, you can't afford. You can't afford it' . . . all the other kids are chiming in, 'he can't afford it.'

While it may not provide an incisive commentary on the black underclass, this brief example of child cruelty does touch upon some of the stereotypes about African-American community. In this way, Murphy supplies humourous black-on-black social critique without putting it into a larger sociopolitical context for his cross-over audiences. Despite their marked cultural specificity, in other words, Murphy's routines did not necessarily threaten white audiences.

As the Buckwheat routine exemplifies, when Murphy did engage with representations of African Americans in popular culture his impressions were encased in routines that only half-heartedly confronted the media mechanisms that perpetuated minstrel archetypes:

> I was standing outside getting ready to come in here and this little Jewish guy came up to me and said, 'Hey, Buckwheat.' There was some brothers standing next to me and they said. 'What did that guy call you. Man? Buckwheat?' Then I started thinking about the Little Rascals – period. Who the fuck thought up the names on that show? Because I am from a predominantly black family and I have yet to run into a relative named Buckwheat. Go to a cookout and say, 'Hi, my name is Ed. What's yours?' 'I'm Buckwheat, man. Yeah Buckwheat, that's my name. No, Buckwheat. I ain't got no last name – Buckwheat, that's it. . . . Don't believe me? Ain't that right, Stymie? . . . I want you to meet my brother. Yo, Farina! [pause] Buckwheat and Farina. . . . You know how

most people are named after their fathers, we was named after our fathers' favourite breakfasts.

The opening of this routine addresses the absurdity of being identified only with a parody of a piccaninny archetype (Buckwheat), but it soon becomes a riff on the issue of naming in its most simplistic form. Consequently, it stops short of actually questioning the ideological agenda informing the representation of black children in *The Little Rascals*. Like much of Murphy's consciously racialized humour, the routine does not endeavour to deconstruct or debunk either issues of race or racial representation. His pronouncements are rooted more in cynical banter than in social criticism.

The uninhibited bravado of *Eddie Murphy's Raw* (1987), directed by Robert Townsend, makes his earlier on-stage persona seem almost self-effacing by comparison. *Raw* undoubtedly played the same role for the second wave of post-Civil Rights era black comics that Richard Pryor's *Live in Concert* (1979) had played for Murphy himself, establishing a model for the Def Jam comic generation that included Rock, Martin Lawrence and Steve Harvey. Like Pryor, the irreverent core of Murphy's humour seemed to capture the imagination of young audiences across lines of race and class.[5] Where Pryor's stand-up managed to push the boundaries of good taste while maintaining his status as an 'equal opportunity offender', Murphy's material seemed to revel in attacks on homosexuals and women (the latter cast as predators looking 'to get half of what's mine').

Indeed, the most interesting material in *Raw* centres on the battle between Cosby and Pryor for his comic 'soul'. Although it begins simply as an opportunity for Murphy to reveal his mimicry skills, this routine develops into a blanket indictment of Cosby (for his 'outmoded' views regarding what a comic can or cannot say) and a quasi-canonization of Pryor (for his 'proselytizing' of outrageous curse-laden humour). Murphy recalls being excited about receiving a call from Bill, but the excitement turns to anger as Cosby chastises him:

(As Cosby) 'You cannot say filth, flarn, flarn, flarn, filth in front of people . . . I can't use the same language that you do but you know what I mean when I say flarn, flarn, flarn, filth.'(As himself) 'I never said no filth, flarn filth. I don't know what you're talking about. I'm offended that you called. Fuck You.' . . . That's when I got mad, he thought that was my whole act – that I cursed and left.

A stream of obscenities follows, culminating with 'Goodnight everybody – suck my dick.' Murphy then turns to Pryor for guidance: 'Richard says, "Next time the motherfucker calls tell him I said he can suck my dick. . . . Tell Bill to have a Coke and a smile and shut the fuck up."' This thus serves both to sever and establish ties with Murphy's black comedic forefathers. The skilfulness of imitations aside, the discourse surrounding 'appropriate' black humour plays out in fairly superficial terms. Cosby is cast as a dinosaur who is out of touch with the 'current' edgy and outrageous humour, which Murphy traces back to Pryor.

Yet, even as Murphy attempts to position himself as a sort of heir apparent to Pryor, the linkage seems weak because the kinship is based more on style than on substance. As Donald Bogle puts it:

It was apparent that Murphy was influenced by Pryor. It was apparent also that he had never understood Pryor's work. For Pryor had gotten inside his winos, junkies or numbers runners, uncovering their vulnerabilities, their troubled histories, and revealing at times their sadness and touching beauty. Murphy, however, seemed to see his various characters as lowlife characters without any innate dignity. . . . And obviously missing from his television skits were the social/political concerns of a Dick Gregory.

(Bogle 1988: 230)

A sort of 'I got mine' ethos informs Murphy's comedy and its apolitical production of black identity. In a *New York Times* article on 'bad boy' comedians of the Reagan era (both black and white), S. Holden defined Murphy's stand-up – in which he curses, mocks and rages without any clear sociopolitical or intellectual agenda – as 'the perfect symbol of post-hip, survival of the fittest humour'.[6]

Although the 1990s would see Murphy forsaking live performance for the movies, his meteoric rise to stardom through the 1980s proved an inspiration for the second wave of black comedians in both media. Chris Rock clearly demonstrates such an influence, and mines the wealth of earlier black humour styles presented by Pryor and Gregory as well. Like Murphy, Rock began his career as a teenager on the New York club circuit. After seeing the 17-year-old Rock do fifteen minutes at New York's The Comic Strip in 1987, Murphy secured a place for him on the HBO *Special Uptown Comedy Express*. This appearance led to Rock being cast, like Murphy before him, as 'the black guy' on *Saturday Night Live*. Despite Rock's insistence that he was 'just happy to be here', he was one of a succession of underused black cast members to experience minimal screen time and few running characters (the notable exception being Nat X). Rock's association with the series allowed him to branch out as a performer, leading to big screen-supporting roles in such films as *New Jack City* (1991). However, his profile for mainstream audiences was enhanced far more by his post- SNL gigs as pitchman: for example, his voicing of 'Lil' Penny' Hardaway, the Nike puppet, or the hostile info guy he did for 1-800-COLLECT.

In a 1992 comedy record Rock raged against the depiction of African Americans in popular culture and the real-life consequences of such mediated assumptions. As the title of the album exclaims, young black men in America today are 'Born Suspect'. The overtly political nature of Rock's comedy achieved even wider currency with his stint as a 'correspondent' for the 1996 presidential campaign on Comedy Central's *Politically Incorrect with Bill Maher*. His sardonic reports from the campaign trail provided a forum for Rock to meld his stand-up sensibility with an incisive sociopolitical critique that obliged audiences to laugh even as they squirmed. Rock's commentary on why Colin Powell could run for office – which was retooled for the 'Roll With the New' show (and quoted on his first HBO special) – directly confronted white liberal sensibilities while not allowing the audience off the hook.[7] Rock unflinchingly tackles whatever he deems hypocritical – regardless of race, creed or colour.

Although white liberals were his target in his first HBO special, *Bring The Pain!*, Rock's initial verbal assault called into question the politics (and the logic) of the black leadership:

Washington DC . . . Chocolate City. The home of the Million Man March. Had all the positive black leaders there – Farrakhan, Jesse, Marion Barry. How did he even get a ticket? It was a day of positivity. Marion Barry at the Million Man March. You know what that means? That even in our finest hour, we had a crack-head on stage.
[A mixture of laughter and boos] Boo if you want – you know I'm right.

Rock's target is not simply Marion Barry, the Mayor of Washington DC who secured another term in office despite a drug addiction scandal because he had remained (at least politically) in the bosom of the black community. Rock uses this scenario to critique such an unconditional solidarity that can defy the logic of self-preservation. Rock's take on the sensational trial and acquittal of O.J. Simpson is similarly designed to take a shot at everybody, regardless of race:

> Black people too happy, white people too mad. Black people saying, 'we won . . . we won . . . What the fuck did we win? Everyday I look in the mailbox for my OJ prize and nothing. [Some folks say] Ooh, it's all about race. This shit wasn't about race, it was about fame. If OJ wasn't famous he'd be sitting in jail right now. If OJ drove a bus, he wouldn't even be OJ, he'd be Orenthal the bus-driving murderer.

As an equal-opportunity chastiser, Rock's comic ire has no *single* target because it recognizes the complexity of race/power relations and their impact upon every aspect of American life. He forces the audience to confront this racial discourse amidst the laughter. In both *Bring the Pain* and his follow-up HBO special *Bigger and Blacker*, filmed at Harlem's Apollo Theater, Rock directly challenges notions of black identity in ways that few black comics have attempted. Like Pryor, his material mines the characters and stories of black community to comment on larger political issues. Like Gregory, he unambiguously states his views regarding the politicized sphere of race relations, whether by underscoring the way the 'war' disproportionately affects the African-American community (particularly young black men) or the burgeoning attitudes towards crime and punishment. His quasi-causal analysis foregrounds the politics of incarceration and the way economic inequities are hooked into it:

> Whole damn country is so conservative. Everybody's saying jails not tough enough . . . jails not tough enough . . . we got to have the death penalty. Jails are fucked up – don't believe the hype. The problem is jails are overcrowded because life is fucked up, too. People are broke. People are starving. Life is fucked up. Shit, life is catching up to jail. If you live in an old project, a new jail is not that bad.

Rock also demonstrates an incisive intraracial introspection in *Bigger and Blacker*. Some of his material explicitly condemns certain social practices within the African-American community, and is clearly inflected by a kind of moralizing that reaffirms middle-class norms ('Dad should pay the bills and keep the lights on so kids can do homework'). His tirade against the impact young single mothers out on the town have on black children – 'If you grow up calling your grandmother "mommy" and your mother "Pam", you're going to jail' – elicits nervous laughter from all segments of his audience.[8]

Among his most controversial material, Rock's 'Niggas *vs.* black people' routine speaks directly to rifts within the black community. 'There's some shit going on with black people right now,' Rock asserts. 'It's like a civil war going on with black people. There's two sides – there's black people and there's niggas. And niggas have got to go . . . I love black people but I hate niggas.' The virulent condemnation of 'niggas' requires a self-critical deconstruction of the historically charged term while forcing the audience (black and white) to recognize issues of difference (in terms of class and social practices) *within* the black community. This tendency towards uncompromisingly critical assessment separates Rock from both Murphy and his Def Jam brethren, by demonstrating his 'ability to set [himself] firmly against the grain, to perceive wrongheaded proscriptions and speak out against them . . . [which] has always been the cornerstone of socially relevant humour' (Watkins 1999: 581). However, it is difficult to make a clear prediction about the political intent of Rock's verbal barbs. While scolding possible sites of institutional racism (criminal justice, schools, media), he refuses to frame such issues in essentialist terms. In response to the audience titters that follow the 'Black people *vs.* niggas' routine, Rock immediately responds:

> I see some black people looking at me – mad. 'Why do you have to say that, brother? It ain't us, it's the media. The media has distorted our image to look. . . .' Please . . . when I go to the money machine tonight, I ain't looking over my back for the media – I'm looking for niggas.

The direct address to his predominantly black audience calls into question any easy assumptions about social problems and issues of representation. Casting himself as both a scathing sociopolitical critic and a devil's advocate, Rock's perspectives on African-American life foreground conflicts central to internally and externally constructed aspects of black identity.[9]

Murphy and Rock represent two strains of black humour that converge stylistically but which diverge significantly in terms of ideological content and their performance of blackness. As Rock himself notes, his humour bears a closer kinship to the socially relevant comics of a previous generation (Gregory, George Carlin and Pryor) than it does to Murphy and his Def Jam progeny (Crisafulli 1996: 1). Interestingly, Murphy in many ways embodies Dick Gregory's prescription for cross-over success: he is a black funny man, not a funny black man. However, this semantic difference is problematized within the context of Murphy's stand-up act, where his particular enunciation of blackness does not inform the content in either a critical or an especially progressive manner. By contrast, Rock's comic persona is built around sociopolitical articulations of blackness, and serves the post-Civil Rights era as the logical extension of Gregory's humour. Once transferred to the big screen, the delineations between the two come into even sharper focus, as do the colour adjustments they have been willing to make to achieve cross-over success.

Comedic colour adjustments: from main stage to big screen

Even though the transition from stand-up to screen was easier for Murphy and Rock than for the previous generations of black comedians, the creation of their mainstream film personae nonetheless required a negotiation of comedic identities. Their film roles correspond to two unique subgenres: the 'fish out of water' film, and the comedy of colour-coded colour-blindness. Both subgenres simultaneously recognize and elide race. The 'fish out of water' comedy and the comedy of colour-coded colour-blindness directly correspond to roles played by Murphy throughout his screen career. The same is true of Rock's Hollywood films thus far. An examination of the black comics' roles within these subgenres reveals how the performances of their comic personae and racial identity are configured according to the parameters of cross-over appeal.

The outsider's struggle to survive and thrive in a foreign, possibly hostile world has always provided grist for the 'fish out of water' film comedy mill – from Buster Keaton's city-bred Canfield heir returning to claim the rural family estate in *Our Hospitality* (1923) to Martin Lawrence's thief turning detective to recover stashed loot in *Blue Streak* (1999). However, this comic staple functions differently when a black comic is placed at the centre of the insider/outsider paradigm. In such cases, black stars are posited in cinematic milieux that are cut off from other representations of blackness, or even from other black characters, thereby placing them in the dubious position of representing the race. Ed Guerrero suggests that: 'One of the reasons for the contextual isolation of the black star or co-star is not too hard to discern because many of these vehicles were originally written for white stars.' For example, the role that catapulted Murphy into superstardom, Axel Foley in *Beverly Hills Cop* (1984), was written for Sylvester Stallone (Guerrero 1993: 126).

Both Axel Foley and Reggie Hammond (48 *Hours*, 1982) are roles that allowed Murphy to incorporate his stand-up persona within a big screen role. Although 48 *Hours* 'literalizes the metaphor of the black image being in the protective custody of white authority', Hammond acts as the embodiment of street sensibility and stand-up swagger (Guerrero 1993: 126). The film operates within the interracial buddy film paradigm by focusing on the temporary alliance forged between surly, experienced cop Jack Cates (Nick Nolte) and small-time criminal Hammond (the 'good' bad guy) in order to catch the latter's former partner. Murphy's character is introduced as a disembodied voice that wafts through the cell block singing along to The Police's 'Roxanne', his fondness for the mainstream pop group signalling a likeable and non-threatening Anglo-friendliness. Playing off the young/old, black/white, criminal/cop dichotomies, the uneasy but amiable alliance of Hammond and Cates acts as a sort of race relations fable that insists we *can* all just get along.

Reggie Hammond displays the signature black machismo of Murphy's comic persona as well as the verbal acuity of his stand-up (particularly when he tells bar-room rednecks that 'I'm your worst fucking nightmare – a nigger with a badge'). Hammond's 'quest for flesh', a running subplot, gives Murphy an opportunity to dip into the sexual dynamo schtick he honed in *Delirious*. By the film's end Hammond is both a hero and a stud: by refusing to grab the money and run he wins the respect of Nolte's character and returns to gaol transformed, if not reformed, by his interaction with Nolte, who embodies the fair side of the white justice system. In turn, the cop allows the criminal to get laid as a reward for 'doing the right thing'.

In *Beverly Hills Cop* and *Beverly Hills Cop* II (1987), Axel Foley mocks but ultimately serves the needs of a white populace. The murder of his white running buddy brings him to Beverly Hills in the original, while the sequel motivates Foley's actions by means of his inflated sense of loyalty to BHPD's Captain Bogamil (Ronny Cox). Foley's methods and his savvy prove to be superior to those of his white cohorts, Rosewood (Judge Reinhold) and Taggart (John Ashton), but his performance of a hard-boiled Detroit cop converts much of the casework into comic antics. Murphy's skill at slipping into multiple characters is used repeatedly, from his angry black man rant at the Beverly Wilshire to his turn as the egregiously fey 'special friend' of the film's villain – which he uses to gain access to a club's private dining-room. His unorthodox methods are eventually lauded because of the fact that, once the case is solved, he will be returned to off-screen (black) space. By using the humour in Foley's cameo of blackness in fundamentally white worlds, Murphy's interloper is constructed as an idealized *and* temporary Other.

Furthermore, perhaps because it was not originally intended for a black actor, BHC occasionally elides and reworks blackness in almost nonsensical ways. As Donald Bogle notes: 'Coming from the streets of Detroit (the very city whose ghettoes had gone up in flames during the race riots of the 60s), the character's friends logically would have been black. But Eddie Murphy is plopped into a white environment in order that a mass white audience can better identify with him . . . It's an unrealistic plot maneuver that reveals Hollywood's cynicism about the major Black star and his audience' (Bogle 1988: 18). Both of Foley's closest childhood friends in BHC are white. Moreover, although there are fleeting hints of a romance between Foley and Jenny (Lisa Eilbacher), he is more or less sexually neutralized despite the swaggering machismo of his step and speech. After all, seeing Murphy woo a white actress would have made the film decidedly less friendly to a mainstream audience. Ed Guerrero points out that 'The source of the energy and tension in all of Murphy's movies is race, and to a lesser degree, class, deriving from Murphy's Blackness as a challenge to white exclusion (but not privilege or domination) . . . and while Murphy gets the upper-hand, the ultimate result of such a challenge is integration and acceptance on white terms in the film's resolution' (Guerrero 1993: 132). Hammond and Foley both clearly exemplify the repackaging of the Black stand-up persona for mass consumption, with Murphy's quick-witted wisecracking and street kid charisma informing the iteration of his screen persona as black comic action star.[10]

Although by the 1990s Murphy appeared to have exhausted this generic type, it is interesting to note that his black 'fish out of water' roles garnered the most critical and commercial success. Ultimately, just as Foley acts as the 'exception' that can be celebrated within a white milieu on a temporary basis, Murphy can be embraced as black comic action hero so long as he does not transgress other mainstream Hollywood boundaries – such as his construction as a leading man. The 'fish out of water' film may seem to problematize the ways in which the black comedian can interject both his comic persona and some degree of cultural specificity into his screen roles, but this is not always the case. In Kevin Smith's independent film *Dogma* (1999) Chris Rock plays a fish out of water among other fish out of water as Rufus, the thirteenth apostle. Without the expectation of a mainstream audience, there is more room for Rock to incorporate his comic persona in the role.[11]

Rock plays a supporting role to renegade angels (Matt Damon and Ben Affleck) who attempt to use a loophole in church dogma to re-enter Heaven. Operating as the film's philosophical centre in a tone very much akin to the comic's stand-up rants, Rock's Rufus tells people what they *need* to know. Rufus agrees to join the holy crusade both to save the world, of course, but also to set the record straight – Jesus was black. When fellow holy crusaders scoff at this revelation, Rufus puts the error into a sociohistorical context:

> Between the time when He established the faith and the Church started to officially organize, the powers that be decided that, while the message of Christ was integral, the fact that he was black was a detriment. So all renderings were ordered to be Eurocentric – even though the brother was blacker than Jesse.

Rufus allows Rock's comic voice to resonate in the character's lines. As the black martyr in this multicultural motley crew, Rock's impeccable comedic timing is well matched by the profane language and scatological moralizing of Smith's film.[12] In this case, the black comedian's stage and screen persona were integrated into film comedy without being diluted beyond recognition. This raises the question of whether the choice to remain outside of the motherlode of cross-over success is the only way for the black comedian to continue to engage issues of race as directly on film as he does in stand-up routine.

Murphy's career answers this question. Even though *The Nutty Professor* (1996) and its sequel *The Nutty Professor 2: The Klumps* (2000) heralded Murphy's return to box office prominence, I would like to focus on *Dr. Dolittle* (1998). This film not only supplies the most extreme sublimation of the controversial aspects of the black comic persona into an unproblematic integrationist fantasy but also marks Murphy's entry into the family comedy genre. Furthermore, the way that race is incorporated or erased in this film demonstrates the marketability of colour-coded colour-blindness. Two principal changes are made in remaking the 1967 film – it is non-musical and a black actor plays the title role. Despite the casting of Murphy, the context of the narrative does not engage black culture and identity in any direct or significant manner. Dolittle's 'gift' of talking to the animals not only becomes a mark of difference but also operates as a signifier for identity. The lost 'gift' that Dolittle had 'unlearned' as a result of his father's desire for him to 'fit in' re-emerges at the point when both his autonomy and his identity are being challenged. A huge corporate Health Maintenance Organization is seeking to buy out Dolittle's practice at the same time as he is striving to teach his daughter to 'fit in'. After Dolittle nearly runs over a dog, Lucky (voiced by Norm MacDonald), his senses are restored: once again, he is able to talk to the animals and to express his own 'individuality'.

Race is both inherent in and absent from the film, with Dolittle's extended family (including wife, two daughters and father) supplying the only black faces in major roles. While actors of colour are among the star-studded cavalcade of celebrity voices (most notably Chris Rock as his daughter's pet guinea-pig, Rodney), the story is set in a predominantly white liberal world in San Francisco. The notion of a white liberal setting is central to the film's elision of race. While one might argue that race motivates Dolittle's father (Ossie Davis) to prescribe conformity as a means of gaining access to the American Dream, it is never explicitly mentioned. Within the context of a cautionary tale that warns against homogeneity (figured as the corporate entity or enforced conformity), racial identity and questions of difference are translated into the 'special gift' of hearing animals speak. Questions about race are thus displaced on to issues of the 'uniqueness' of individual identity and the struggle between the individual (small business owner) and the corporation. Dolittle's gift, which *could* mark him as Other, is constructed not as an obstacle to achievement or assimilation but rather as a type of uniqueness (read: rugged individualism) that has consistently been part of the mythology of the American Dream. In this way, racial identity, coded as uniqueness, slides past otherness into the realm of a mythic, idealized middle-classness. The clear villain of this film is the corporation, personified by the HMO president (Peter Boyle), which is an embodiment of soulless homogeneity and mediocrity. The film's plot may reward the return of the individual's uniqueness (Dolittle opens a dual practice for animals and humans, which will undoubtedly be a lucrative one) but it is also in the business of smoothing out individual difference. It is especially ironic that a tale which professes to celebrate the expression of individual gifts requires Murphy to dilute his comic persona almost beyond recognition. As far as his big screen persona is concerned, this struggle for the comic soul of the new family-friendly Murphy sees Cosby rather than Pryor as the victor. In Murphy's John Dolittle, the profane and culturally specific aspects of his stand-up are replaced by a Cosbyesque integrationist fantasy in which race is no problem at all.

Indeed, Murphy's comic persona plays only an ancillary role in many of his most recent films, as the voice of the puny dragon in Disney's animated feature *Mulan* (1998); as the mild-mannered Sherman Klump, his egomaniacal alter ego Buddy Love and the entire Klump clan in *The Nutty Professor* films; and as action star Kit Ramsey and his geeky brother Jiff in *Bowfinger* (1999). Interestingly, some of these characters seem to quote different impersonations from Murphy's old act: the Klumps, for example, appear to be refugees from his family cookout material. Yet only the 'posse'-laden Ramsey and the hypersexualized Buddy conflate the on-stage and off-stage public personae of the young Murphy and feed directly from the attitude (if not the content) of the *Raw* years – and these figures are played as parody. Murphy's performance of black identity through machismo has been thoroughly domesticated.

The year 2001 saw the release of Chris Rock's first big studio venture, Paramount's *Down to Earth*. Arguably, the comic potential was great, with Rock doing double duty as writer and star in a film directed by Chris and Paul Weitz, the white indie wonder boys responsible for the *American Pie* films (1999, 2001). This remake of Warren Beatty's *Heaven Can Wait* (1978) – itself a remake of *Here Comes Mister Jordan* (1941) – features Rock as Lance Barton, a stand-up comedian who dies before he can 'kill' at Harlem's Apollo Theater and is then reincarnated in the body of a murdered fifty-something white millionaire, Charles Wellington. The question of whether or not the uncompromising stand-up persona of Rock would translate into a PG-13 Hollywood vehicle was answered within the first twenty minutes of the film: the answer was yes *and* no. Despite Rock's characterization of the film's humour as 'race neutral', cultural specificity inflects the film throughout – particularly in terms of Lance/Wellington's relationship to popular culture and, of course, stand-up. Soon after his reincarnation as Wellington, Lance requests a television in the mansion that has BET (Black Entertainment Television). Later, the film presents alternating images of Lance (tall, skinny black man) and Wellington (short, pudgy, white) as he rides in the Rolls, jamming to Snoop Doggy Dogg's 'Gin and Juice' while flashing the three-fingered sign for 'Westside'.

Rock's stand-up act is metered out over the course of the film. Lance/Wellington's first stand-up gig directly lifts the 'black mall vs. white mall' routine from *Roll with the New* ('there's no shit in a black mall except sneakers and baby clothes') with the comic twist that such material is now voiced by an elderly white man – to a stunned reaction from the club's black audience. Coming from Rock, this routine serves as a critique of corporate America's perception of the black community as a collection of pregnant women and wannabe athletes. But when it is delivered by Wellington, a privileged white male, the material is compromised because it now emanates from a source of enunciation for the very assumptions Rock critiques. Rock's act also informs the social conscience that Wellington develops as he determines to save Brooklyn Community Hospital for the community, inspired by the urgings of the activist (and love interest) Sontee (Regina King). His answer to the hospital Board of Directors regarding uninsured patients is a tirade straight out of *Bring the Pain*:

> Insurance. . . . Insurance ain't enough for people. I don't even know why they call it insurance. They should just call it 'in-case-shit-happens'. I give a company money in case shit happen. Now if nothing happens, shouldn't I get my money back?

With an opening weekend of $18 million and the number two slot in domestic box office, *Down to Earth* promised to deliver cross-over success for Rock – but at a cost.[13] As one critic noted, 'Like many of Pryor's movies (*Brewster's Millions*, *The Toy*), *Down to Earth* takes pains to soften and bland out its star's more scabrous characteristics' (Turan 2001: 1). Another reviewer simply states that 'Mr. Rock's fans . . . are going to want a movie with the same acidulous funkiness that he brings to his stand-up, they are not going to get that' (Mitchell 2001). Or, as one of my fellow moviegoers commented on the film's opening night in Ann Arbor, Michigan: 'It was aw'ight but . . . it wasn't funny like I thought it'd be.'[14] In the process of mainstreaming Rock's stand-up humour for a studio film, the race issues that motored his biting social critique now provide the set-up for a string of running gags. There is little difference in the type of laughter elicited when Lance celebrates his inability to hail a cab – 'I surely am a black man again' – and the 'Homey's' punch Lance/Wellington receives after his impromptu duet with DMX's 'Ruff Riders'. By streamlining Rock's abrasive and edgy performance within a mainstream Hollywood narrative, *Down to Earth* delivers humour that could be described as race *neutralized* rather than race neutral. Although racial difference is interwoven throughout its narrative, the film deals with race relations as evasively as the integrationist fairy tale of *Dr. Dolittle*. The literal colour-coding of these films supplies mainstream audiences with comforting but empty signifiers for race in America, wrapped up by happy endings that celebrate inclusion and acceptance. 'Funny is funny,' they seem to say, 'regardless of race, creed or colour.'

Who is laughing mad now?

> In the case of |film| comedy, the tendency is to imagine the comic as outside of history, an essential force . . . |C|omic tradition is imagined as self contained, never losing its essential identity to the contingencies of a merely arbitrary history.
>
> Dana Polan[15]

I would argue that Dana Polan's assertion about comic tradition can never apply to the African-American comedian. Rooted in an explication of the social conditions of African-American life, black humour carries an inherent critique of cultural and racial inequalities. Implicitly or explicitly, such humour explores the conflicting (and conflicted) allegiances of being black and American. The 'essential identity' of the black comic is always supervised by the history of race relations in America – from what venues one may perform in, to the assimilationist negotiation of blackness in mainstream media show-cases. As in the Civil Rights era, and earlier, issues of race continue to inform daily life in black America – in terms of media representation, social mobility and political agency. How, then, could they not play a role in its humour? In a *New York Times* interview the week before the opening of *Down To Earth*, Chris Rock commented on what it meant to be a black comedian:

> Being a comedian is like being in a boxing ring but when you add the subject of race, it's like you get to use a bat, too. Few guys can't resist using that bat. But then journalists start analyzing it and talking to me like I'm Kwesi Mfume |the president of the NAACP|. I don't need that gig. All I care about is being funny.
>
> (Malanowski 2001: 27)

Even though Rock's comment reveals a desire for a comic tradition that is 'outside of history', it nonetheless acknowledges the power that black humour offers to the 'bat' of social critique.

Is it unfair to expect black comedians to operate within a pedagogy informed as much by cultural criticism as it is by the need just to 'be funny'? Yes, but I would maintain that it is necessary nonetheless. This necessity is illustrated by the colour adjustments that take place in the mainstreaming of the black comic persona for Hollywood comedy – and in the miniscule number of black actors or black themed films that are actually deemed able to 'go wide'.

On stage, the black comic retains the ability to get the audience laughing while slipping in sociocultural truths. The boundless promise of social screen comedy, however, remains unfulfilled as the performance of Blackness continues to be diluted for mass consumption. Pryor, Murphy and Rock, who have all revealed great potential for providing insights into black identity and culture, lose their critical edge when their personas are reformatted for the big screen. As long as conventional wisdom dictates that sardonic, cultural critique cannot play well at the Cineplex, the underbelly of race relations and racial inequity in post-Civil Rights America will not be the stuff of which Hollywood comedies are made. So . . . who is laughing mad now?

Notes

1 A longer version of this study includes analysis of both the historical influences on the African-American comedian (stretching back to the Chitlin' Circuit) and a more expansive view of the contemporary black comedians (including male and female members of the Def Jam generation). In future work I hope to focus specifically on Whoopi Goldberg, a black comedic actor who supplies one of the most complex cross-over success stories in contemporary American film.
2 When Pryor hosted the 'cutting-edge' Saturday Night Live in 1975, the show was broadcast with a seven-second delay for fear of what the unpredictable comic might do with a platform that was both live and national. The only other instance when the time delay was implemented in the twenty-five-plus-year history on SNL was with Andrew Dice Clay in 1990.
3 Even Cosby, Leonard's co-writer and producer, panned the film.
4 There is no little irony in the fact that Cosby, known for his mainstreamed version of blackness, scored big screen success in a film that supplied a slice of black life to white audiences (without interrogating the sociopolitical contexts of the milieu) while Pryor's greatest commercial successes used black identity as a comic accessory to racist constructions of urban black culture.
5 By 1987, Murphy could 'open' a movie . . . something that only a handful of black actors before or since have been able to do. Along with that power – fuelled by box office success – came the elevation of Murphy as the founding member of the 'Black Pack', a term he coined at the press conference for Beverly Hills Cop II. Between the late 1980s and early 1990s Murphy and his 'pack' – which included Robert Townsend (Hollywood Shuffle, 1987), Arsenio Hall (The Arsenio Hall Show, 1989–94) and Keenan Ivory Wayans (the future creator/producer of In Living Colour, 1990–94) – were seen as the new wave of black comedy.
6 Holden regards Murphy's comedy as the accompaniment to an age when 'As the political climate turned more conservative and materialistic, hip irreverence turned sour, and the wink in the eye of comedy became a sneer' (Holden 1988: 1).

7 'White people say they'd vote for him because they think it's the cool thing to say. . . .
"Sure, I'll vote for him" (punctuated with a dismissive 'yeah, right' chuckle).'

8 In fairness, Rock also takes to task the young fathers – 'niggas [who] always want some
credit for some shit they are supposed to do . . . [he says] "I take care of my kids" . . . you're
supposed to do that you dumb motherfucker.'

9 Rock employed this cultural critic approach on his Emmy-nominated HBO series *The Chris
Rock Show* (1997–2000). It provided a new venue for numerous African-American comedians
and musical acts (with Grandmaster Flash as the series' musical director/DJ), as well as
black activists/leaders – from cultural critic Cornell West, to figures who had been targets
of Rock's comic critique (including Reverend Al Sharpton and Marion Barry).

10 Intriguingly, some aspects of Murphy's stand-up act that had generated so much ire
were excused within the context of a 'guy' film. The misogyny that informed much of the
material about women in *Raw* also found its way into BHCII – as exemplified by the
repeated 'it's a dick thing' ethos in the marital advice Foley offers to Taggart (a slightly
sanitized version of Murphy's 'Cumin Hard' routine) and by Brigitte Nielsen's character,
referred to simply as 'the big bitch', whose shooting acts as a collective reassertion
of masculine solidarity.

11 Although not strictly an example of the 'fish out of water' film, Rock's supporting role as
Lee Butters in *Lethal Weapon* 4 (1998) offers a variation on how the black comedian can
be used within the action comedy. While his role acts as a sort of narrative garnish to the
already established interracial buddy paradigm, the character of Butters is constructed
as a college-educated black detective who acts as an alternative to Riggs (Mel Gibson) and
Murtaugh (Danny Glover), the old school 'cops who don't play by the rules'. Cast as the
'kid' with the veteran partners, Rock's role is a fairly thankless one yet he still exhibits
low-dosage glimmerings of the comic's stand-up persona.

12 In another independent film, Neil LaBute's *Nurse Betty* (2000), Rock's turn as the sardonic
hitman provides another example of a choice of role that – in terms of character voice, if
not character construction – also exemplifies continuity between comic and screen
persona.

13 At just over $64 million in domestic and foreign box office, *Down to Earth* turned out to be
Paramount's seventh highest grossing film in 2001: http://www.the-numbers.com/movies/
2001/DWN2E.html

14 On 16 February 2001 I was seated in a large theatre in the local Cineplex with a crowd that
was decidedly more integrated than it had been the previous summer when I saw the
black comedian concert film *The Original Kings of Comedy* (Spike Lee, 2000) in the same
venue. Although I did not have the opportunity to ask the young African-American male
what he meant, his comment seemed to speak to the 'blanding' that the *Times* reviewers
on both coasts address.

15 Quoted in Karnick and Jenkins 1995: 265.

References

Anonymous (2000): 'Biography', *Whazzup with Dick Gregory*, http://www.math.buffalo.edu/~sww/
gregory/gregory_dick.html (accessed 12 December).
Berger, P. (2000): *The Last Laugh: The World of Stand-Up Comics*, New York: Copper Square Press.

Bogle, D. (1988): *Blacks in American Films and Television: An Encyclopedia*, New York: Garland Publishing.

Crisafulli, C. (1996): 'Q & A with Chris Rock', *Los Angeles Times*, 5 June, Calendar F: 1.

Guerrero, E. (1993): *Framing Blackness: The African American Image in Film*, Philadelphia, PA: Temple University Press.

Holden, S. (1988): 'Comedy's Bad Boys Screech Into the Spotlight', *New York Times*, 28 February, Arts & Leisure: Section 2.

Karnick, K. Brunovska and H. Jenkins (1995): 'Introduction: Comedy and the Social World', in Karnick and Jenkins (eds) *Classical Hollywood Comedy*, New York and London: Routledge.

Malanowski, J. (2001): 'Not to Say This Is A Better Movie Than Beatty's', *New York Times*, 11 February, Arts Section, 27.

Mitchell, E. (2001): '*Down To Earth*: He May Be In Heaven but He's Dying at the Apollo', *New York Times*, http://www.nytimes.com/2001/02/16/arts/16DOWN.html (accessed 16 February).

Reid, M. (1993): *Redefining Black Film*, Berkeley: University of California, 1993.

Turan, K. (2001): 'This Time "Earth" Can Wait', *Los Angeles Times*, 16 February, Calendar: 1.

Watkins, M. (1999): *On The Real Side: A History of African American Comedy from Slavery to Chris Rock*, New York: Lawrence Hill.

Low Blows?

13

Theorizing performance in post-classical comedian comedy

PHILIP DRAKE

Recent Hollywood cinema has seen a surge in the popularity of comedian comedy. Films such as *Dumb and Dumber* (1994), *Ace Ventura: Pet Detective* (1994), *The Mask* (1994), *Kingpin* (1996), *The Nutty Professor* (1996), *Liar Liar* (1997), *There's Something About Mary* (1998), *Deuce Bigelow: Male Gigolo* (1999) and *Me Myself and Irene* (2000) have offered audiences the pleasures of 'low' physical comedy. New comic stars such as Jim Carrey, Chris Farley, Mike Myers and Adam Sandler (and existing stars such as Eddie Murphy and Robin Williams) have all performed in commercially successful films that have taken the bodily performance of the star as their primary focus rather than more conventional forms of narrative motivation. This has led a number of cultural commentators to argue that the phenomenal recent success of films featuring physical gags, pratfalls, jokes about bodily functions and the loss of bodily control have been part of an increasingly prevalent 'dumbed down' sensibility in popular culture that embraces stupidity at the expense of more cerebral pleasures.[1]

My aim in this chapter is to focus on a number of 'dumb' performances by Jim Carrey – arguably the most high-profile of contemporary comedians – in order to explore more general questions about the theorization of screen performance. In doing so I will also argue a broader point – namely that the pleasure we experience in performance, especially comedic performance, highlights the serious inadequacy of models of narrative upon which film studies has been built. I argue that greater consideration of the complexities and pleasures of performance can help us to address the interaction between audiences and texts in the active process of making and remaking meaning.

Understanding performance

What is performance? As any cursory reading of an introductory performance studies text reveals, it is emphatically not simply either 'acting' or 'what the performer does'.[2] Instead, performance is a particularly slippery and contested term. It refers both to a theoretical approach and to a practice. Graham Thompson has defined performance as a 'mode of assessment of the "textual/character/actor" interaction'.[3] This definition is useful because it emphasizes that the performer signifies in any given moment according to several regimes of fictionality. First, s/he is a textual character within the diegetic world constructed by the film and positioned within this for us by the filmic apparatus. At the same time, however, s/he is also an actor performing a role, and we are aware of the skill and craft displayed in the construction of the performance. If the performer in question is a star, as at the centre of comedian comedy, this signification is yet more complicated. The star image circulates outside of the text; their signifiers are informed by previous roles and subsidiary texts, as well as the recognition in a particular culture of their status as celebrity. Hence any moment of star performance simultaneously invokes multiple semantic frames – of fictional character, of star persona, and of generic codes and conventions. At any particular moment, then, we might see, for instance, Jim Carrey performing as (1) Ace Ventura, the fictional character in a narrative film, (2) Jim Carrey, celebrity and star, (3) Jim Carrey, traced through other fictional characters from other performances, and (4) a physical 'body' comic, thereby evoking comparisons to other performers (such as Jerry Lewis). There may, of course, be many more semantic frameworks in addition to these. These 'recognitions' require particular kinds of decoding skills (as well as decoding positions) which are culturally specific, the most obvious being perhaps the recognition of the star as a celebrity in the first instance.

Thompson's definition of performance is useful because it acknowledges the centrality of interpretation (and therefore an audience) to the embodiment of a performance, but without ignoring the complex encoding process. Performance, in his terms, is not just the intersection of the text/actor/character but its *mode of assessment*. This is the fundamental relationship between text and audience that marks out the performative from the everyday. Audiences bring to any 'moment' of performance their own cultural capital, sets of expectations, taste formations and memories of previous encounters. Hence to recognize a performance *as a* performance is always already to decode it in some way, to assign it particular values and align it according to our cultural capital. No discussion of performance – academic or otherwise – is 'untainted' by these processes of decoding. The pleasure we derive from watching the performance of a favourite star is partly that of recognition and familiarity, rather than simply those of identification with a particular character within a film narrative.

How, then, do we make sense of performance? Is it purely subjective? I suggest that our evaluative discourses posit preferred (and possibly hegemonic) epistemological frameworks – what the sociologist Erving Goffman terms 'frames' – through which performances may be decoded.[4] At the same time, performances are 'keyed' through such conventions as mode of address, performance style, typecasting, genre and so on, to give particular ways of making sense of the events on screen. A performance in this sense is not simply a text; it is a layered social experience, an interaction between audience and text, where meanings are contingent upon the interpretive schema placed upon the star performance by a particular audience. This is not, though, a simplistic normative process; in fact, as any exiting filmgoer will attest, frames may be negotiated or rejected according to the decoding tactics of the audience. For instance, a camp reading may develop a tactic of reading against the preferred meaning of the text.[5] A bored and distracted spectator may produce a disengaged reading that fails to establish any kind of primary framing. The consequence of this is that frame analysis of screen performance is simultaneously a matter of text, audience and context.

The difficulties encountered in the study of screen performance, however, are not simply of theoretical definition but also one of adequate frameworks for analysis. The analogue nature of screen performance (which depends upon subtle gradations of gesture and voice), mediated through the extra-narrative signifying function of the star, has long presented difficulties for hermetic models of formal analysis. This is not simply a lack of precise, critical terms through which to analyse performance, but also from how to account for what performance does – the *affect* of performance. This is perhaps one of the reasons why performance analysis has presented such problems for film studies. To describe the particular facial expression of an actor – the broad grin familiar in the idiolect of Carrey, for instance – and particular gestures and movement, does not say much about the meaning of the performance. The idiolect of the star offers pleasure in its familiarity that resists theoretical elaboration as a formal system. These pleasures are individualized through our experiential memories of other performances, as well as those imbricated within narcissistic fantasies of identification, mastery and idealization.[6] To talk of performance is to speak personally, to write oneself into one's research – forms of writing resistant to the scientism of structural or formalist analysis. Furthermore, film performance is mediated through the cinematic apparatus and the operation of other sets of codes (the signification of *mise-en-scène*, camera placement, editing, sound). Screen performance is therefore ontologically complex: it is both unified (in presentation) and fragmented (in execution), present (on the screen) and absent (in another time and space). Moreover, it is available to us only through a technologically mediated enunciative apparatus (projector and sound system, television set).[7] This has meant that the analysis of performance in film presents significant difficulties that do not apply to other media forms, such as the stage – where performance and audience usually share the same time and space.[8]

I now want to look more closely at performance in comedian comedy. Drawing upon Jim Carrey's physical comedy, I want to consider exactly what we mean by 'dumb' performance and what is at stake in its interpretation and critical evaluation.

Post-classical comedian comedy

Steve Seidman uses the term 'comedian comedy' to delineate the formal conventions of comic performance in classical Hollywood cinema.[9] The model he proposes offers a suggestive framework for considering the work of comedians as dissimilar as Buster Keaton and Woody Allen in relation to specific genre conventions and the expectations they set up. Seidman argues that comedian comedy has historically formed an important tradition in Hollywood cinema and that its characteristics may be traced across different texts. First, the comedian film is centred on the performance of a particular actor/performer, whom we recognize as a star, and whose star persona circulates outside of the immediate narrative. Second, comedian comedy self-consciously, and often flamboyantly, acknowledges the comedian's role as a performer rather than subsuming their performance to the protocols of realist character construction. Where an actor's performance is conventionally thought of as being determined and directed through narrative agency, the 'tradition' of comedian comedy 'ostends' – or foregrounds – the comedian as a performing sign within the framing context of the filmic performance.[10]

Seidman contrasts this process with the classical realist mode of Hollywood narrative, which generally attempts to efface performance by providing a goal-orientated narrative as the motivating causal force. In classical realism, this formulation suggests, the actor's performance is determined and directed through narrative agency. The star persona attached to the actor/performer is subsumed by that of the character they are playing. In contrast to performance in comedian comedy, realist screen acting usually uses a representational rather than presentational address and maintains a level of ostensiveness – the register of the performance – appropriate to narrative demands. Seidman suggests, then, that we might see comedian comedy as either working in opposition to classical Hollywood conventions or, alternatively, as working within and negotiating these conventions, taking on some classical elements and refusing others.

I want now to reconsider this supposed opposition between performance and narrative, as it has fundamentally shaped approaches to comedian comedy and has also, to some extent, marginalized the useful writing on performance in comedy. Questions of performance in other forms of narrative cinema have focused on a much narrower definition of perfor-mance, which is usually seen as deriving from the authorship of the film (as in acting discourse) rather than from a relationship between a particular text and a particular audience. My argument is that analysis of performance in comedian comedy not only offers a more sustained treatment of the concept, but can also add to our understanding of star performance across other genres.

Performance and narrative motivation

Throughout this chapter I deliberately use the phrase 'comic performance' instead of 'comedy performance' because I am referring to a mode of performance that is *specifically* comic, rather than one that is rendered comic through its narrative context. This distinction is, in my view, worth retaining, although in practice it may be rather more analytical than observable. The narrative context of comedian comedy often supports and sets up the performance, providing enclosures in which it can take place with narrative justification. For example, there is frequent use of the narrative conceit whereby the protagonist suffers from a split personality, a device which helps to emphasize the disjunction between social conformity and eccentricity. This, of course, opens up a large number of possibilities for physical comedy through the comedian's embodiment of dual personae, and a large number of post-classical 'dumb' comedies have drawn upon this Jekyll-and-Hyde scenario for their humour. The most obvious is the 1996 remake of Jerry Lewis' *The Nutty Professor*, in which Eddie Murphy plays both Sherman Klump and his alter ego Buddy Love (and indeed nearly all of Klump's family). The conflict between the two is visually embodied as a battle between their respective physical selves, with computer-generated effects enabling rapid morphing between these two bodies. Like most high-concept films, *The Nutty Professor* provides a justification for these transformations – the secret formula – that may be flimsy in terms of the motivational conventions of realist narrative but which nonetheless provides an explanation that is just adequate enough to sustain causal narrative logic.[11]

The Jim Carrey comic vehicle *Me, Myself and Irene* uses a narrative device to motivate performance – a multiple personality disorder that establishes an opposition between nice guy cop Charlie and his ostentatiously nasty alter ego Hank. As with *The Nutty Professor*, the show-down between the two selves takes place through physical conflict (and hence physical comedy). Once more there is narrative motivation for his transformation – Charlie forgets to take his medication – but again the excessive consequences are clearly motivated by conventions outside of classical realism. If we were to compare, for instance, the motivation of Carrey's transformation with that of James Mason (playing a character in a similar situation) in the classical Hollywood drama *Bigger than Life* (1956), the distinction becomes clearer. The motivating rationale of 1990s 'dumb' or 'gross' comedy is not psychological realism but the hyperbolic justification of the gag sequence, which has its own internal narrative structure. Where *Bigger than Life* deals with an identity in crisis, *The Nutty Professor* and *Me, Myself and Irene* frame identity as a matter of (mere) performance.

Writing on *Me, Myself and Irene*, Kent Jones argues that the 'dead air' of comedy – the space and time before and after a gag – is crucial in shaping the momentum of this narrative structure.[12] The expectation of what the next sequence might bring – will it top the last gag in bad taste? – is the key to the pleasure that audiences derive from the film. However, the performance sequence is often keyed within the diegesis too. As with the musical, a convention of comedian comedy is the placing of diegetic enclosures within narrative that provide space for ostentatious performance. The court-room scenes in Carrey's earlier film *Liar Liar* (1997), for instance, serve to place the character he plays centre-stage and provide him with time and space in which he can perform to an audience (both diegetic and implied). The performance can again be explained partly by means of a narrative device (Carrey plays a lawyer who is unable to lie), but the credible sufficiency of this motivation remains questionable.

Seidman suggests that comedian comedy belongs to a non-hermetic tradition that directly acknowledges the spectator and which enunciates 'look at me perform!' Contrasting this with classic realism, he argues that – like cartoons and comics – comedian films provide us with the pleasure of watching the breakdown of classical narrative structures, offering a 'narrative exposition that is "spoiled" by actors who "step out" of character'.[13] Interestingly, Seidman suggests that many comedian stars entered the film industry from other media, such as vaudeville, comedy clubs, radio and television. This is also the case with the contemporary performers – including Carrey, who was both a stand-up comic and ensemble member of the television comedy sketch show, *In Living Color* (Fox, 1990–94), and the numerous performers whose film careers were boosted by appearances on the US sketch show *Saturday Night Live* (NBC, 1975–). These forms have tended to support a more presentational mode of performance and have, unlike Hollywood cinema, historically been characterized by a direct mode of address (often live, or with the appearance of liveness) and a willingness to refer to the fictionality of the performance.

Comedian comedy explicitly adopts aspects of this presentational mode of performance, with performers able to represent a character in the fictional narrative while at the same time signifying as a star, outside of that character. Furthermore, in comedian comedy the stars can often refer to their performance, or change the framing of the performance (by addressing the audience, for example), without breaking the primary frame in which the performance takes place. Indeed, bathetic shifts from moments of comedy to pathos (and back again) are a staple of such comedy. However, to argue that narrative is either 'spoiled' or 'subverted' by comic performance is, I suggest, problematic for several reasons. First, it assumes that narrative operates independently from performance, when we might argue that narrative and performance work together. Narrative and performance are less opposed than Seidman claims, and comedian comedy usually integrates ostentatious performance using some form of narrative device (however flimsy). Second, Seidman's argument disregards the possibility that the narrative conventions of comedian comedy might actually be based on, or license, this supposed transgression. By foregrounding its production and artificiality the comedian comedy text may be less a 'deconstruction of its signifying practice', as Seidman suggests, than a means of fulfilling the requirements and conventions of a specific genre where terms conventionally associated with realist performance – such as 'authenticity' and 'sincerity' – have very little explanatory force.[14]

The usefulness of the term 'comedian comedy', then, is that it helps us make a distinction between comedy that is oriented around the performance of a comedian, and narrative comedy in which the context or situation provides the humour. I have tried to suggest, however, that these distinctions are not in themselves rigidly fixed. In fact, star performance in comedian comedy tends to dominate narrative and present itself as spectacle. At the same time, I have argued that the comedian film has tended to maintain what might be termed 'sufficient' realism to allow performance sequences to be tied, however schematically, to narrative and causal relations.

The opening scene of Carrey's film *Ace Ventura: Pet Detective* (1994) is helpful in making these distinctions clear, because it establishes Carrey as both a central character and a physical comedian (evoking the performance style he refined on *In Living Color*). The scene ostensibly shows Jim Carrey playing a mail delivery man *en route* to deliver a large box marked 'fragile'. Soon, however, Carrey begins to mistreat the box rather than handling it with due care and attention: he throws the package around, exaggerating his bodily movements and smiling goofily at the amazed onlookers. His smile – a key signifier in Carrey's idiolect – re-keys the performance with insincerity, marking it as too excessive for realist acting (he sticks out his teeth and curls his top lip across them while turning around in a distorted bodily movement). Ace/Carrey throws the package until whatever is inside seemingly breaks, then plays football with it along a corridor before delivering it to its owner. The sequence therefore develops into a virtuoso piece of physical comedy, drawing attention to itself as spectacle. Carrey's comic persona is emphasized by the carefully choreographed action, such as when he dances around the package before flipping it over his head – which has the effect of transforming an ostensibly mundane object into an expressive performance tool.

In the same scene, however, there is another mode of performance taking place. This is the reaction of onlookers to the scene, who operate as background to the star performance. While they do not motivate the narrative – the camera follows Ace/Carrey throughout the scene – they react to him in astonishment, as if they are committed to conventions of classical realism. The film thus establishes a dual register of verisimilitude. There is the performance frame that applies to the Carrey/star performance, which is characterized by its ostensive, presentational address and its ability to create enclosures in which we admire the performance *as* performance. At the same time there is another set of conventions and expectations that apply to the supporting characters, who are committed to the cause–effect of narrative and an effaced, representational mode of acting.

Such divisions in modes of performance are common in contemporary comedian comedy. Many films appear to be able to maintain different modes of performance in operation at the same time, without causing any narrative confusion. In fact, such balanced heterogeneity of performance modes can help to sustain a sufficient realism, because the presence of non-recognizable actors in subsidiary roles serves to anchor the signifiers of the star to the text and to the diegetic world. The realist performances thus help establish the auratic authority of the star, and to legitimate their framing as spectacle. In comedy the gulf between these modes of performance may be wide, and it is fairly common for texts to switch between modes rapidly (which is also part of the pleasure in other genres such as the musical and melodrama).

As Steve Neale and Frank Krutnik have argued, the star comedian is therefore able to become 'an anomalous and privileged figure within the world of the film . . . able to step outside its boundaries, and able to play with its rules and conventions'.[15] This is often manifested as an opposition between the eccentricity of the comic performer and the social conformity of the supporting characters. Much 1990s 'dumb' comedy, and many of Carrey's films work with this distinction. In *Ace Ventura: Pet Detective*, for example, his character is positioned outside of the conventional and institutional structures of the police force (which is, significantly perhaps, ultimately shown to be corrupt). Similarly, Steve Seidman notes the frequency with which film comedians are associated with animals and children, which serves to emphasize the 'counter-cultural' drives of the character.[16] In the *Ace Ventura* films, for example, the Carrey figure is obviously separated from the adult world through his connection to animals, with whom he can communicate.[17] In *Dumb and Dumber* he enacts childish pranks upon others, as well as mimicking, pulling faces, sulking, belching, and making gags about flatulence and urinating in public. Using the narrative conceit of infantilism and the inability of the character to integrate into adult society, Kristine Brunovska Karnick and Henry Jenkins suggest that the performer is given opportunities for 'broad' comic performance.[18]

Physical comedy, ostentation and pastiche

It is worth looking at *The Mask* in more detail, as it provides frequent narrative enclosures in which Stanley/The Mask/Carrey can perform ostensively, and in which he has to shift abruptly between different modes and registers of performance according to the 'character' he is playing. First, Carrey plays Stanley, a nice but dull bank clerk who is rendered in a hyperrealist performance style (that is, connoting a slightly exaggerated, insincere realism). Second, in the guise of 'The Mask', he plays a cartoon character who operates within the conventions of animation. The latter is inflected not only through Carrey's star image and idiolect (the Carrey-isms through which we can link the two characters) but also, courtesy of the special effects, through the anarchistic mode of performance familiar from Tex Avery cartoons.[19] However, despite shifting between different modes of performance, with different framing conventions, the film does not lose expressive coherence. This is because we are presented with a narrative justification for the shift: when Stanley puts on the mask he becomes his exaggerated self, The Mask. The object of the ancient mask thereby provides a narrative reason for the transformation, operating as a keying device for the reframing (or laminating) of the performance – allowing multiple verisimilitudes to coexist within the narrative without any confusion or apparent contradiction.

The set-piece in the Cocobongo Club offers a good illustration of these shifting modes of performance. In this remarkable sequence, Carrey (as The Mask) dances increasingly wildly with Tina/Cameron Diaz, before Dorian, the club owner (and villain of the film) attempts to shoot him. Tina/Diaz, it has been established, adopts a broadly realist mode of performance that is subservient to narrative.[20] Carrey, on the other hand, is given licence within the film, with many set pieces serving to frame his performance (and the special effects) as spectacle. Upon being shot at by Dorian, he bends and stretches his body, as a cartoon character would, to avoid the bullets striking him. At the same time he does a number of impressions – first a bookmaker, then a bullfighter, then a Cossack, then Elvis and finally a Hollywood gun-slinger. The rapid shifts between the adoption of these personae are concealed by the special effects: Carrey's figure is blurred when The Mask moves at rapid speed allowing the film to laminate the body of Carrey with computer-generated effects. The series of impressions ends when The

Mask, as the Hollywood cowboy, is shot in the chest. The performance mode he adopts is a pastiche of a scene familiar from the classical Hollywood Western when one of the protagonists is shot. Carrey/The Mask, already positioned on a literal stage, falls into the arms of one of Dorian's sidekicks, croaking, 'You've got me partner . . . hold me closer Ed . . . It's getting dark.' The intertextual references here are clearly keyed as a heightened pastiche of the heroic death of the Hollywood cowboy, yet the performance is layered yet further by its framing within the film. As Carrey/The Mask/The Cowboy performs, an audience appears in the film and the performance turns into a parody/pastiche of the Academy Awards ceremony, with Carrey, as The Mask, holding an Oscar for the performance. At this point Dorian and his sidekicks turn towards the camera, adjusting their jackets and ties and smiling as if at the Awards gala. This frame is held momentarily, before Carrey resumes the role of The Mask.

Constantly shifting between modes of performance, and doing so with knowing intertextuality, this sequence sets up multiple frames that shift between what Richard Maltby and Ian Craven have termed 'autonomous' and 'integrated' modes of performance.[21] The first refers to a situation where bracketed sequences of performance – which, like the above sequence, often take place before an internal audience – are able to manipulate time and space, momentarily disrupting realist causality. The latter refers to modes of performance that remain subject to narrative and framed within a representational address.

Henry Jenkins has argued that although there is always some distance between character and star image, comedy focuses on this gap while realist cinema attempts to efface it.[22] The recognition of the star *as a star* is, then, a generic convention of comedian comedy. Star acting simultaneously plays with levels of meaning by providing a layered performance. To a greater or lesser degree, depending on the ostentatiousness of the performance and our recognition of the star, we may be aware of both the autonomous and integrated elements of the performance at the same time, without this necessarily disrupting our understanding of what is going on. In *The Mask* we are often unable to distinguish easily where the performance of Carrey ends and the special effects begin. Clearly, such realist concepts as authenticity, sincerity and internal coherence – terms prominent in discourse of value that circulate around screen acting – hold little explanatory power for these modes of performance.

Body comedy and cultural value

> When he's in a scene, and he's in most, no one else in the cast has a hope of catching your eye; some haven't even a hope of making themselves heard. Where all is excess, nothing is finesse.
>
> Alexander Walker reviewing *Liar Liar*, *London Evening Standard*, 1 May 1997

Having discussed the generic demands placed upon performance in comedian comedy, and specifically in the performances of Carrey, I want to conclude by touching on the relationship between comic performance and cultural value. As the comment above by film critic Alexander Walker illustrates, the centrality of star performance to comedian comedy clearly dominates its primary framing. More than perhaps any other genre, pleasure in comedian comedy relies on our pleasure in watching the star performance.[23] The pleasure of one spectator in performative 'excess', such as that of ostensive body comedy, is to others (such as Walker) indicative of a lack of finesse, a disruption of the values embodied and upheld by teleological modes of performance.

This kind of cultural discrimination is familiar territory: throughout the history of cinema the politics of comedy, and of comic performance, have caused much debate and disagreement. However, ironically, while contemporary 'popular' critics such as Walker have often dismissed body comedy as excessive, a number of other critics have celebrated exactly this aspect of performance. Brecht, for instance, admired the epic mode of performance adopted by some comic performers, in particular Chaplin, and suggested that the 'gestic acting' of comic performance was sometimes able to critically draw attention to itself as artifice and to comment upon the presented character's behaviour.[24] Antonin Artaud, Salvador Dali and Roland Barthes similarly admired the anarchistic performances of the Marx Brothers.[25] The critics of *Cahiers du Cinema* famously lauded the performances of Jerry Lewis for its elasticity, inarticulateness, stylisation and quotation.[26]

At the same time, however, Lewis' performance, once labelled 'spastic comedy' due to its physical inarticulateness (an effect, of course, of the skill of Lewis' bodily control), was also considered by many critics – rather like Carrey's – to be 'low' 'dumbed-down' performance, and provides an interesting historical comparison. This contradiction – body comedy as both something 'low' yet also celebrated for its transgression of conventions – has characterized academic discussion of the politics of comedy too. Much of this has centred around a discussion of whether comedy may be considered as a 'progressive genre'.[27] I have insufficient space here to consider this debate in full, but a brief outline is instructive. The progressive genre debate considered whether the transgression of social conventions and the rejection of the governing codes of realist behaviour in comedy call into question taken-for-granted social hierarchies, or whether these might actually function as what Umberto Eco calls an 'authorised transgression', working to reinforce the hegemony of dominant conventions.[28] Proponents of the former view often used (and sometimes historically abused) Mikhail Bahktin's notion of the carnivalesque in support of their argument. The attraction of Bahktin's theory lay in his delineation of the carnival as a parody of social ritual, an inversion of social hierarchies and involving a loss of bodily control. Screen comedy often celebrates these instances of social disruption – the urine-drinking and laxative gags in *Dumb and Dumber*, for instance, are amusing precisely because they work outside of social conventions, utilizing social embarrassment to comic effect. However, in his essay, 'The Frames of Comic "Freedom"', Umberto Eco casts doubt upon this utopianism, suggesting that comedies, far from subverting conventions, actually 'remind us of the existence of the rule' and our identification with it.[29] The subversiveness of comic performance, he argues, is licensed by its framing: the cause–effect relations of social action no longer apply in the comic world and neither, too, do such concepts as social transgression. Neale and Krutnik agree with this, arguing that in comedian comedy, 'subversion' and 'transgression' are 'institutionalised generic requirements'.[30] They suggest that, rather than opening up the text to a critical reading, the self-reflexivity of comic performance may actually reinforce and renew the generic conventions of comedy.[31]

Quotation and intertextuality are all conventions of post-classical comic performance. We are not surprised to see a pastiche of *The Silence of the Lambs* (1990) in *Dumb and Dumber*, or when the catchphrase 'Alrighty then!' from *Ace Ventura: Pet Detective* is quoted in the later film *The Cable Guy* (1996). Comic performance is frequently layered with such knowingness, and this is indeed part of its pleasure. Epistemological complexity may also be reflected in the audience's engagement with performance in comedian comedy. Although laughter is often thought of as a response to something we find humourous, the nature of laughter illustrates the doubleness of power in comedic performance. We can laugh with or laugh at something, depending on our orientation towards the text. To laugh, then, demonstrates an active engagement with the performance. However, to laugh is also partly to lose an element of self-control, it often feels like an involuntary physical response (although this bodily response may be culturally determined: the cultural specificity of humour and our social-ization into the codes that are being invoked will partly determine its effectiveness). The stand-up comic and television comedian Jerry Seinfeld once suggested that 'to laugh is to be dominated', a concept emphasized by the stand-up phrase 'to work the audience'.[32] Yet in film comedy laughter may also unite an audience, without the fear of embarrassment (of being made an unwilling spectacle) that live stand-up comedy, for example, might entail. It also cues a recognition of the fictionality of the performance, questioning classical accounts of the cinema as a place of socially sanctioned voyeurism. With comic performance characterized by its exhibitionism, and its willingness to ostend itself, our place as onlooker is acknowledged.

One of the main problems with the progressive genre debate, then, is the assumptions it makes about texts, in particular about the formal conceptualization of potentially disruptive elements. Direct address to camera, for example, which is common in comic performance, is often read prescriptively as rupturing the closed text and foregrounding the production of performance. This assumption that a particular formal device will generate a particular meaning tends to ignore the shifting nature and cultural specificity of such meanings. While quite rare in Hollywood cinema, such devices are common to other popular forms, particularly television, where they are not regarded as disruptive. Furthermore, this formalist argument avoids a consideration of the audience in such a process: the politics of comedy are here an effect of the text rather than of an audience which may opt to decode these signs in part according to interpretive frames that are determined outside of the text.

As I have outlined above, much critical writing on screen performance assumes a hierarchy of performance, with questions of realism and realist modes of acting privileged over comic performance and over other modes of performance that make use of hyperbole and ostentation. Comic performance often draws attention to itself as a performance, with the result that the systems of identification set up in realist cinema are less secure. The pleasures offered by comic performance may have more to do with recognition and play, rather than with identification. As John Caughie has pointed out, this may be related to the admiration of virtuosity, with 'the spectator's appreciation, as a spectator, *from the outside*, of the skill of someone performing'.[33] Often comedian comedy, particularly post-classical comedian comedy, places its audience as witnesses to the performance, willing conspirators in its gag structure. Questions of identification and character may be less relevant here than those of recognition, play and the return of familiar pleasures. In *Liar Liar* Carrey's character is asked by his son whether if he pulls a face it will stick. He self-consciously answers, 'Absolutely not. In fact, some people make a good living that way.' This answer indicates a reflexive awareness in Carrey's performance of his own status as a star, and popularity as a physical comedian, and is typical of the knowingness that 1990s Hollywood cinema assumes in its audience. The often flimsy narrative premise of comedian comedy – often criticized for its dumbness – may ultimately be less important to our reading of and pleasure in these films than our investment in, and recognition of, the idiolect of the performer and the knowing references they make to their own star image.

Notes

1 Films often cited as symptomatic of this tendency include Carrey's films, those directed by the Farrelly brothers, as well as recent teenage 'gross-out' comedies such as *American Pie* (1999) and less specifically comedic films such as *Forrest Gump* (1994).

2 Although 'acting' and 'performance' are often used interchangeably, performance is a much wider concept than acting, as it also conceptualizes the relationship between audience and performer. I use the term 'acting' to refer to the particular kind of performance centred on the construction of character, although this is admittedly rather unsatisfactory. A useful introduction to performance as a theoretical concept is Carlson, M. (1996): *Performance: A Critical Introduction*, London: Routledge.

3 Thompson, G. F. (1985): 'Approaches to "Performance"', *Screen*, Vol. 26, No. 5: 78–90.

4 Goffman, E. (1974): *Frame Analysis*, Boston, MA, Northeastern University Press.

5 Though of course a camp reading may now be one of the dominant frames for decoding star performances, particularly in the ironic 'knowing' Hollywood cinema of the 1990s.

6 See Jackie Stacey's nuanced account of cinematic identification in star–audience relations in Stacey, J. (1994): *Star Gazing: Hollywood Cinema and Female Spectatorship*, London: Routledge: 126–75.

7 See Krutnik, F. (2000): *Inventing Jerry Lewis*, Washington, DC: Smithsonian Institution Press: 123–5.

8 See Brewster, B. (1991): 'The fundamental reproach: Bertolt Brecht and the cinema', in Burnett, R. (ed.): *Explorations in Film Theory*, Bloomington: Indiana University Press: 191–200.

9 Seidman, S. (1981): *Comedian Comedy: A Tradition in Hollywood Film*, Ann Arbor, MI: UMI Research Press.

10 In his book on film acting James Naremore uses the term 'ostensiveness' to describe the enunciative quality of the star performance, and posits a scale that runs between representational to presentational modes of performance. See Naremore, J. (1988): *Acting in the Cinema*, Berkeley and Los Angeles: University of California Press: 34. See also Umberto Eco's fascinating analysis of ostentation, drawing upon C.S. Pierce's famous drunkard in Eco, U. (1977): 'Semiotics of Theatrical Performance', TDR: *The Drama Review*, No. 21: 107–117.

11 On high concept see Wyatt, J. (1994): *High Concept: Movies and Marketing in Hollywood*, Austin: University of Texas Press: 1–22.

12 Jones, K. (2000): 'A Class Act', *Film Comment*, Vol. 26, No. 4 (July/August 2000): 28–32. Jones goes on to argue that this is resolutely an inheritance of a vaudeville tradition, firmly located in working-class representation.

13 Seidman: *Comedian Comedy*: 55.

14 Ibid.

15 Neale, S. and Krutnik, F. (1990): *Popular Film and Television Comedy*, London: Routledge: 105.

16 Seidman: *Comedian Comedy*: 64–71.

17 The same trope is appropriated and expanded by Eddie Murphy in the 1998 box office hit *Dr. Dolittle*.

18 Karnick, K. B. and Jenkins, H. eds. (1995): *Classical Hollywood Comedy*, London: Routledge: 161. Note the importance of infantilism to roles played by Tom Hanks, Steve Martin, Robin Williams and the lead characters of the *Wayne's World* and *Bill and Ted* films. It is also striking that these are all male, and that similar female comic roles are hard to recall.

19 See Norman Klein's interesting analysis of the fit between Carrey's 'elastic' performance and that of the Tex Avery cartoon character. Klein argues that these new forms of visuality have given rise to a hybrid cinema of animation, CGI and bodily performance. See Klein, N. (1998): 'Hybrid Cinema: The Mask, Masques, and Tex Avery', in Sandler, K. S. (ed.): Reading the Rabbit: Explorations in Warner Bros. Animation, London: Rutgers University Press: 209–55. See also Magid, R. (1994): 'ILM Magic is Organised Mayhem', American Cinematographer, Vol. 75, No. 12 (December 1994): 50–60, for an analysis of the special effects in The Mask.

20 Throughout the film Tina/Diaz is objectified quite self-consciously by the narrative – for instance, her lingering, slow-motion entrance at the start of the film operates almost as a parody of Hollywood fetishism, so overdetermined is its presentation of her as an erotic Other.

21 Maltby, R. with Craven, I. (1995): Hollywood Cinema, Oxford: Blackwell Publishers: 249.

22 See Jenkins, H. (1992): What Made Pistachio Nuts?: Early Sound Comedy and the Vaudeville Aesthetic, New York: Columbia University Press: 132.

23 In my discussion with friends and colleagues about Carrey's films it is clear how strongly opinion is divided over the qualities of his performance idiolect.

24 See Brecht, B. (1964): Brecht on Theatre, London: Methuen: 50; and Rouse, J. (1981): 'Brecht and the Contradictory Actor', Theatre Journal, Vol. 36, No. 1: 34.

25 See Jenkins: What Made Pistachio Nuts?: 9.

26 See Johnson, C. and Willemen, P. (eds) (1973): Frank Tashlin, Edinburgh: Edinburgh Film Festival: 117–122, and a discussion of this in Jenkins: What Made Pistachio Nuts: 12–13.

27 For further discussion on the genealogy of the progressive genre concept see Barbara Klinger (1995): '"Cinema/Ideology/Criticism" Revisited: The Progressive Genre', in Grant, B. K. (ed.): Film Genre Reader II, Austin: University of Texas Press: 74–90.

28 Eco, U. (1985): 'The Frames of Comic "Freedom"', in Sebeok, T.A. (ed.): Carnival!, Berlin: Mouton: 1–9.

29 Eco: 'The Frames of Comic Freedom': 6.

30 Neale and Krutnik: Popular Film and Television Comedy: 4.

31 Ibid. The ambiguous status of the stereotype in comedy is symptomatic of the problem: does the foregrounding of stereotypes in comedian comedy consolidate their position as hegemonic representations or call them into question?

32 Jerry Seinfeld, quoted in Borns, B. (1987): Comic Lives: Inside the World of American Stand-up Comedy, New York: Simon & Schuster: 20.

33 Caughie, J. (1981): 'Terms of Realism', in Gledhill, C., ed.: Film & Media Studies in Higher Education: Conference Papers, London: BFI: 117–30.

Select Bibliography

Agee, James (1974): 'Comedy's Greatest Era', in Mast, Gerald and Marshall Cohen (eds): *Film Theory and Criticism: Introductory Readings*, New York: Oxford University Press: 438–57 (originally published in *Life* magazine, 3 September 1949).

Anderson, Christopher (2001): 'I Love Lucy: U.S. Situation Comedy', *Encyclopaedia of Television*, Museum of Broadcast Communications website, <http://www.mbcnet.org/ETV/I/htmlI /ilovelucy/ ilovelucy.htm>.

Babington, Bruce and Peter William Evans (1989): 'Joking Apart: Three Comedians (Bob Hope, Mae West and Woody Allen)', Chapter 6 of their *Affairs to Remember: the Hollywood Comedy of the Sexes*, Manchester: Manchester University Press: 95–178.

Bakhtin, Mikhail (1984): *Rabelais and his World*, Bloomington: Indiana University Press.

Balio, Tino (ed.) (1995): *Grand Design: Hollywood as a Modern Business Enterprise*, 1930–1939, Berkeley: University of California Press.

Barr, Charles (1967): *Laurel and Hardy*, London: Studio Vista.

Beach, Christopher (2002): *Class, Language, and American Film Comedy*, Cambridge: University of Cambridge Press.

Borger, Len (1978): 'Harold Lloyd: The Comic Persona of the All-American Boy', in Reilly 1978: 181–90.

Boskin, Joseph (ed.) (1997a): *The Humour Prism in 20th-Century America*, Detroit, MI: Wayne State University Press.

Boskin, Joseph (ed.) (1997b): *Rebellious Laughter: People's Humour in American Culture*, Syracuse, NY: Syracuse University Press.

Carroll, Noel (1990a): 'Buster Keaton, *The General*, and Visible Intelligibility', Chapter 7 of Peter Lehman (ed.) *Close Viewings*, Tallahasee: Florida State University Press: 125–40.

Carroll, Noel (1990b): 'Keaton: Film Acting as Action', in Carole Zucker (ed.) *Making Visible the Invisible: An Anthology Of Original Essays on Film Acting*, Metuchen, NJ: Scarecrow Press: 198–223.

Carroll, Noel (1991): 'Notes on the Sight Gag', in Horton 1991: 25–42.

Cohan, Steve (1999): 'Queering the Deal: On the Road with Hope and Crosby', in Ellis Hanson (ed.) *Out Takes: Essays on Queer Theory and Film*, Durham, NC: Duke University Press: 23–45.

Crafton, Don (1995): 'Pie and Chase: Gags, Spectacle and Narrative in Slapstick Comedy', in Karnick and Jenkins 1995: 106–19 (originally published 1988).

Curry, Ramona (1996): *Too Much of a Good Thing: Mae West as Cultural Icon*, Minneapolis: University of Minnesota Press.

Dale, Alan (2000): *Comedy is a Man in Trouble: Slapstick in American Movies*, Minneapolis: University of Minnesota Press.

Doty, Alexander (1990): 'The Cabinet of Lucy Ricardo: Lucille Ball's Star Image', *Cinema Journal*, Vol. 29, No. 4 (summer 1990): 3–22.

Doty, Alexander (1991): 'The Sissy Boy, The Fat Ladies, and The Dykes: Queerness and/as Gender in Pee-Wee's World', *Camera Obscura*, nos. 25–6 (January–May): 125–43.

Durgnat, Raymond (1969): *The Crazy Mirror: Hollywood Comedy and the American Image*, London: Faber & Faber.

du Pasquier, Sylvain (1970): 'Les gags de Buster Keaton', *Communications*, No. 15: 132–45.

Everson, William K. (1978): 'Harold Lloyd: The Climb to Success', in Reilly 1978: 168–75.

Fischer, Lucy (1991): 'Sometimes I Feel Like a Motherless Child: Comedy and Matricide', in Horton 1991: 60–78.

Gunning, Tom (1990): 'The Cinema of Attractions: Early Film, its Spectator and the Avant-Garde', in Thomas Elsaesser (ed.): *Early Film: Space, Frame, Narrative*, London: BFI: 56–62 (originally published 1986).

Gunning, Tom (1995a): 'Crazy Machines in the Garden of Forking Paths: Mischief Gags and the Origins of American Film Comedy', in Karnick and Jenkins 1995: 87–105.

Gunning, Tom (1995b): 'Response to "Pie and Chase"', in Karnick and Jenkins 1995: 121–2.

Hamilton, Marybeth (1996): *The Queen of Camp: Mae West, Sex and Popular Culture*, London: Pandora.

Horton, Andrew (ed.) (1991): *Comedy/ Cinema/Theory*, Berkeley: University of California Press.

Jenkins, Henry (1986): 'The Amazing Push-Me/Pull-You Text: Cognitive Processing, Narrational Play and the Comic Film', *Wide-Angle*, Vol. 3, No. 4: 35–44.

Jenkins, Henry (1990a): '"Shall We Make it for New York or for Distribution?" Eddie Cantor, *Whoopee*, and Regional Resistance to the Talkies', *Cinema Journal*, Vol. 29, No. 2 (spring): 32–52.

Jenkins, Henry (1990b): '"Fifi Was My Mother's Name!": Anarchistic Comedy, the Vaudeville Aesthetic, and *Diplomaniacs*', *The Velvet Light Trap*, No. 26 (autumn): 3–27.

Jenkins, Henry (1991): '"Don't Become Too Intimate with That Terrible Woman!" Unruly Wives, Female Comic Performance and *So Long Letty*', *Camera Obscura*, 25–6 (January/May): 202–23.

Jenkins, Henry (1992): *What Made Pistachio Nuts? Early Sound Comedy and the Vaudeville Aesthetic*, New York: Columbia University Press.

Johnson, Catherine Irene (1981): *Contradiction in 1950s Comedy and Ideology*, Ann Arbor, MI: UMI Research Press.

Karnick, Kristine B. and Henry Jenkins (eds) (1995): *Classical Hollywood Comedy*, New York: Routledge.

Kehr, Dave (2000): 'The Lives of Jim Carrey', *Film Comment*, Vol. 36, No. 1 (January–February): 12–15.

Kerr, Walter (1975): *The Silent Clowns*, New York: Knopf.

King, Geoff (2002): *Film Comedy*, London: Wallflower Press.

Knopf, Robert (1999): *The Theatre and Cinema of Buster Keaton*, Princeton, NJ: Princeton University Press.

Krämer, Peter (1988): 'Vitagraph, Slapstick and Early Cinema', *Screen*, Vol. 29, No. 2 (spring): 101–3.

Krämer, Peter (1989): 'Derailing the Honeymoon Express: Comicality and Narrative Closure in Buster Keaton's *The Blacksmith*', *The Velvet Light Trap*, No. 23 (spring): 101–16.

Krutnik, Frank (1984): 'The Clown-Prints of Comedy', *Screen*, Vol. 25, Nos. 4–5 (July–October): 50–9.

Krutnik, Frank (1994): 'Jerry Lewis: The Deformation of the Comic', *Film Quarterly*, Vol. 48, No. 4 (autumn): 12–26.

Krutnik, Frank (1995a): 'The Handsome Man and His Monkey: The Comic Bondage of Dean Martin & Jerry Lewis', *The Journal of Popular Film & Television*, Vol. 23, No. 1 (spring): 16–25.

Krutnik, Frank (1995b): 'A Spanner in the Works? Genre, Narrative and the Hollywood Comedian', in Karnick and Jenkins 1995: 17–38.

Krutnik, Frank (2000): *Inventing Jerry Lewis*, Washington, DC: Smithsonian Institution Press.

Krutnik, Frank (2002): 'Sex and Slapstick: The Martin & Lewis Phenomenon', in Murray Pomerance (ed.): *Enfant Terrible!: Jerry Lewis in American Film*, New York: New York University Press.

Krutnik, Frank (2003): 'Fools, Freaks and Geeks: Hollywood Comedian Comedy' (forthcoming article).

Leider, Emily Wortis (1997): *Becoming Mae West*, Cambridge and New York: Da Capo Press.

Louvish, Simon (1999a): *Man on the Flying Trapeze: The Life and Times of W.C. Fields*, London: Faber & Faber.

Louvish, Simon (1999b): *Monkey Business: The Lives and Legends of the Marx Brothers*, London: Faber & Faber.

Louvish, Simon (2001): *Stan and Ollie: The Roots of Comedy*, London: Faber & Faber.

McCaffrey, Donald (1968): *Four Great Comedians: Chaplin, Lloyd, Keaton and Langdon*, New York: Barnes.

Maland, Charles (1991): *Chaplin and American Culture: The Evolution of a Star Image*, Princeton, NJ: Princeton University Press.

Mast, Gerald (1976): *The Comic Mind: Comedy and the Movies*, New York: Random House.

Matthews, Nicole (2000): *Comic Politics: Gender in Hollywood Cinema after the New Right*, Manchester: University of Manchester Press.

Mellencamp, Patricia (1983): 'Jokes and their Relation to the Marx Brothers', in Stephen Heath and Patricia Mellencamp (eds): *Cinema and Language*, Frederick, MD: University Publications of America: 63–78.

Mellencamp, Patricia (1986): 'Situation Comedy, Feminism and Freud: Lucille Ball', in Modleski, Tania (ed.): *Studies in Entertainment: Critical Approaches to Mass Culture*, Bloomington and Indianapolis: Indiana University Press: 80–95.

Mellencamp, Patricia (1992): *High Anxiety: Catastrophe, Scandal, Age and Comedy*, Bloomington: Indiana University Press.

Mitchell, Glenn (1997): *The Marx Brothers Encyclopaedia*, London: Batsford.

Mulvey, Laura (1975): 'Visual Pleasure and Narrative Cinema', *Screen*, Vol. 16, No. 3: 6–18.

Musser, Charles (1990): 'Work, Ideology and Chaplin's Tramp', in Robert Sklar and Charles Musser (eds): *Resisting Images: Essays on Cinema and History*, Philadelphia, PA: Temple University Press: 36–67.

Musser, Charles (1991): 'Ethnicity, Role-playing, and American Film Comedy: From *Chinese Laundry Scene* to *Whoopee* (1894–1930)', in Lester D. Friedman (ed.): *Unspeakable Images: Ethnicity and the American Cinema*, Urbana: University of Illinois Press: 39–81.

Neale, Steve (2000): *Genre and Hollywood*, London: Routledge.

Neale, Steve and Frank Krutnik (1990): *Popular Film and Television Comedy*, London: Routledge.

Neibaur, James L. and Ted Okuda (1995): *The Jerry Lewis Films: An Analytical Filmography of the Innovative Comic*, Jefferson, NC: McFarland.

Palmer, Jerry (1987): *Logic of the Absurd: On Film and Television Comedy*, London: British Film Institute.

Paul, William (1994): *Laughing, Screaming: Modern Hollywood Horror and Comedy*, New York: Columbia University Press.

Rapf, Joanna E. (1993): 'Comic Theory from a Feminist Perspective: A Look at Jerry Lewis', *Journal of Popular Culture*, Vol. 27, No. 1 (summer): 191–203.

Reilly, Adam (ed.) (1978): *Harold Lloyd: The King of Daredevil Comedy*, London: Andre Deutsch.

Rickman, Gregg (ed.) (2001): *The Film Comedy Reader*, New York: Limelight Editions.

Robertson, Pamela (1993): '"The Kinda Comedy That Imitates Me": Mae West's Identification with the Feminist Camp', *Cinema Journal*, Vol. 32, No. 2 (winter): 57–72. Expanded version in Robertson, Pamela (1996): *Guilty Pleasures: Feminist Camp from Mae West to Madonna*, London and New York: I.B. Tauris: 23–54.

Robinson, David (1985): *Chaplin: His Life and Art*, London: Collins.

Rowe, Kathleen (1995): *The Unruly Woman: Gender and the Genres of Laughter*, Austin: University of Texas Press.

Rutsky, R. L. and Justin Wyatt (1990): 'Serious Pleasures: Cinematic Pleasure and the Notion of Fun', *Cinema Journal*, Vol. 30, No. 1 (autumn): 3–19.

Sanders, Jonathan (1995): *Another Fine Dress: Role-Play in the Films of Laurel and Hardy*, London: Cassell.

Seidman, Steve (1981): *Comedian Comedy: A Tradition in Hollywood Film*, Ann Arbor, MI: UMI Research Press.

Sennett, Mack (1990): *King of Comedy*, San Francisco: Mercury House (originally published 1954).

Sikov, Ed (1994): *Laughing Hysterically: American Screen Comedy of the 1950s*, New York: Columbia University Press.

Watkins, Mel (1999): *On the Real Side: A History of African American Comedy from Slavery to Chris Rock*, (2nd rev. edn), Chicago, IL: Lawrence Hill Books (originally published 1994).

Willemen, Paul (1973): 'Tashlin's Method: An Hypothesis', in Claire Johnston and Paul Willemen (eds): *Frank Tashlin*, Edinburgh: Edinburgh Film Festival.

Winokur, Mark (1996): *American Laughter: Immigrants, Ethnicity, and 1930s Hollywood Film Comedy*, London: Macmillan.

THE LIBRARY
GUILDFORD COLLEGE
of Further and Higher Education

Index

THE LIBRARY
GUILDFORD COLLEGE
of Further and Higher Education

Guildford College
Learning Resource Centre

Please return on or before the last date shown
This item may be renewed by telephone unless overdue

03 Jul 08
1 0 JUL 2012

Class: 791.43028 KRU

Title: Hollywood Comedians, the Film Reader

Author: KRUTNIK, Frank

WITHDRAWN

141712